T0209268

The Ends
of the Earth

The
Ends
of the
Earth

—— essays ——

W.S. Merwin

COUNTERPOINT

Berkeley

"The Wake of the Blackfish" first appeared in *The Paris Review*; "Reflections of a
Mountain" first appeared as "Aspects of a Mountain" in *Shenandoah*; "The Tree on
One Tree Hill" first appeared in *Manoa*; "Snail Song" first appeared in *Orion*; and, a
section of "Name in the Sand" first appeared in *The New York Review of Books*.

Library of Congress Cataloging-in-Publication Data is available.

ISBN 978-1-61902-748-0

Interior design by Tabitha Lahr

Printed in the United States of America

COUNTERPOINT
2560 Ninth Street, Suite 318
Berkeley, CA 94710
www.counterpointpress.com

Printed in the United States of America

for Alastair Reid

Contents

The Ends
of the Earth

The Wake of the Blackfish:
A Memoir of George Kirstein

Late in March, in the year I would turn thirty, he wrote me a letter about sea monsters.

He and I had never met, and he addressed me, on the stationery of *The Nation* magazine, formally, with a colon after my name, and signed himself George G. Kirstein, over his title, Publisher.

He began and ended his letter by speaking of some poems of mine that *The Nation* had been publishing, to do with the sea. It was a subject that had occupied my imagination since childhood, and some of the writings of Conrad, first discovered in a book that was a present from my mother on, I think, my thirteenth birthday, in the coal-mining town far from the sea where we were living then, had wakened in me the craving to write. But my actual experience of the sea, apart from a couple of Atlantic crossings, was limited almost entirely to some sailing in summer with friends almost as inept as I was, on an old Dutch fishing boat off the south coast of England. The dilapidation of the neglected vessel (she had been named *Curlew* at some wishful moment in the distant past) and our own lack of skill and knowledge, along with the miserable weather, the cold rains and fogs, and the complicated tides and currents of the south coast, impressed and greatly magnified the time and its details. They were not extensive but they were, and they remained, immediate, and they came to focus years of reading and daydreaming about the sea into the writing of the poems that had occasioned George's letter. He said that the subject of the poems spoke to a prejudice of his own. "The sea is one of my passions and I have spent a considerable part of my life on it."

He particularly wanted to say something about a poem of mine that recounted a sighting of a sea monster, a presence disputed among those who had seen it. I need hardly say that I had never beheld a sea monster, and my piece was a complete fiction. But according to George, the poem was "particularly real to me because I experienced it." And his letter suddenly took on the ageless tone of innumerable sailing yarns. "I was bound for Halifax from Boston in my old forty-foot yawl and was off watch in the middle of the night. The boy at the wheel was drowsy because, as you know, the light on the binnacle has a hypnotic effect. Suddenly there was a loud intake of breath just ahead of the bow and the monster disappeared into the black ocean. What had happened, of course, was that we had nudged a sleeping blackfish, but the discussion has never ended as to whether it was the monster or whether we saw it." In the poem the "discussion," after a long sighting in a familiar place in broad daylight, led to an ultimate doubt of the habitually accepted distinction between the waking world and the world of sleep—or whatever is the waking world's obverse. It was not a doubt that George would ever have entertained or admitted, and it may have been one of the many possibilities that he closed off more and more curtly with age. By the time he wrote me he had long since evolved a bluff manner designed to repel, as a general rule, sustained speculation about any such matters. It was one of the outer reaches of an extreme reticence where feelings were concerned. A publisher who sends a letter to someone whose work he has been publishing, whether or not they may have corresponded before, is not, on the face of it, committing an act of dangerous self-exposure. But I realized later, and most of all since George's death, how exceptional it must have been for him to do such a thing, including its introductory bit of personal history. Of course he wrote all the time to people he did not know, but seldom, I think, to artists or to poets even if he had published them, simply because he liked their work. He was shy about poetry and he pretended to know nothing about it. But the truth was that he had majored in English at Harvard and had written his thesis on Hardy's *The Dynasts*. Yet he had come to affect a plain downright businessman's and man-of-action's presumed ignorance—a sympathetic ignorance, to be sure—about a number of things. About the arts in general, and as a matter of course about "modern poetry." With music he had gone further, and he flatly declared, as a kind of tic, that it made no sense to him, and that he could not tell one piece from another. And yet at Harvard he had sat for hours on end listening to Kirkpatrick practicing Bach.

If his writing to me as he did was in fact as eccentric for him as I suppose, I imagine that it was one of a considerable number of departures from habit which followed more or less naturally from the new phase in his life that had been marked by his buying and, indeed, taking over *The Nation* magazine only a matter of months before. I did not know much about the background of that decision, and for that matter seldom found it easy to elicit consecutive biographical information about George. I expected that he may have been somewhat more free with accounts of himself with some of his own contemporaries. There was, after all, a generation between us. I know that the business side of the decision was something he approached with confidence based on an impressive variety of administrative and financial experience, but I never knew—of course I never knew—how much money he had, and once I learned that he "had money" it seemed to me that I should not know any more about it than that. His own feelings about money were intricate, as I would come to realize. They included contempt and attachment in indeterminate shadings. "Money," he told me once, much later on, "is something that everybody is neurotic about." He liked to make it plain if, for example, the matter of some private expense was raised, that while he thought little of money or its hypnotically entangling effects, he had enough of it to live as he pleased, with no financial anxiety and to own a forty-foot yacht and do things like buying *The Nation* magazine when the spirit moved him. And he told me more than once that he had not started out rich. His father, he said, had thought it would not be good for the boys to have too much at the beginning, and he started them out with $25,000 each and that was that. "And I did not put the rest together by trusting deadbeats," he said to me years later, referring to my own foolishness in putting my savings in the custody of a glib welcher, a friend of friends, in California, and losing it as a result.

On one of George's first jobs he had been in charge of the horses (he knew nothing about horses and I doubt whether he had ever been on one) for one of the big film companies, MGM I believe, that made westerns in Hollywood. He had been a floor manager at Blooming-dale's for a while. He talked with some experience about the selling of garden furniture. He had worked long and devotedly in labor relations and had written a book about it, and during the war had served on the War Labor Relations Board under Roosevelt. For some years he had been executive director of the regional board of the Hospitalization Insurance Plan. All of his actual business enterprises, he once told me, had done very well for him. That was the way he put it, too, as though he had been, more than anything else, lucky. It had come to him naturally.

That was the way things had happened to his own father, too, from the way he described it. Clearly he admired his father, who must have had an abiding influence on him. George told me that his father, as a young man, had been the manager of a professional baseball team, and in later years had been the partner of Lincoln Filene, at Filene's Department Store, in Boston. Lincoln Filene himself was obviously a strong and original person, and George's father, the younger man in the partnership, had probably learned a great deal from him. The currents of progressive liberalism of the 1880s and '90s, the European-American immigrant ferment represented by writers such as Carl Schurz, had appealed to the daring and iconoclastic idealism in both men, and George was proud to tell me that they had made Filene's one of the first large business enterprises in Boston, certainly, and indeed in the whole country, to turn the stocks of the company over to the employees, and have the workers really own the business. In so doing, George admitted, Filene and George's father were far ahead of their employees, many of whom were shocked by the proposal and opposed to it and its responsibilities.

I did not realize until some time later just how distinguished a figure George's father had been, in the Boston of the early years of the century, but I knew that the combination of skeptical, secular, no-nonsense liberalism and a reforming yet essentially prudent view of the functions of the social order had been there as an extremely impressive example in George's childhood and had provided a basis for George's values in politics and in many other aspects of his life. One could hear it from the way George spoke of him, and evidently it was so, even though his father must have seemed essentially out of reach. He was so much older than George—but most human relations, for George, appeared to belong to distance.

In any event, the business part of the decision to buy *The Nation* was not hard to imagine, later. It was the part that had to do with *The Nation's* character—a magazine seriously concerned with intellectual and artistic opinions and events—that was more daring, more intricate and shadowy. At Harvard George may have been following his own real interests, or he may have been trying to resolve his inevitably contradictory feelings about the influence of his brother Lincoln, his elder by a few years, whose dazzling career there was well-known to everyone who was interested in the arts. Among Lincoln's achievements, as many who are acquainted with the era know, was the magazine *Hound & Horn,* which Lincoln founded in his sophomore year, with R.P. Blackmur editing and contributing. With its first issue the review was recognized as one of the most distinguished publications on literature and the arts in the country. Lincoln himself wrote and painted brilliantly and easily. And Lincoln had known, and knew, just about everyone who had to do with the arts—certainly in that part of the world—and it must have seemed to George that Lincoln also knew pretty much everything worth knowing about them. Lincoln was not bashful about conveying such an impression. His tolerance of his much younger brother's emergent impressions was probably distant at best. His patience with interests and opinions other than his own was not something for which he was known then or later. George, with no single driving original talent, must have felt that the world of the arts, and to a great degree the arts themselves, had been pre-empted by Lincoln, and that in that sphere, above all, he was constantly in Lincoln's shadow.

And besides Lincoln there was Mina, some years older than her brothers, and Mina too had constituted herself a patrician authority on the arts that interested her, on culture in a grand and somewhat brittle sense, on social requisites, and she was already on the way to becoming the scholar who would edit Proust's letters and write a life of Bizet, as well as several lighter accounts of privileged decors. She was closer than George to either of his parents, his busy father, or his mother who had been brought up to wealth and a familiarity with the arts in Europe and the United States, and to a love of opulent furnishings. In George's references to her—they were little more than that—she sounded somewhat cold and autocratic. He spoke as though it was really Mina who had brought up both Lincoln and himself, as though their mother was not much with them, or with him, during those years. But Mina, by the time she was overseeing George's upbringing, was already busy making a social milieu for herself in Boston, and George had felt out of place among her interests and associates.

He had discovered that he liked to sail. His life of sailing had begun in Marblehead, where the family spent their summers, and his father may have had something to do with the choice of his first boat. Neither Mina nor Lincoln, he noted more than once, was in the least interested in boats or in sailing. His memory of the years of Mina's unofficial guardianship had crystallized into an image of the day when his childhood was almost over, and George, aged thirteen or so, had contrived to sink his boat in Marblehead Harbor. It must have been quite thoroughly sunk, even if not in very deep water, and I am not sure that he ever told me the immediate fate of the boat itself. The part of the occasion that remained most vivid for George and always brought back to him a flicker of wry pleasure was the recollection of him stomping home, dripping the foul mud of the harbor bottom, his clothes soaked with it, his topsiders squelching and slopping, and the rest of him burning with adolescent rage and humiliation, and flinging open the door to find Mina in the act of serving tea to a—perhaps the names are still there in a diary. Obviously his sister's face rose before him each time as he stood there again, dripping in the doorway and in that connection too he told me a little about the carpets—even though it was the summer house. And by comparison, something about the elegance of the house in Boston.

Considering the influence of his family on him during those years it is not surprising that George turned to boats and sailing, but it is perhaps remarkable that he kept any interest in the arts at all. He seems to have reached beyond the more immediate presences of Mina, and for a while of his mother, and of Lincoln, and their pronounced certainties, and to have drawn perhaps more than he knew upon the figure, more remote than any of them, of his father, who let him alone to make up his own mind, as neither George's mother, nor Mina, nor Lincoln ever did, if they paid any attention to him at all.

And George's father no doubt took at least a polite interest in the arts, an administrative and practical interest—he was for years president of the Boston Public Library—but he was also involved not only in business but in civic matters and to some degree, indirectly, in local politics. George told of a delegation of businessmen, which included Lincoln Filene and his father, that had called upon a newly elected mayor of Boston. We had been talking about the delinquencies of the city of Boston, which George always insisted was the most corrupt city in the United States. It was a subject to which George warmed periodically, and it was a distinction that he claimed without qualification for his native town, something beyond dispute and eternal. Chicago was as nothing, by comparison. The corruption of Boston, the impossibility of decent government there, had become a benchmark for George, against which he could measure the relative difficulty of decent government or honest and responsible journalism, or upright civic behavior, anywhere else, and we returned from time to time to one of the most flamboyant figures produced by the peculiarity of Boston, Mayor Curley, who had run one of his legendary mayoral campaigns from jail. Curley indeed became so garish a symbol of the aspect of Boston that George had fixed upon, that I always imagine it must have been Curley himself who had received the delegation of businessmen George told about. But even Curley's career, interminable as it must have seemed to many, could scarcely have gone back far enough for that, and so there must have been an earlier figure with the prerequisites for the part. The story, in any event, is that the delegation, once the doors were closed, told the new mayor that they were only too well aware of the temptations of their city, and that they wanted an honest mayoral administration. They said they realized that anything of the kind would involve a mayor's passing up opportunities of a shady nature which from time to time would appear in his path. And they said they wanted to compensate him in advance for his abstinence on such occasions. They wanted to make an honest administration worth his while, and to that end they were there to offer him (this was in the early years of the century) a quarter of a million dollars. And he had laughed at them.

Whatever its basis in history, and whatever apparent naïveté it suggests, the story reveals some of the things that George continued, stubbornly, to believe. One was the possibility of combining, even in circumstances of inevitable corruption, business enterprise with civic responsibility, and responsibility of a personal and at the same time somewhat quixotic sort. Though the mayor in the story laughed and the delegation apparently got nowhere, its very existence was the kind of thing that kept the country from being more rotten and destructive than it was. And the delegation had been formed in this case not of penniless reformers but of affluent and successful members of the business community. George saw private wealth in a variety of ways, some of them inconsistent and some of them fluctuating, but somewhere he clung to the belief that it was a public trust, even that it was owned on sufferance, and that it entailed a moral obligation to benefit the public in some way. The obligation could be ignored, of course, and often was, but that was simply one of the many prevalent forms of irresponsibility with which we were all familiar. George did not apply this assumption like a rule—I was surprised sometimes to notice how tolerant he seemed to be of the mindless self-indulgence of some of the rich he knew—but it figured among the grounds for his contempt for the heedless conduct of others, from time to time. I do not want to suggest that George's character was simply a reflection of family influences, but his were uncommonly imposing, and I think that in his views of civic and political responsibility his father prob-ably was a model that he never seriously questioned.

His father was a reader and combined a respect for books with his sense of civic purpose by serving, as I have said, as president of the Boston Public Library. George's love of Mark Twain and of biogra-phy were obviously set in motion by his father, who read both con-stantly, sometimes aloud. His father may have had something to do, also, with fostering George's lifelong liking and admiration for Eng-land and the English, though the nautical history of England cer-tainly nourished both, later on. If George's relation to the more visual and physical arts was at best hesitant by the time he entered Harvard, he was a confirmed reader of history and of English literature. His private exploration of the arts—as independently as possible from the comments of Mina and Lincoln—must have been in poetry, leading him to enthusiasm for the work of John Livingston Lowes (some of which, of course, focused on Coleridge's great nautical ballad) and on Hardy's long sea poem.

But I doubt whether it ever occurred to him at Harvard that he would ever do anything after college that was in any way involved with literature. He had friends in publishing, but if he ever consid-ered that, it may still have seemed uncomfortably close to Lincoln's world, and anyway, most of George's friends in publishing houses were in Boston, which George wanted to leave. His sister and brother appeared to have constituted themselves the artistic representatives of his generation of the family. His father did not try to influence them, but according to George he thought they were both completely crazy (though they were both so young when he died that the opinion itself must have been a leaping to conclusions). George suggested that Mina and Lincoln had more or less consigned to their younger brother the role of ordinary businessman. It is hard to imagine George ever having been simply pushed into something and staying there against his will. Somewhere along the way he must have adopted a view of himself that was basically similar to theirs, and he settled into the part without, clearly, altogether disliking it. Over the next decades the main field of his knowledge and activity was labor relations, the arbitration of labor disputes, and his leisure was spent sailing in the summers. He made enough money doing what he thought he ought to do to be able to live as he pleased.

George said that it came as some surprise to Mina and Lincoln when they learned, in the mid-fifties, that he was planning to buy *The Nation*. He may have been assuming some of their response to his deliberate breaking out of the course to which he felt they had more or less relegated him. He thought they considered it somewhat presumptuous of him to take over a publication that devoted a section—even if it were only "the back of the book"—and one with a long and distinguished history to the arts. He had expected, and he noted, their skepticism and their patronizing. He quoted Mina saying, "What do *you* know about running a magazine?" and what she meant, he said, was "What do you know about editing anything to do with books and the arts?" He thought he would try. He was approaching fifty. It was what he wanted to do, and it gave him a field in which to exercise his interests in politics, history, economics as well as what he thought of as an outsider's appropriately limited interest in the arts. The history of the magazine, which was nearing its centennial year, had also attracted him. It had been a part of educated conversation all his life, and its place in the minds of liberal Northerners at the time of the Civil War and during the decades that followed it had probably had something to do with *The Nation's* indispensable place on the list of publications that George's father consistently read and generally approved. In deciding to buy *The Nation* George was at once, and quite deliberately, maintaining a connection with much that he honored and felt indebted to in the past, and adopting a new relation to it and to an indeterminate number of other things. This was the man who had written to me about nudging the vanished blackfish.

He wrote to me again some six weeks later to say that he planned to be in Boston in early June to attend a Harvard reunion, and would like to meet if it were convenient, and see whether we might make some "sailing plans for the summer on my boat . . . along the home shores instead of the waters around England."

The man who climbed the five flights of stairs to the top floor apartment where I was living on West Cedar Street in Boston had short curly gray hair, thin on top, and as I saw when he reached the landing outside the door, a face starting to flow downward, with a large rounded nose and embedded eyes, mournful and prepared to be amused. He was wearing what must have seemed appropriate for Harvard at reunions: one of those open-necked knitted cotton short-sleeved shirts that seem to have been around forever, signifying the same kind of occasions. And he was carrying a six-pack as a present.

I have since seen a photograph of George as he had been only four years before that meeting, and I was struck by how much his appearance had changed in that short time. In the picture his hair was dark and he still had it all. The meltdown of his face had not even begun. It was still smooth and probably not very different from the way it had looked when he was a student at Harvard. In the picture he was already a little broad across the middle, but by the time he got to the top of the steps on West Cedar Street he had acquired a pronounced bulge at the waistline. But he was not helplessly out of breath, though he was a heavy smoker. Almost everyone seems to feel that many flights of stairs require comment, born of fatigue or embarrassment or resentment. I think George simply said, "Must keep you in shape," and came on in, scarcely trying to hide his curiosity about this oddity living in Boston, where George had grown up.

And it is still hard to imagine what he saw. If he had been looking for the sort of place where he or many of his friends might have lived, the apartment would certainly have appeared to him to be quite impossible. Starting with the stairs. Starting before them, at the entrance, which was just past the really old and acceptable red brick houses on Beacon Hill. This building was a yellow brick job dating from well into the present century—probably about the same age as George. I never noticed in him much imaginative relish for buildings, outdoors or in—much feeling for architecture or the decors and furnishings and accretions that people grew, part deliberately and part unconsciously, around their lives. So to him I suppose the place was unimaginable. At the time I thought it was just fine. Five relatively large rooms on the top floor, and from each of them a view of the Charles River or the roofscapes of Beacon Hill. I had been led to it the summer before, within hours of setting foot in Boston, and the finding of it had seemed a triumph. My guide (though only to the street door and not up the five flights) had been a short, sagging, out-of-breath woman, a kind of spirit of Beacon Hill, where she had lived all her life and now ran a real estate business of sorts, an informal, word-of-mouth apartment-renting agency out of her own small flat on the Hill, which was stuffed with old family furniture, its floors deep in ancient and rather dirty hooked rugs, the walls invisible behind shelves of old books, glass paintings, marine paintings, cases of crumbling mounted butterflies, and large, dark, unidentifiable still-lifes behind glass.

Smelling a little of stale bath salts and her cats, she had thrown a shawl over her blouse, though it was August, and puffed ahead of me down the stairs and along the street, and then had handed me the key at the street door and gone home to wait. Not for long. Even through the dirty panes the light from the river filled the empty rooms, and I went straight back to sign the lease, in which I agreed to pay seventy-five dollars a month.

Though I had never lived in Boston, the move there represented to me a kind of homecoming. Seven years I had spent in Europe, with feelings about the States changing and revolving. The urge to get back to the States was generated in part—and more than I was then ready to admit—by the deepening frustrations and claustrophobia of an unfortunate marriage in England. But besides that I felt a need to renew contact with something—I was not sure what it was, but I thought of it as being my own. Yet I did not want to go back to the States to take up an academic career, as so many of my friends had done. Finally in 1956, I was offered a grant of three thousand dollars to spend a year in association with The Poets' Theater in Cambridge, and try to write a play. It was just what I wanted, and the five empty rooms and their echoes seemed like the beginning of everything.

I furnished them, a little reluctantly at first. Some things came from the Morgan Memorial and some from the piles of furniture that people in those days regularly tossed onto the sidewalk for the dump truck; and some were odds and ends lent by friends. George stood in a front room that looked down onto West Cedar Street, and seemed uncertain where to sit down. There was an old green chaise lounge from the Goodwill Industries, and a rather small rocking chair. Finally he lowered himself into a wicker armchair—or what looked like a wicker armchair. Actually it was the remains of another rocking chair that had lost a rocker and finally washed up onto a roof-top across the street, where it leaned against the chimney for a month or so while I admired its undiminished dignity, its easy acquaintance with the weather; and one day meeting someone from the building, I inquired about it and was given it for carrying it away. Its other rocker was removed, the accumulated soot was scrubbed from the wicker, something was folded to make a cushion for the seat. George no doubt found it a little lower than he had come to expect an arm-chair to be, but then, at that moment he had decided that he did not know what to expect. Chairs were lower.

Chronologically, of course, that was the youngest that I would ever see George. But as I recall that meeting I see that he was younger, at that moment, in other senses, than he had been for some time. The trip to Boston as the new publisher of *The Nation,* the Harvard reunion, the time of year with the prospect of the summer's sailing, new departures of all kinds, had infused him with a youthful buoyancy and an openness to the unfamiliar, both of which I glimpsed more and more rarely in later years.

He had come to Harvard, he told me, to try to drum up money for *The Nation,* and he was meeting a series of people who were in town for the reunion, as well as residents of Boston and Cambridge. He told me a few of the names. He was asking, he told me, for contributions "in five figures, and not the lowest five figures," and he was getting them. He talked of some of his plans for the magazine, its temper, it position, the audience he hoped to reach.

And we talked about Richard Blackmur, who we discovered was a mutual friend. Blackmur had been my own mentor in college. I had revered the low-keyed luminous acuity of his insight, which played constantly over everything literary and non-literary. He was certainly the most perceptive and spacious literary intelligence I had ever been close to, someone of a profound, private, and—I believed—reliable, indeed oracular wisdom, however useless it may have been to him in his own life. I have never seriously doubted that that was so. It was Blackmur, I learned later, who made it possible for me to stay in graduate school studying romance languages (supposedly) when the more conventional members of the faculty had quite properly determined to boot me out.

George had known Blackmur when they were both young men: They were nearly of the same age, with Blackmur the elder by a couple of years. Just enough, perhaps, at that time in their lives, to lend a certain substance to the air of seniority which I imagine—and I have heard—cloaked Blackmur at every stage of his life. The age difference may have been further emphasized by the fact that Blackmur was working for George's brother Lincoln, on *Hound & Horn.*

There was then, and there has been ever since, something legendary about *Hound & Horn,* a kind of iconographic status that can be accounted for only partly by the quality of the writing published, the roster of contributors, the level of distinction that it maintained, or even the length of its existence, which was not so short as to present no continuity at all but brief enough to add to its posthumous reputation some of the romantic lustre associated with poets dead in their youth. No doubt there was something legendary about Lincoln himself, at Harvard, which contributed to the attitude toward the magazine, at the outset at least. And there was clearly a very different kind of legendary quality about Blackmur himself. I had heard vague references to it from the handful of people I had met who had known Blackmur in his somewhat ancient youth. To George, Blackmur must have appeared as a foil to the elaborately connected Lincoln—Blackmur, penniless and a preternaturally curious outsider, a born exile fascinated by the rococo convolutions of power, living a few steps away from the Harvard Common but preferring to educate himself rather than formally matriculate at the college, Blackmur already writing an essay a day, already seeing himself as the "conservative nonconformist," the secular conscience. Blackmur in the years that would inform his later commentary on Joyce's young hero in *Portrait of the Artist as a Young Man* and *Ulysses* with a perception, sympathy, and occasional impatience that seemed to come from firsthand experience. Blackmur already allured by the Adamses and Henry James.

He could talk, George said (and so did everyone else) about anything, and at any length, in his low measured voice, as though the intricacy of the subject amused him—about neap tides in Maine, the mating mores of grasshoppers, Rabelais, and the Rabelaisian functions of the human body. He talked slowly, rolling the syllables like lozenges, examining the ramifications of the subject as he went, opening avenues and associations (no wonder he loved Coleridge). Not at all like Lincoln's rapid-fire delivery of unquestionable opinions and final judgments. But Blackmur, inbred New Englander though he was, was an oddity in the world of Harvard, and evidently was so regarded by the regular and the regularly aspiring academic community. Some of that regard must have haunted him then and complicated his feelings about his role as an outsider. There was no doubt something unmistakably patronizing in the manner of the Harvard establishment and its devotees, including perhaps Lincoln himself, and I could sense it at moments in George's references to the Blackmur of those days: a flicker of wondering amusement. Clearly he had thought of Blackmur as a phenomenon impossible to emulate, and yet he had considered Blackmur's cranky independence, his intransigent but respectful position outside the establishment, as altogether exemplary. I realized then and later that his early friendship with Blackmur must have helped him to decide that my own way of living was more or less comprehensible. He did, in fact, have a genuine and deep regard for what he took to be independence, and he admired what seemed to him indifference to wealth, possessions, status, and general opinion. But at the same time he welcomed a precedent. Everyone does. For George it had particular importance. He was, as I came to realize, in most of the immediate aspects of his own life, a very conventional man.

We talked of sailing—the literature of it. Conrad, Eliot writing of the coast of Maine, Blackmur and the lobster fishermen, and of more practical plans. He was excited about the summer ahead, a youthful excitement. The excitement is still there in the letter he wrote about meeting in June, to sail from Mamaroneck up the New England coast. After reassurances about nothing much being needed by way of clothes, he said:

> *I will meet the 12:44 at Stamford on Friday . . . My rough plan, after spending an evening with chart and dividers, is to meander in a desultory way towards the Cape Cod Canal entrance, reaching it on Wednesday or Thursday. Then we will sail across the Gulf of Maine directly from the Canal entrance to Monhegan Island . . . Sea-gull Local #463 of Mamaroneck has been communicated with and they intend to alert Monhegan Local #436 of the arrival. The idea of this is to give the little men with the fog machines plenty of time*

*to get down on the points and do their stuff. I can practically
hear them now, saying, 'It's all right for volume, Jake, but
we gotta put more yellow in it.' It's always fun to aim for
Monhegan and wonder what in the world you will hit. Be
assured we will hit something, though, as it is almost impossible to miss the coast of Maine.*

Several of my literary friends in Boston who knew rumors about
Lincoln, Mina, and George, threw up their hands at the idea of such
a venture, especially in such company. None of the people I knew was
acquainted with any of the Kirsteins firsthand, but evidently there
were orthodox views about them, based upon unimpeachable prejudice. The angularities of Mina's and Lincoln's behavior were generally
known and had become more or less canonical, because Mina and
Lincoln, as everyone agreed, were interesting. George, on the other
hand, was referred to as though he were still the muddy young man
who had burst, in such a rage, upon Mina's tea party.

That clear sunny afternoon just past mid-summer was the first
time that I had actually set foot in the commuter land of Connecticut and Westchester County—those household words. George and
a woman friend of his picked me up out of the emerging throng of
weekenders and drove me past the colonial-style entrances and tended
lawns to the old Boston Post Road, and Mamaroneck, which (after
years in Europe) I was startled to hear referred to as a village. Taylor's Lane turned abruptly from among the diners and filling stations,
dipped at once among the tall reeds of a marsh, and climbed into the
woods beyond it. In there, George told me, was hidden the old house
where Ethel Barrymore had lived. The sunlight dappled the green
undergrowth as though it were still spring in those woods that must
have been allowed to return after the first and no doubt the second
growth had been cut off, before the present century. Another quarter
of a mile or so and the sheen of water appeared on our left. The mill
pond, George told me, which extended all the way to Rye (wherever
that might be). A short causeway led out into the still water, to a small

island topped with a house that looked as though it belonged in a movie. That was Believe-It-Or-Not Ripley's, or it had been. Empty now. Beyond the mill pond, the open water of the sound, and on the horizon, in the flattering distance, Long Island. We passed one very beautiful big old plain farmhouse, belonging to another neighbor and close friend of George's, slipped through a gate under big trees, and stopped at the back of George's house, at the end of the mill pond, where the long stone dam crossed the mill race. George's house had been the mill.

During his last years George wrote a history of it, which turned into a small history of the community. The mill, which had operated most profitably as a pumice mill, was very old. It was also exceedingly plain. Its plainness, in fact, was its only real elegance. A box, of no particular proportions, with a smaller box tacked on one side across the mill race. There was no special grace in either the building itself or the windows set into it around two stories. The clapboard painted white, the shutters red.

But the front of the house faced onto several acres of grass and old apple orchard, and to one side of the open green was a low sea-wall. Beyond that, a narrow rocky cove opened into the sound, brushed by sails in the distance. The miles of mill-pond behind it, the mill-race flowing under one end of it as the tides changed, the inlet and the sound in front of it—obviously the person who chose such a place was someone who wanted to be near water. The house, as I came to know it, revealed other things about its owner.

Anything about the interior that might have showed that it had once been a mill had long since gone. The house had been thoroughly domesticated, and remodelled several times. It had once belonged to Ezio Pinza, and as I recall it had afterwards passed into the hands of a man who had eventually killed himself there, in the downstairs sitting room where George sat and read in the evenings at home. One of George's superstitions was that he had none. I think he said that it was Pinza who had the place done over so thoroughly, changing the way the rooms were laid out, boxing in the old ceiling beams with pine. On the ground floor there was a big entrance hall with wide wooden stairs, and off to the right the sitting room over the sea wall, with its fieldstone fireplace; on the other side the guest bedroom (one of three—everything panelled in the same kind of pine.

The long living room upstairs, looking out over the sound, and the dining room overlooking the full length of the mill-pond, made a single long, light, spacious room. Everywhere the furniture was comfortable, commodious, and dull. It brought something of the department store with it. There were few signs of a woman's attention. George's marriage had ended some years before he acquired The Old Mill, and his women friends after that had had little influence on the house. The nautical motif was rather heavy. Clocks set in brass capstan wheels, that rang the hours in ships' bells. Ship patterns on the bedspreads and curtains, on the plates at the table, and the lampshades. The real distinction, apart from the light, the space, and the views of water, may have meant little to those guests of George's who were not addicted to maritime art: There was a fine series of Japanese prints of ships (gifts, I think, from Lincoln) on the stairs, and in the main rooms a number of large ship models, some of considerable age, including a few remarkable wooden bas-reliefs of ships on carved and painted seas, which had been presents from Mina.

Out in the offing, at the mouth of the inlet, George's thirty-eight-foot yawl, *Skylark*, rode at her mooring. George had acquired *Skylark* soon after the war, and she had not been sailing for more than a few years, but for some reason she was referred to familiarly or fondly as though she were much older, a kind of heirloom. It may have had something to do with the old standards of craftsmanship with which she had been built—vintage work, from before the war. Certainly it conveyed some of the affection, and perhaps some sense of vulnerability, that George felt for her.

We loaded the luggage, and the groceries for the next few days, into a tender, and ferried them out to *Skylark* and settled in. George's friend who had come with him to the station pushed off in the boat.

The sound was still as we stowed things away for the trip, but by the time we had finished a breeze had sprung up. It was not the northwester that had been promised by the weather forecasters, with blue skies and bright sun. Instead, it was swinging in from points farther south, and there were mats of low overcast above the island in the distance, but it was a good breeze nevertheless, and fair weather had been prophesied. In the latter part of the afternoon we slipped the mooring and made sail from Mamaroneck, heading for a small harbor on the Long Island shore that George called the Sand Spit.

I could see why he liked the place as we approached, in the long mid-summer evening light. An arm of sand bar enclosed a deep narrow basin of calm water, a kind of curving lagoon surrounded by rather steeply shelving beaches. Only one other boat was there as we made our way in through the channel and dropped anchor, but as we sat in the cockpit having supper one more followed us, and another made it in with the last light. Their portholes glowed for a while, but the little harbor was remarkably quiet.

But early in the night the wind began to pick up, and it rose until the stays were whining. George seemed to be suffering from some kind of digestive disorder and I heard the hand pump in the head gasping and belching, and then doing it again in a while. Each time the accompanying note in the rigging was louder and more shrill, and the motion of the boat swinging at anchor was more pronounced. George was sleeping in the bow, and my bunk was in the central cabin. I saw him slip past several times and go up on deck, cigarette burning. Once I asked whether everything was all right and he grunted.

The wind was howling when I woke at first light, and George was up in the cockpit.

"What a night," he said. He pointed to two of the other boats that had dragged their anchors and were almost up on the beach. He had come up on deck in the night to check, and had let out more anchor cable. One of the other boats had nearly collided with us in the dark. Our own anchor had held better than theirs, and we were swinging on the long cable. We had some breakfast, standing in the wind, and listened to the marine forecast. There had been a little surprise for the weather people. A hurricane had been moving along the New England coast, laying about itself as it went, but that had been a few days earlier, and the storm, according to the meteorologists, had blown out to sea and away. But apparently it was not so. There had been an atmospheric change of mind. The promised northwester had not come in strongly enough, or something unforeseen had happened, and the storm had come back, thumping against the coast, not invading it, but obviously not ready to leave. The wind that had been howling most of the night was as loud as ever. Outside the channel, beyond the sand bar, we could see surf breaking almost over the bar. All sorts of small craft warnings were in effect. We were not exactly a small craft, and George thought the wind would probably drop a little after sunrise. We could put out the other anchor and stay where we were, or we could get out of there, which George decided to do.

When breakfast was put away we broke out a jib, and George started the engine. We eased up on the anchor and hauled it aboard, and then headed out through the channel into the surf. *Skylark* climbed over the breakers like a dory, and we made it, wet and well shaken down, and there we were, out in the whipped, gusty, uncertain temper of the sound, a very different place from the one we had crossed in the evening light. We seemed to be the only boat out there. But in fact, outside the breakers the waves were not particularly high. The sky was blue, and the sun was bright on the blown spray. We headed east up the sound under full sail, running before the wind, listening to the marine operator, and occasional accounts of boats in trouble, vessels dismasted. But the wind seemed fairly steady and we kept a good distance from all charted navigational hazards, and after a while as we boiled along and the morning warmed up, it all began to seem normal. George not only left me at the wheel but went below and busied himself stowing things and studying the chart.

I must have been up there alone for a couple of hours in the sun and wind and I began to realize that I had not had much sleep the night before. My eyes were beginning to sting with the glare and the constant fine blowing spray. Far ahead of us, in the haze that hid the horizon, I could make out something that appeared to be a vessel, but its shape looked very improbable. I watched it through the binoculars, but I could see no hull, down in the haze. There appeared to be three masts, moving together. But, as the image grew, they looked like square-rigged masts, there were yard-arms. And they were moving into the wind, without a stitch of canvas that I could see. A little closer, and the image was definitely that of a square-rigger, and a very old-fashioned one at that. I began to run over what I remembered of the story of the Flying Dutchman. Finally I called George, with some hesitation, because it sounded so unlikely.

"There's something strange heading this way."

"Yes."

"A square-rigged vessel."

"Yeah."

"Looks very old. A brig, maybe. Or even some kind of galleon."

"A what?"

"Galleon."

"Yeah."

"Coming straight for us. Into the wind. With no sails up."

"What were you drinking last night?"

He appeared in the companionway and said, "You ought to wear sunglasses in this glare."

"You look."

He took the glasses and looked where I pointed, and then went on looking for a long time. Then he started to laugh, and handed the glasses back.

What the haze had hidden from me until then was the tug, far in advance of the apparition, towing it. The vision itself, as it came closer, turned out to be the *Mayflower*—the replica, that is—being towed to New York after its much-publicized voyage across the Atlantic. Slowly she disappeared behind us, bucking and rolling as she went, and back there, as she vanished, heavy clouds were beginning to build. By the time we nosed our way, in mid-afternoon, among the rock islands of a small archipelago named The Needles, off the Connecticut coast, the wind had shifted south and had begun to lash us with heavy rain.

George and, as I recall it, the marine operator, assured us that the wind would drop after sunset. But in fact it rose higher, and then higher, and the rain sluiced across the portholes all night. By morning the sky was clearing but the wind was as rough as ever and the waves were higher. We broke out the anchor in the last of the rain and headed on up the coast. By late afternoon the sound was quiet and smooth and we slipped into a harbor like a mirror on the island of Cuttyhunk, and spent the evening talking and reading, chatting with the geese that came cruising out to us looking for handouts. The island was bathed in golden mid-summer light, and the storm had gone at last—we thought.

But next morning the wind was back, and our exit from Cuttyhunk was not quite as wild a ride as the departure from the Sand Spit, but the swell out in the sound was high. And so it went, on up the coast, to Marion, Massachusetts, and then the Cape Cod Canal: bright, clear, sunny days, whipped by winds, with dark clouds haunting the southern horizon, and occasional squalls of lashing rain. We chugged through the canal, with terns wheeling and diving around us, and emerged at the northern end in late afternoon. George decided to make a night run across the gulf of Maine, heading for Monhegan Island. Even though, he said, the wind would probably drop completely after sunset, and we might have to motor a good part of the way.

But as Cape Cod receded behind us, the wind really began to get serious, hitting us from the southwest, with occasional gusts from the southeast. The daylight faded; we lost sight of the shore, and the clouds along the southern horizon darkened and rose over us. Out of the lee of the Cape, the sea turned mean, and flung us from one wave to crash into the next one. We learned—too late to do much about it—that the hurricane that supposedly had died out several days earlier had still not left the coast, and the winds of the past few days had been small rearguard actions that it had set up to give us the idea of what we had missed. But what was now overtaking us was a freak return—not, fortunately, of the full force of the hurricane, but of its death-throes.

They were quite impressive enough. Huge waves, from several quarters astern, broke clear over the cockpit. The wind became increasingly erratic, with heavy gusts followed by moments that seemed airless. We shortened sail—George shortened sail, while I stayed at the wheel—and so the night lurched on. In the center of it was the binnacle light, and under it the compass card dancing like a kite. If whichever of us was not at the wheel lay down on the bench in the cockpit, it would only be a moment before a wave broke over us, or a violent roll pitched him off onto the deck. We hurtled forward as though falling downstairs, and struck the troughs between waves as though they were floors. When I was at the wheel there were sickening instants when I thought that the compass card had spun ninety degrees and more, and that we were out of control and about to be swamped broadside. In a moment when we could hear each other I asked George whether it was always like this when the wind dropped.

It did, in fact, drop a little, shortly before sunrise. I was at the wheel again as the first light began to seep into the sky. The swells seemed as high and heavy as ever, but imperceptibly they had grown more regular, and so had the wind, which lightened steadily with the approach of dawn. As the gray sea became visible I saw a trawler not far ahead of us, heading out to sea. Our courses looked to me too convergent for comfort and I called George, who had gone below by then, to tell him.

"Ram the bastard," George called back. "He'll soon learn." Evidently he too thought that the storm was past. A moment later he appeared in the companionway looking noticeably older than the day before.

"Jesus, your eyes look red," he said. He stood in the companionway looking slowly around the horizon, and then, after pointing out the direction in which I should expect the first glimpse of Monhegan Island, he turned in for a nap. An hour or so later, when my watch was about finished, he peered up out of the cabin again and asked, "Seen Monhegan yet?"

I could see nothing in the direction I had been watching, except waves and the blue sky.

"Not yet," I said.

"Funny" he said. "It's nine o'clock. We should have seen Monhegan by now."

He came on up, reached for the glasses, turned toward the bow. Before even raising the glasses, he said, "There's Monhegan. Right there."

"Can't see a thing," I said. My eyes were so tired that it was a long moment before I could make out the shape of the steep island, which under ordinary circumstances would already have been visible for most of an hour. We had breakfast in the cockpit, sailing past under the gray cliffs and the lighthouse, and on to Tenant's Harbor, a quiet anchorage among a few lobster boats. And sleep.

By the time we were ready to wash up and wander around the few streets of Tenant's Harbor, a low overcast had drifted in from the sea, and a light rain was falling. We clambered onto the wharf, watching two men in the lobster boats unloading their catch, and walked on up into the town, telling each other what we knew about lobstering and the lives of lobstermen, Blackmur's poems about lobstering, and the progressive overfishing and destruction of marine flora and fauna along the Atlantic coast by new techniques bent to familiar motives. The streets were empty. Frame houses tucked behind lilac bushes, under old trees. Lace curtains drawn all the way across the ground floor windows. On our way to the main street to buy a paper, George told me that on that day a woman who had been his companion for several years, and from whom he had separated a year or so before, was getting married. He said very little about it. As I remember she had wanted to marry George, but she had wanted marriage more than he had, and they had parted as a result. I learned a little more about his private life—he spoke of his marriage that had come apart while he was away in the South Pacific during WWII—but only a little, and it was clear that George was not prone to talking about such things.

But by the end of the trip, or my part of it, a few days later, I had a fairly clear, if still very sketchy, notion of the nature of George's history with women from his college days on. He liked the company of women, but his manner with women in general was rather old-fashioned: courtly, and likely to be unconsciously patronizing. His views were conventionally sexist, far more than he would have admitted. I found it troubling, and more so as I came to know him better and could see that the fixed attitude that was there in most of his dealings with women was inseparably tangled with his own emotional inhibitions, his profound difficulty in expressing, returning, or even tolerating open displays of affection with women with whom he was involved. As we walked through the streets of Tenant's Harbor I saw that what I had at first supposed to be a simple fatigue was also depression: the thought of the wedding, and its place in his own story, moving in upon the day and wakening his own ignored, suppressed, conflicting feelings, his regrets and complex resentments.

The remainder of the trip had its small events. Rocks draped in basking seals. The beauty of the coast, the rock islands and the stands of forest. The birds. George liked to listen to the ball game, mid-afternoon. I am so without interest in organized sports that I usually do not even know what kind of game is being referred to, and the elaborately excited nasal gabble of the sports commentator seemed a terrible intrusion upon the quiet of the coast, the shushing of the waves, the voices of birds and seals. It brought back a world of barber shops. If I was not at the wheel, usually I went up forward of the mast, with a book and a pair of binoculars. But by the end of the trip I had learned something, not about baseball, but about the temperamental ways of Ted Williams', and his effects on his detractors and admirers. I even suspect that George himself was as captivated by Ted Williams behavior as he was by the game itself. It was certainly what he returned to, when the game was over.

And we talked more about political matters, events in the news and what they seemed to portend, than I had ever done with anyone. During my years in Europe I had followed the news, much of the time rather vaguely, and my reading of newspapers in general has always been erratic, depending on what has been going on. But I had come back to the States with an appetite for the life of the place, and I had begun to read not only a couple of national papers and *The Nation*, but some of the local sheets. (There was one tabloid called the *Mid-Town Journal* that I used to pick up, not just for the lurid items that purported to be news and were so obviously retouched in the telling as to sound utterly unreal, but for the rococo flourishes of its peculiar journalistic style, which went in for such heavy alliteration that it blurred what meaning remained, as the music fogs the words of a libretto. The content of this crusading sheet eddied around the nefarious doings of the metropolitan area, and focused, with lubricious righteousness, on the functionings of the underworld. I forget whether it was published weekly or twice a week—the issues tended to be rather repetitious. A single headline remains with me intact. No number of the paper was complete without its account of a raid on a house of ill-repute, and the regular rhetoricians must have been taxed to find new ways to announce the latest triumph of decency. This one, in large letters, trumpeted, "Bags Brothel Boss And Babes.")

The ruminations with George about what was happening in the country and in the world became a single conversation that we fell into at the beginning, as something already familiar, and resumed over the years as though it had never been interrupted. The tenor of it was frequently somber and seldom optimistic, but it was pierced by George's vein of black humor. It was a quirky gift, delighting in outrageous twists and exaggerations, sometimes plain silly adolescent, downright atrocious, but there were times when George seemed one of the funniest people I had known.

By the time I left George, and *Skylark*, in Camden harbor, where my place was taken by an old friend of George's, a fellow officer on a troop ship in the South Pacific in WWII, the conversation, its tone, and I suppose its limitations, had come to be taken for granted. Such things often do not survive the circumstances that brought them about. In this case the running dialogue was the staple of a friendship that survived many changes in both of our lives. As for *Skylark*, when she was put into drydock at the end of the season, it turned out that an impressive number of her oak ribs had been cracked in that night crossing of the Gulf of Maine.

The trip itself, of course, became part of the family fund of allusion, and some of the conversation and some of its tone passed into the correspondence that really began after that sail was over. The last time I saw George, almost thirty years later, he handed me—I realized that he felt some urgency to do so—a box containing the whole of the correspondence between us. I winced as I looked through my own letters, the earlier ones in particular. There was, to begin with, the usual shock at hearing one's own voice. But worse than that was the bumptious manner, the current of facetious banter incorporating snatches of imitations, affectations, adolescent inanity. It was easy enough, even after three decades, to recognize the sources of some of the imitations. "Chum," as a form of address, I had picked up from Berryman, who clearly had picked it up from somewhere else. I was a little surprised at it all, even though I knew that those letters were full of family monkeyshines that would be embarrassing to reread. But the brashness on the one hand, and the ponderous and marble jawing on the other, were unpleasant to rediscover in all their indelibility. It was the adolescent quality that was as startling as anything else, for in fact I was in my thirties already when the earliest of those letters were written. I am sure that I was, in fact, far less mature at the time than I liked to believe. The correspondence and the friendship allowed me to reveal some of the nonsense that was usually more soberly attired. Later I imagined, as we do, that having finally outgrown things they disappeared. In any case, the embarrassment itself at the rediscovery is really vain and foolish, a clinging to an image on a bubble.

I suspect that the adolescent tone is an indication of something else that friends of George suggested to me over the years: He became, from the beginning, a paternal figure for me, and acted toward me in some ways as a parent for the rest of his life, though both of us would have shied away from putting it that way. When my wife read the letters recently she suggested that George had suddenly come to represent for me the parent with whom, long after childhood, I had a good time, and that as a response I regressed happily to the showing-off and the antics of adolescence, out of high spirits and a feeling of liberation. I was also presenting what I took to be a sympathetic imitation of George's own humor, which was not above a certain undergraduate turn. The letters are relaxed and imprudent, and yet it is remarkable, on looking through them and recalling the years they evoke, to notice how much was never mentioned in them, or was mentioned only in passing, or long after the fact.

Things, for instance, having to do with what would be termed our private lives, particularly emotional attachments with other people When I began to read through the letters I was struck by what was unmistakably affection. It was not openly expressed, heaven knows—George signed his letters "Yours." My own silly banter was one of the manifestations of the affection, and the very promptness and attentiveness of George's letters, particularly during the sixties, was another. But though the letters display an obvious confidence in many shared interests, enthusiasms, dislikes, they are not really intimate. Which is something else they share with a certain sort of parental relation—the sort that I was used to, and from all I know the sort that George had known. It would never have occurred to me to speak to either of my parents about girls, my feelings about them, or anything that happened with them. I assumed that they assumed that such things did not exist at all, or existed only as distant surreptitious interests that would be embarrassing if named. It would have been unthinkable to raise such a subject with my own father when I was growing up. And with my mother—once when I was about sixteen, I think, she asked me solemnly never to do anything I could not tell her about, and then told me that she trusted me. So when opportunities arose, they were far from home and never divulged.

And George spoke to me occasionally, with evident approval, of certain relationships of his own, relatively close associations centered around work, or business, or some interest such as sailing, that he had had for years with individuals about whose private lives he knew nothing at all. He was repelled by public displays of affection of any kind. The surprising thing, it might seem, is that there is as much personal warmth in the letters as there is. But of course George was not as remote or forbidding as he pretended to be, even in his last years when he had withdrawn until his old friends found it hard to talk with him about any personal matters at all. The real warmth of his nature had been deeply suppressed very early, but it had survived, along with a mordant wit and a rather louring charm, and it was why George had friends around him who were fond of him until he died.

No doubt the accepted exclusion of emotional intimacy, or of reference to certain emotions (for indignation, straight or burlesque, and other feelings about public events, and admiration of natural or artistic phenomena were permissible) led to awkwardness, as it had led to remoteness from parents, and it helped to turn the facetious exchanges, as time went on, into the twitches of a mannerism. The impulse to greater candor that was natural in the situation was frustrated, and emerged, if it did at all, stunted and distorted beyond recognition. About personal matters, the letters are stiffer than our conversations were. It was obviously even harder to write back and forth about such things than it was to talk about them.

And of course the letters cover only the periods when George and I were some distance apart, often with an ocean between us. But during those years I spent a great deal of the time—more than half of most years—abroad. Soon after the first cruise on *Skylark* I returned to Europe, grudgingly. My English wife, to whom I was then married, had been away from England and her London house for longer than she wanted to be. She invoked her aging mother. The marriage itself was hopeless, and the return was a death blow to it, but I was not yet ready to admit as much to myself. It would be years before I could discuss the matter with anyone. That sort of thing had never been mentioned in my family either, though my parents stared out of opposite windows. Divorces were things that simply did not happen among people we knew, and my father always refused, as a minister, to marry anyone who had been divorced. There is no allusion to the unraveling current of my marital situation in the letters. Instead, there are dutiful references to the health, opinions, and activities of the woman to whom I would remain legally married for some years to come.

As for George's own life of the heart, he said, at the time of that first cruise on *Skylark,* that Miss Right was probably one of the seals who lay sunning on the rocks or swam close to the boat to gaze up out of the water. It was those huge soulful eyes, he said, that he would not be able to resist. Miss Right's name was Phoebe. All seals were named Phoebe. After I left *Skylark* George wrote to me that he had met Miss Right just outside of a herring net and that they had conversed for "virtually an entire afternoon, and she explained to me the difficulties of breaking down fish weirs."

Soon after the trip, though, he met Jane Cianfarra at one of the parties which he so seldom attended. Jane was beautiful, gentle, and tragic. She had been married to a New York *Times* correspondent in Rome and had been returning with her husband and two children on the *Andrea Doria.* The prow of the *Stockholm* struck the *Andrea Doria* at night in the fog, knifing directly into their cabin, cutting it in half. She had never seen her husband or infant again, and her small daughter had been found unconscious the following morning on the bow of the Swedish vessel. She had scooped up at the moment of impact. Jane herself had been pinned under wreckage, with both legs broken, and was rescued by an Italian steward.

Jane's fragility, for George, was one of her endless attractions and he paid court to her with a certain awe and no great hope of success. But the courtship did continue, and he even managed to entice her out sailing with him briefly before *Skylark* was taken out of the water for the winter. The attention, and perhaps even the sailing, may have been just what she needed, and Jane accepted the proposal that George had wanted to make from the start. They were married that same autumn, and Jane seemed to settle at once into The Old Mill. For someone scarred she was very easy to be with, and George was completely devoted to her.

Before Christmas he wrote, "Jane wanted to send you a candle which we saw in a hardware store about four-and-a-half feet tall and two feet in diameter, which had been marked down and was for use on the lawns of factory buildings to show that they welcomed Christmas. I put my foot down, though, having seen your apartment, because you wouldn't have been able to get it in." The day after New Year's he wrote, "We went by the store again the day after Christmas and the candle is only $2.95 now. Seems very reasonable, and if you only add the $25 express charges, it seemed to Jane a real bargain."

We had booked passage on the *Flandres* for Plymouth, England, the following March. "We are both very sorry to be going," I wrote to George a couple of weeks before the move, "naturally in some-what different ways." Jane helped to shepherd our assorted trunks and gypsy baggage through on their way from Boston to the pier.

She and George were about to leave for England too, and they got there not long after our own return to a cold London spring. George, Jane, and I spent a few delightful days driving through southwest England—Bath and Cornwall. We arrived at Stonehenge on the day they raised the first of the fallen stones. George bought every book he could find on the subject and seemed to have read them all by dinner time. He was a happy man.

That year I was in Europe all summer and George and Jane sailed, mostly by themselves. Despite the catastrophe in her history Jane turned out to be an enthusiastic and extremely capable sailor—except for fogs. George's letters were full of incidents of their summer sailing far up—or far down—the coast of Maine. During those months I was gradually but steadily captivated by the half-ruined farmhouse in France that I had bought four years earlier with a tiny legacy that I had been left by a maiden aunt, and my own letters were full of details of the place. And we wrote to each other about pieces for *The Nation*, and about the events in the papers, with which George, as always, was better acquainted than I was.

I did not get back to New York until the autumn of 1960, but I saw George and Jane on other visits of theirs to Europe. Then for several years I contrived to spend the winters in New York, living on the Lower East Side, much of the time on my own. George, of course, found the location, the address, the apartments unimaginable, but accepted them with the fond tolerance with which a parent might indulge an incorrigible child. Like much of the rest of my life, they were consigned to the category of bohemian eccentricity, crazy but inevitable.

He felt he had to make similar accommodations for my clothes. His own were altogether conventional and mine were often less formal than he thought the circumstances warranted. On one trip in Europe together he fussed almost every evening because I had brought no sport jacket but only a knitted cardigan, and he was worried that the country restaurants might not admit us. From time to time I was lent a tie. In time he repeated with relish the tale of our walking down Madison or Lexington, in New York, at around three one afternoon and going into a series of almost empty restaurants where we were told they could not seat us. He claimed it was my jacket (I was wearing a tie that day). I suggested that the hour might have had something to do with it, but he preferred his own explanation, which forced us, he insisted, to have a very bad lunch in the end.

Poetry itself, much of it, slipped into the inexplicably eccentric category at times. His way of speaking of some of it survives, for instance, in a paragraph about St. John Perse:

> *Everyone here in literary circles says that my sister's friend Leger is the greatest poet since the greatest poet. As you probably know, his* Seamarks *has just been published. I like the sea, Bill, and the title had the sea in it, so I tried to read it. I feel like one of the fools who don't think* Hamlet *is a great play, but in the quietest possible voice, as I hide my head in a comic book—which I can understand—I have to confess that I don't like* Seamarks *very much. Indeed, I think the children who tell you about their really imaginative images are somewhat more interesting and even more exciting. Any-*

way, Time *magazine agrees with Mina and I believe even
the reviewer who is reviewing the book for* The Nation *says
it is great. I have a little difficulty with the reviewer too, but
perhaps you can explain it to me when you see it.*

The tone persisted when George and Jane and I went to the theater together, which we did about once a week when I was in New York by myself. Pinter, whose plays Jane and I loved, drove George into flights of eloquent incomprehension. And Genet:

I had a little difficulty at The Balcony *by Genet, which
Jane and I saw the other night. It's a play about a whore-
house and there's a bishop and a general and a judge in
it, except they are not really bishops, generals, or judges.
They are shoe salesmen, railway clerks and fish peddlers
who dress up like other people for kicks. We got that far
pretty well which was the first act but then—the second
act. It seems that they really turned into bishops, generals and judges and coffins keep coming in the doors on the
corners. Jane thought it was symbolic of the triumph of
Franco in Spain. I thought it showed the tough financial
plight of whorehouses. You see, there is a wide range of
interpretation that can be put on Genet's work but right
in the second act the range of interpretation narrowed as
the audience got smaller and smaller. Each pair of eyes saw
a different thing but there were fewer and fewer eyes and
finally I could see nothing.*

My barely surviving marriage apparently was entered in the category of artistic eccentricity, along with my apartments and clothes. He referred to it, when he did at all, as though it were quite what he would have expected. But then the whole subject of marriage was one that he had dismissed years earlier, deciding that it was on the whole a terrible institution—except for his being married to Jane.

I loved living on the Lower East Side. But the farmhouse in France, the small village, the open countryside, drew me back—I missed them when I was not there. And I missed New York when I was in France, and there was no solution. When I was away, George wrote to me with admiration about the beginnings of the black civil rights movement. The date of the letter was April 27, 1960:

> *The truth is, that an entirely new spirit has come over the young in this country even during the last year or so. The most refreshing evidence of it is the sympathetic picketing which is going on in virtually every college in America to support the Negro cafeteria sit-down students who are struggling for equality in the South. The Negro students themselves are taking the leadership and I can assure you that they are any-thing but soft. They are being jailed, fined, beaten, harassed and generally made as miserable as possible.*

Their actions led him to reflect on the new generation altogether. "Personally, I think that a generation which has led the world through a depression and the worst war in history and up to the brink of another one should retire gracefully and soon."

I had already become involved in the peace movement in England and had written about the third Aldermaston march for *The Nation*. Back in the States, I edited the poetry for *The Nation* for a while in 1961 and continued to write articles about anti-nuclear protest for *The Nation*, and then a long piece for *The New Yorker* about the "Everyman" demonstration in San Francisco in the spring of 1962. *The New Yorker* was inching cautiously toward political comment. Their first real coverage of the growing black movement had been James Baldwin's superb *The Fire Next Time*, and the "Everyman" essay was to be the first writing they would publish on the anti-nuclear movement. It was set up, the galleys were corrected, and less than a week before it was scheduled to appear, the Cuban missile crisis was announced. Immediately *The New Yorker* killed it. I was told that at such a time it would be inappropriate. I called George to tell him and he said, "We'll give you the Christmas issue."

Living in downtown Manhattan, the reverberations of the Cuban missile crisis seemed to become part of the neglected architecture itself. On the street corners and in the bars I heard the usual louts and loud-mouths declaring that "we should have dropped the bomb on them long ago." Literary friends who described themselves as liberals insisted that Jack had done a fine and essential thing, and perhaps he had. Others who had always made a point of taking no interest in "politics" called up at odd hours to ask whether I thought we would be bombed. I began to be pursued by the thought that if in all this madhouse, someone were to ask me what I thought would be a good way to live, I would not have a very clear answer, and it seemed to me that it was time to try to find one. The farm in France, of which I had grown inordinately fond, appeared to me more than ever to be a piece of great good fortune. I realized that I did not know how to grow a single thing that I ate every day, and I decided to go back there and try to learn to grow food in the garden—something all my peasant neighbors knew how to do.

The decision coincided with George's beginning to talk of leaving *The Nation*. I have a clear, obscurely uncomfortable image of his first raising the subject. He and Jane and I had stayed late at *The Nation*, which was then down on Sixth Avenue below Fourth Street. We were in George's car, and had performed some errand of Jane's, I believe, in the Village, and we were driving on the short block of Tenth Street, east of Greenwich Avenue, past the Jefferson Library. We stopped at the red light and as it turned green and we swung left to head uptown, George announced that he thought it was time for him to sell *The Nation*. The car was full of tobacco smoke. I remember how the back of the car seat looked, and the Ansonia Pharmacy and the laundry as we passed. George said he had had the magazine for ten years and that was enough. He said he hated being in the city, the filth, the violence, the racket. He said he would be quite happy sailing in the summer and reading the complete works of Jefferson, and maybe writing a book.

He did not sell the magazine at once. But the subject returned in his letters that summer and in the months that followed. In fact it was more than three years after that before he sold *The Nation*. And his letters about the American scene remained as intent and unawed as ever. He wrote with a familiar distaste of the brew-up for the 1964 presidential election, in letter after letter, and with only a few days to go, he summed up his views of the spectacle:

> *This country is performing its quadrennial ballet about the forthcoming election. The somewhat irreverent Episcopal Bishop of Washington last week said, from his pulpit, that the American people were confronted with a ghastly choice. They could either elect a man so stupid that he endangered not only the peace of the nation but whatever domestic tranquility survived through our current tensions, or we could select a crook whose ethics were so appalling that on an annual salary which had never exceeded $25,000 a year, he was able to amass a $10,000,000 fortune. That bad Bishop was referring to none other than Lyndon B. Johnson who is my candidate for the presidency . . .*

The following spring we traveled again in Europe. George had suggested an "Ajax box-top trip" with himself as Ajax the host, and he wanted to be told where to go. So he and Jane came to the farm at Lacan, with a rented station wagon, and from there we drove through the Gorges du Tarn to Provence: Nimes, Arles, Avignon, Aix, Les Baux, La Camargue. George's inhibitions about poetry and contemporary writing extended to French food. We stopped together for a picnic ("You pick it out") and the market of Aix offered up the treasures of the south to fill our filets. When the contents were spread on the grass outside the bird sanctuary on La Camargue, George sampled a shaving of this and a taste of that, and finally seized upon a liver sausage and moved it over beside him protectively. "I don't think you'd like it," he said, as he spread it lavishly on his bread. He said it was kind of like liverwurst.

From France we loaded ourselves onto the boat to Corsica, a rough night passage that kept Jane awake and unhappy; and then we drove around Corsica for days. Jane was delighted to be back in southern Europe again. Everyone was. George kept saying that it was something that he would never have done on his own, and that it was the first time he had liked France. The landscape, the wine, the meals, the wedding party to which we were invited (and where they got us, George included, to sing "Drink To Me Only With Thine Eyes"), started him talking about his brother and sister, until the laughing became dangerous on the winding mountain roads. As for Ajax, George insisted afterwards that it had not cost him a cent. One outing on the way back had taken care of the whole thing.

> *We took off, as you recall, in a lovely drunken haze of good feeling about our successful cruise in Corsica, and landed in Nice soon afterward. Jane could only think of the Negresco, so we proceeded to what must be the world's lushest hotel. There were green velvet spreads on the bed and red satin on the walls, crystal chandeliers and Jeezel it wasn't like what we had been staying in at Corsica at all. After a few more drinks, we proceeded to the municipal casino where there was a game going on with a roulette wheel and with the green cloth with numbers on it which I have seen in casinos. Other than the fact that the tools of the trade seemed to be the same, I was unable to gather any similarity between this game and others I have played at various pleasure spots. I put my little money on the number zero a number of times in order to find out what the game was like. The little white ball fell in the zero on the wheel three times in succession and people shoveled great wads of francs at me. At this point I explained to Jane that I didn't know this game, and we left. The following day we took what must be the world's most endless airplane journey back to the States.*

By the latter part of that year (1965), in preparation for selling *The Nation* to James Storrow and retiring, George started to gather material for his book on "The Rich":

> *I have not had a great deal of time to study those rich with the intensity that I would like. I have, however, begun compiling the clips of their more outstanding suicides which occur at least once a month. The most recent was the heir to the Heinz money who said in his farewell letter, 'there is no place for me here . . . , I'm kind of philosophical, you see, and the book is going to be kind of philosophical too. It's going to have weight and substance and it's going to be thoughtful. It's going to be controversial too and by the time I'm finished with it I'll be thoroughly ashamed of it. But it will sell like mad. It's that same awful story of the three successive zeros at the roulette table at Nice.*

The sale of *The Nation* was announced at the beginning of 1966. The *Times* and *Newsweek* wrote what he called "respectful stories" about the magazine and his years there. He admitted that "in a way I am proud of my stay at *The Nation.*" Mentioning the press comments on his influence he said, "Maybe I made the sheet part of the establishment, but I would rather think that dissent is a little more acceptable these days due to the lunacy of the actions of the most powerful nation on this or any other earth."

He and Jane spent much of that winter sailing in the Virgin Islands. *Skylark,* now an aging wooden vessel, was not best suited for sailing in the Caribbean, and six months after the sale of *The Nation,* George sold *Skylark* too, and bought, in Maine, a fiberglass Bermuda 40, which he and Jane christened *Shag.* Early in 1966 George's beloved Newfoundland dog Skipper died suddenly. George refused to be "sentimental" about it, but the loss grieved him, and Skipper's death, the parting with *Skylark,* and the sale of *The Nation* must have reflected each other uncomfortably. He continued to work on his book about the rich, and his research filled him with a kind of gruesome hilarity.

He remained convinced that the book would "sell like mad," and his publisher, Houghton Mifflin, shared his optimism. He had some of the same mixed feelings about it that he had about money itself. The book was bound to succeed, he said, simply because of its subject: Being rich was something everybody wanted to know about. He was somewhat concerned as to what he would do with the money, which he said he did not want. Give it to Harvard, perhaps. But in fact *The Rich* was scooped, as Houghton Mifflin explained to George, by another book on the same subject whose publisher and author had learned of George's book and hurried to get theirs out first. The earlier book got all the reviews, and when George's came out shortly afterwards, it was largely ignored.

It bothered him, more than he would say, of course, and it dampened whatever ardor he may have had for writing, and discouraged his already shaky faith in his abilities in that direction. And in so doing, it confirmed his lifelong suspicion that Mina and Lincoln's assessment of his talents had been right. He planned other books, or talked of them, but with no great expectations about their reception anywhere. The one he came to work on most steadily was a modest and rather plodding series of reminiscences of sailing, but he was not even under any illusions about finding a publisher for it.

Since the spring of 1963 I had been living year round at the old farmhouse in southern France, but in the fall of 1966 I returned to New York to be present at the rehearsals of Lorca's *Yerma*, which I had been commissioned to translate for Lincoln Center. With that return I resumed the pattern of spending part of the year in New York and part of it in France. I saw more of George but of course wrote to him less. And there was almost no indication in the letters of the continuing dissolution of my marriage and the disturbances that accompanied it. George knew of other relations of mine, but he seemed to prefer to believe that, odd and remote though the marriage obviously was, it represented something stable in my life, and it was as well for it to remain there. Beyond that he appeared to pay no further attention to it.

Besides, to judge from his letters and the time I spent with him and Jane, George was as happy in his own marriage as he was capable of being. In the autumn of 1966 I spent some time with them outfitting the new Bermuda 40, on the Miami River, and taking her out for her shake-down cruise among the Keys, and the time confirmed this sense of their life together.

In the years of my shuttling back and forth between rural France and downtown Manhattan I had invariably spent the summers on the farm, but in 1968 I decided to come to New York for the summer. Carolyn Stoloff offered me her tiny charming, but very hot apartment on West Eighth Street in the Village, across from the old Eighth Street Bookstore, and I saw George and Jane fairly regularly when they were in Mamaroneck. That summer I noticed a change in George that disturbed me. His marital contentment seemed unimpaired, but he grumbled and snarled about the young, about the student sit-ins at Columbia, the SDS, the long hair, the middle-class kids who were too spoiled and lazy to work—the "youth," in fact, whom for years he had been urging to dissent, and who at last were dissenting. The change seemed to have come over him quite suddenly, in the course of the winter. We argued about it. About George the editor who had followed with empathy the nuclear protests, the black civil rights movement, the first waves of campus unrest, and about what had happened to him. I had expected him to rejoice as I did in what seemed to me the long overdue groundswell of youthful recalcitrance. What form did he expect it to take, after all?

I realized as we talked that the change in him was more disturbing than I wanted to believe, and that it represented something that had been happening in George since he gave up *The Nation,* and before— something that had been part of the impulse to give it up. It was an angry rejection of some of the very things that he had professed but with which he was not entirely at ease and did not know why. It was a symptom of old inconsistencies, and of age itself, and of a never assuaged sense of complex betrayals. It made him sound like some of the very people of whom he had spoken for years, with contempt, and it revealed some of his own mixed feelings about those people and their world. It seemed as we talked that our new and deepening disagreement must be unreal, that it must be some passing impatience and frustration, and that the values he had evoked for so many years would surely reinstate their perspective. But at the same moment I was aware of an abyss opening between us, across which, if it remained there, it would become harder and harder for us to hear each other.

In July I returned from a few days' visit to my parents in western Pennsylvania. I had driven back, in ten hours, in the secondhand car that I had bought that summer with George's guidance, and I let myself into the hot apartment and called up The Old Mill to let them know I was back, and to talk about the visit. A woman's voice answered the phone, as Jane usually did. It did not sound like Jane, but I heard only "Hello," and asked, "Jane?" It was the German housekeeper, who recognized my voice and said, "Mrs. Kirstein is dead."

She went on at once to explain that Jane had died suddenly in the night, two nights before. Mr. Kirstein had found her dead in the morning. He had called me but of course I was not in New York, and at the moment he had not been able to lay hands on the number at my parents' house. He had called up his old wartime shipmate in Ohio, and had flown out there a few hours after Jane's body had been taken from the house. I called him there in Ohio and arranged to meet him when he came back.

His upbringing, his lifelong habits, the images on which he had modelled his behavior and his sense of himself, prevented him from being able to express his grief, which must have been the most devastating feeling of which he had ever been aware. I could not leave him alone at The Old Mill, and I virtually moved out there from New York for the first few weeks, and after that spent several days a week there, through the summer. George was stunned and overwhelmed by his loss, and the inability to let out his grief in tears or ceremony or even, for long, in candid talk, was inseparable from a categorical rejection of the possibility of suicide, which for George was a proof of weakness. He spoke about that from time to time, and I could see how his grief, for want of other forms of expression, was taking that of anger, and he did not yet know what he was angry at—at life itself, at himself, at Jane and his love for her which held him helpless. He was angry—and revolted—at the thought of being a figure of grief, an object of pity or of visiting his own pain upon the company of friends, and he spoke to very few people. But he did go and spend some days with Mina, who he said was sympathetic—he said it as though it surprised him, when indeed the occasion may have been good for Mina.

And then, abruptly, he flung himself into a series of brief sexual relationships, one right after the other, some of them with old friends—and clearly including old friendship—and some with women he had just met. They were of all ages and there seemed to be no similarity of appearance or temperament. He knew more or less what he was doing, and more or less what to think of it. That winter he returned to the Virgin Islands to pack up the house that he and Jane had rented there. I joined him at Christmas for a few days. The run of promiscuity led him to several affairs there, one of which, in the early seventies, evolved into a final, brief marriage.

As for my own marriage, a few months after Jane died, my wife and I had agreed to separate—something which indeed did not represent a marked change over the actual situation of the preceding few years, but simply rendered it more or less formal. She had sold her own house in London, and also her mother's apartment there, after her mother died, and she had bought another farmhouse ten miles from mine in France. She never lived there, but preferred to stay in mine. I returned to the farm in the summers and stayed in another building on the property as I had done for some time. But my summers in France grew shorter, and I kept a pied-à-terre in New York, in the Village, on Waverly Place.

And from 1970 until 1973 I went to Mexico in the winters, and lived in San Cristobal de La Casas. In those years George spent almost as much time in the Virgin Islands as in Mamaroneck. He invited me down there sailing regularly, but my life was already complicated enough with travels between New York and France, and New York and Mexico; the years seemed to have been broken into fragments, each too small, and it was hard to welcome the idea of breaking further pieces off any of them.

In 1972 both of my parents died, my father in June, before I was to leave for France, and my mother in September, just as I was about to return. I had left my VW bus (used for the trips to Mexico) out in a garage at George's, and drove back and forth to the house in western Pennsylvania where they had lived, packing things up, disposing of their possessions. Often, coming and going, I spent a day or so in Mamaroneck with George.

The next year, in France, I settled into the empty farmhouse ten miles from my own at Lacan, and late in the summer I was joined there by Moira Hodgson, who had been my friend in New York and Mexico for five years. George, by then, had embarked upon his last marriage, and his new wife, Pauline, wanted to travel in Europe. George suggested being Ajax again, as he had been on the trip to Provence and Corsica eight years before. This time the itinerary was in northern Italy: Milan, Padua, Verona, and a week in Venice at the Danieli.

In Padua Pauline had a gallbladder attack, and she was an invalid for the rest of the trip. George insisted on eating as though the carefully chosen dining places were no different from the Italian restaurants on the Boston Post Road in Mamaroneck. Night after night he ordered veal parmigiana with a side order of spaghetti, after several scotches on the rocks, and never touched the wine. And it rained and rained—and we loved being there, and wandered endlessly under umbrellas, with guide books or without them, trying to get lost.

George's marriage survived one appalling Christmas at The Old Mill, and broke up in the course of the following year. George was suitably shamefaced at his own rashness, which had led him, at his age, into what should never have been a marriage at all, and he unburdened himself of some of his self-reproach while carrying out orgies of brush-cutting and clay-pigeon shooting at some distance from the house. He did not think it was at all funny at the time. But we talked more candidly about his life then than we had been able to do since the summer after Jane died. Of course the collapse of the rather frantically inflated illusions of his last marriage left him once again alone with the unresolved grieving for Jane, with his anger at her loss, and with a sense that his life was purposeless and empty. He was, as he plainly said, in love with a dead woman. He began an unremitting campaign to remove the crab grass from the lawn in front of The Old Mill.

He had given up the idea of marriage but he was lonely And he was lucky to meet one day, by chance, an old friend, Frances Whitney, who was not interested in marriage either, was free and independent, and besides, George said, "utterly crazy." Which meant, it turned out, that she was principally interested in modern dance, in making light-show sculptures and costume jewelry, and to some degree in quasi-occult matters. They became inseparable companions—a peaceful relation that lasted for the rest of George's life.

In 1979 and 1980 I found myself in a financial mess. I had entrusted most of my savings and the half of my parents' savings that I had inherited to the friend of a friend already mentioned, who had promptly lost it, under cover of talk. In the meantime I had put down what money remained on a piece of land, on the first steps toward building a house on it, and on moving my books and papers from France. Suddenly there was no money and I found myself with a half-paid-for piece of land, a partly-finished house that I could not live in or put my things in, and debts. George helped out, as did my sister and other friends, until I could scramble out of that one, and repay them, and he was delighted to be able to tease me about my foolishness.

I was living in Hawai'i by then, but I saw him for part of each year, when I returned to New York, and my relation with him remained, on the surface, unchanged. But our lives and interests seemed to grow more and more divergent, and when I saw him I was disappointed at how little we seemed to be really talking to each other. I thought he was like an aging and withdrawn parent, unoccupied but distant and at times morose. As far as I could see he was interested in little—sports on TV, the biographies of generals or politicians—and it was hard to entice him to do things together, to spend evenings in town, to talk at any length about subjects that we agreed on.

After I moved to Hawai'i in the mid-seventies, I was at last divorced. George stubbornly refused to visit Hawai'i. He took to spending winters in Florida, with Frannie, where he sailed less and less. His health was beginning to fail him, and at last he sold *Shag* and took up golf instead of sailing.

There was a breath of the old warmth in early 1982 when I returned to New York and met Paula, and introduced her to him. "You have a jewel this time," he said, and he spoke of her and behaved toward her with a total unreserved admiration that I had seen him express for no woman besides Jane. Paula and I returned to Hawai'i in 1983, and I saw George on our trips back to New York several times that year. My last picture of George was taken at our wedding party just before Christmas. He looks as though he is having a good time. His fondness for Paula and his approval of the marriage was a kind of confirmation of our affection for each other that had been there, virtually unspoken, for so many years.

A few times, after the winters in Florida, he and Frances sailed up the inland waterways on a chartered boat, and he wrote still with obvious pleasure about the trips, the country, the waterway, the birds, as he did of the human fauna in Florida. But ill-health was bearing him down and it shadowed his letters. He sailed for the last time in 1985, on the New England coast, and regretted it. "The trip was windless, cold, fog, rain. . . . My pledge [to never get another sail boat] is now carved in stone in a special place in my brain."

That year Mina died, and not long afterward he had a heart attack—apparently a small one, but a warning. He said nothing about it, and both Jane's daughter Linda, who lives in Texas, and I were cross with him about that. Paula and I had begun trying to lure him and Frances out to Hawai'i instead of Florida, but he was clearly not going to countenance any further changes in his routine:

If you think that ad you sent us about the new development on Maui made our mouths water you should be surrounded, as we are, by the glamorous ads, brochures, TV pictures etc. of Florida's retreats for the aged. Hot and cold running blonds, jacuzzis, swimming pools, two golf courses to choose from for each one in his 'golden' years, no wind at all, uniformly warm, but not hot, weather, plus nearby culture, art libraries, and the wonderful stimulating company of the other octogenarians.

At the same time:

At least one good thing about being mildly apprehensive about health in Florida is that you are not unique. The TV is overcome daily with good advice for the incontinent, the arthritic, the denture wearer, or those unfortunates with pains in the back, liver, spleen, or you name it. As far as my own health is concerned, I guess it's improving. I'm back to walking two miles a day, hitting some golf balls not very hard and generally prospering. As you will learn to your dismay, the aging process is a pain in the ass. Mina kept warning me, until I lost patience, what a bore it is to be old. All I can say is that although rarely correct about most things she was right about that.

But he was still interested, back in Mamaroneck, in a friend's fight to keep a neighboring yacht club from jamming up the cove with a marina. It was a rearguard action in which George had been involved for a number of years, and temporarily at least, it was succeeding. "It would be a real tragedy," George wrote, "if his [the club owner's] dream of parking another fifty boats at the mouth of the cove died. What I always say is, 'You can't stop progress, but you can sure as hell slow it down.' What do you always say?"

In early April of 1986 we returned from a week away on the Big

Island of Hawai'i during which I found myself thinking about him a great deal. We had spoken on the telephone several times that spring, after his heart attack, and I was anxious about him. Telephone conversations with him had never been very satisfactory He was usually impatient to get off the phone, and I am not fond of the instrument. Most of the time we used it only to arrange to meet. But I wanted to talk to him. Those last conversations had been brusque and frustrating. I had been writing him a letter in my head. A message was waiting for us when we got home, saying that he had died two days before, as we had been sitting out an awesome thunderstorm on Hawai'i. He had just got back to Mamaroneck from Florida a week or so earlier, and had been feeling generally wretched. But he had gone for his favorite walk, through the marsh west of The Old Mill, which he and a neighbor had bought in the early seventies and turned over to the Nature Conservancy in memory of Jane. He and I had walked there on my last visit to Mamaroneck. It is the long tidal estuary of a small stream, and though it is near human habitation, it is full of birds, wildlife, marsh flora, and is surrounded by remnants of old orchards run wild. He had fallen at the entrance to the marsh, where neighbors found his body a little later.

I was sometimes puzzled by the durability and strength of our friendship, on both sides. Obviously, something of it fitted no patterns and no conceivable expectations. Besides being a friend through all those years, he led me to other friendships that I value—something, on the face of it, surprising for someone who found it so difficult, so embarrassing, to show or even to admit affection. But a number of his other friends remained bound to him with admiration and deep fondness for many years. One for whom George felt unlimited regard was Robert Penn Warren. George and Warren obviously delighted in each other's company and they had sailed together on a chartered boat, in Greece, in the seventies. After George died I wrote to Mr. Warren about it, and he wrote back with characteristic generosity:

A more remarkable man than George I never knew, nor a man to whom I was more temperamentally drawn. Though I suppose that this would have seemed improbable in the light of some abstract definition of the two of us. Later on I was somewhat surprised to hear Vann Woodward say the same thing about George. Vann thought that he was a great discovery—a kind of man he had been looking for all his life.

I was glad that Mr. Warren also said, "somehow we have grown to associate your presence with his presence." There is no one to thank.

Reflections of a Mountain

I went from Venice to the Virgin's Holy Mountain of Athos, with only two nights between.

One would expect such a passage to provide contrast so entire and abrupt as to shock—a leap between opposites. And the contrast was there, everywhere. My ears were still echoing the slosh of dark canals and the anonymous bubbling of crowds in the Piazza San Marco when I began to hear the wind in the chestnut forests that unroll from under the ravens' stone ridges. The reflected water-light of autumn shimmering along facades of palaces built on mud, the evanescent vanities, deceptive lightness, and elusive confidences of the Queen of the Adriatic, marvels of composed acquisition, possessiveness that claimed even the sea year by year, as the sea now claims it, and took marriage as its figure (not by chance was *Othello* set in Venice), an ancient republic whose power and greatness were represented by elected prisoners, a city all leaves and no trees, in late September, had not been veiled but enhanced by the sleep of travel, when I came on foot, alone, around a high bend, and saw, in the early light, far to the southeast, through the woods, the bare shadow rising thousands of feet in one line out of the sea, to the marble point which some have taken to be the exceeding high mountain where the devil showed Jesus all the kingdoms of the world and the glory of them, and which many believe to be, with its northern approaches (including the spot where I was standing), the site that the Mother of God had received for an earthly garden of her own. At a glance it would seem that the two places must have little in common except the planet and its turning, but on the way between them thinking about them reveals other links. Both Venice and Athos make reverberating statements about existence, its dimensions and its treasures, and both look beyond us. Neither of them belongs to our century, yet both formulate a sense that clearly is shared by all periods but that seems characteristic of the present and its furnishings: a vertiginous touch, the feeling of stepping-stones sinking under the feet they help to cross.

Venice, of course, is sinking literally, borne down by its triumphs, succumbing to its own monuments. As the wooden pilings driven deep into the silt and clay have rotted under the marble, more marble has been added to the pavements, raising levels but increasing the weight. On the canals, white marble steps that once led up to landing stages now lead down under the polluted water and disappear. Delivery barges, the curtained launches of the rich, high-powered diesel water-taxis, the nifty speed-crafts of the perennial adolescents with much to prove and motors to prove it with, one after the other send waves ricocheting back and forth across the narrow channels. Annually the waves splash farther up rotting doors and slide deeper into rooms, bringing bits of driftwood, cans, disposed plastic conveniences, black bags of garbage that have slithered off collection scows, oil slicks, detergents, all the latest effluvia. The stone along the waterline is being eaten away. Cracks climb from it into the masonry. Tall belfries lean this way and that on their softening foundations. During the high tides around the autumn equinox the Piazza San Marco, and the streets near it, flood. The lagoon backs up through the drains in the well-laid pavements. It rises into the gorgeous Basilica of Saint Mark itself, where the saint is represented again and again crossing water, and the most prominent dove in the porch ceiling is Noah's. On some days the flood fingers sections of the mosaic floor.

Boardwalks laid on trestles allow files of tourists to proceed slowly back and forth across the squares and into the church and out of it. Gondolas made fast to jetties appear to be riding at moorings out in the lagoon. Opinions differ regarding how fast the city is subsiding, but it seems certain that the rate is accelerating as the pilings rot. At the same time, surface—not just the water surface, but all that is superficial: the visible, the outside, the garment, the public, the act of display—has always been integral to the nature, the architecture, and the life of Venice, and if Venice can be preserved even piecemeal, no doubt it will be effected by elaborate, expensive, public attentions, and in order that Venice may continue to be seen. Athos is another matter. There too wealth has mattered, and accumulation has been practiced: Kings and queens have built monasteries, endowed them, repaired them, protected them, and added to their treasures. And there too the visible artifacts—frescoes, illuminated manuscripts, architecture, and sculpture—are prized and admired, and some of the ikons are revered. But whereas Venice clearly profits, and may in the end be salvaged by tourists and their money, for Athos they and what they represent merely contribute to the gathering destruction. For the essence of Athos and the element that threatens it are both invisible.

Geographically the way to it is through Greece. Three peninsulas, set like fingers of a hand, run southeast from the district of Chalkidikis into the Aegean Sea. The mountain stands at the end of the one farthest to the east, that points toward the island of Lemnos. The peninsula is some thirty miles long, most of it high and rocky, though there is a narrow bit at the northern end where it drops almost to sea level. It is claimed that sections of a faint furrow, between the two shores there, mark the course of a canal that Xerxes, sailing to attack Greece early in the fifth century BC, ordered to be dug, rather than risk the terrible seas at the foot of the mountain: An entire fleet had been lost rounding the headland a few years before. South of this dubious memorial the land rises in low hills for a few miles and then heaves up into sharp folds running toward the summit. At the start of this century the boundary of the Holy Community of Athos lay considerably farther north than it does now. The Greek government has expropriated a number of square miles of the gently sloping base of the peninsula—much of its best farmland—and turned it over to farmers and to other forms of exploitation. Compensation, in the form of a small regular subsidy, was promised to the monasteries whose land was taken, and they depend on it. Its continued payment is now in doubt. The monastic community, by the terms of its charter, governs itself. But in fact there is a connection with the Greek state which does not seem altogether to content either party. The visitor's first contact with it is likely to be in Thessalonika, at police headquarters. According to the Treaty of Lausanne of 1923, and the Charter of Athos of 1924, drawn up jointly by Greece and the monastic community, the monks are Greek subjects, the Greek penal system extends to Athos, ecclesiastical administration is left to the representatives of the twenty monasteries, and there are ecclesiastical police empowered to refuse admission to visitors. Perhaps even fifty years ago pilgrims could arrive on the Athenian peninsula under no colors but their own, and remain there without credentials until their deaths, as some are said to have done. In the ancient tradition, the guest had been sent from heaven and should be received as though he were Christ. Now papers are required, in triplicate. They must be supplied by the Greek police, and necessitate a visit to another office across town and further confirmation from the authorities on Athos. Until recently there was virtually no time limit imposed on visitors. Now, due in great part to the annually developing number of tourists, a week is the maximum, unless the monastery representatives choose to extend the permit, and normally a visitor is not allowed to spend more than twenty-four hours in any one monastery

The road has helped to make, or at least implement, the difference. For centuries the journey to Athos was long and exacting. It took more than curiosity, a few hours, and the price of a bus ticket to get anyone, on foot or muleback, across the hundred-odd miles of inhospitable mountains between Thessalonika and the base of the peninsula. In the past few years the road has been gouged and tarred all the way to the present boundary, which once lay well within the monastic domains. For most of the journey it winds steeply through chestnut woods and over barren slopes, connecting a few shrines and small towns, passing under ruined castle walls at Aristotle's Stagira, where a sign in both Greek and Roman letters points off the road to a white statue: the shape of a beard and a gown. A regular profile, facing the sea, against a blank sky as the bus turns; he looks quite new. The Philosopher, you know. In these towns, a monk told me later, they have football stadia but no libraries. Hill villages set among orchards sagging with ripe apples, the cracking boughs weighed down onto old walls and spilling over them, awash with October sunlight. Dahlias, geraniums, calendulas. People sitting out at tables in the shade of grapevines, the remaining leaves turning translucent after the grape harvest. Dogs gliding through the shadows of the tables. Towels hanging beside open doors. Families facing the bus as though they were grouped for daguerreotypes. Firewood. Television aerials. Hens under lines of laundry. Piles of new red hollow bricks, white mortar, raw roof tiles. Erissos, down on the Aegean shore, is entirely modern—the ubiquitous housing (southern European version) that looks as though every room might be the bathroom. The old town was totally destroyed in 1932, by an earthquake that killed many of the inhabitants. A little way down the coast, set back from the shore among trees, beyond little fields and pastures with tethered cows and donkeys, are the domes of a tiny church, an outpost of Athos, and farther along, overlooking the sea, a bare cement construction, a hotel. There are few cars on the road, but the developers have plans. From the first rather tentative-looking hotel the road rises and crosses the peninsula to the next long bay. Between one year and the next a huge masonry receptacle has been completed there, on the rocks above the water: a sweeping drive, suburban lighting, liveried evergreens, the architecture of a clinic on a postcard, or a chic sector of the Atlantic Wall. And the name, Eagle's Palace Hotel (true), in English so that there may be no mistake. One is assured that it is the first of many. On the shore below, from the small quay at Tripiti, fishing boats cross to the island of Ammouliani. A few minutes later the road descends to the coastal village of Ouranopolis, the end of the line—so far.

The approach to the village is lined with half-finished multi-layered constructions: the hotels of next year's resort. But the building that still dominates the place is the thirteenth-century tower of Prosphori, on the rocks by the shore. It was once a dependency of the monastery of Vatopedi, and it may mark the site of pagan Dion. At the beginning of the last century it must have stood almost alone, by the water. There is a small old house beside it, that has been run for some years as an inn, and facing the sea are the vestiges of a few other cottages converted to shops and eating places. I had seen the town last in September, the year before, and in that month the season, though waning, was still in swing: Many of the tables under the pergolas and in the few restaurants were occupied by Germans—I was told that that nation's penchant for Greece had been turned to account by the proprietor of the new attentively landscaped beach hotel at the edge of town, who had connections with travel agents in Germany. More and more busloads of mixed Germans were confidently expected every year. A foreigner is addressed in German as a matter of course. But on the first of October, still, the high life goes home. Most of the tables are put away, most of the restaurants close, the antique dealer returns to Thessalonika, and doors are left open toward the sea so that women with cats at their feet can get the afternoon sun to their needlework. Most of the village was built after World War I, to house two groups of settlers of Greek ancestry brought from Turkish Asia Minor under the provisions of a League of Nations arrangement for resettlement of populations. In the year since I had seen it, a startling number of the remaining structures from that original period, and the lanes between them, had been removed to make way for hotel launching pads. But in October the locals still sit under the vines of the one open cafe, the half-inch of retsina in their glasses glowing with the long light off the sea. Beyond the tables, the wharf, and the sand of the shore. When I had left my things in the inn I walked down the empty beach past a hauled-up fishing boat, a truck out to pasture, a shuttered hotel, a jumble of fallen rocks running into the sea. Birds in the thornbushes, conversing about evening—pipit, wagtail, or lark voices, the glassy trill of some finch, none of them quite familiar, but the ancient words clear. Shadows swirling on the darker side of rocks, and then on the side from which the light was draining. The sun descended into gold-bordered clouds. The last breeze died. The blinking of a buoy on one of the small rock islands was echoed finally, more steadily, by a few lights thin as stars, over Ammouliani, where I have been told there is no electricity The peninsula beyond it, to the west, faded into the dark sea. This one was sacred, once, to the sea-god, and its peak was named for his son. Suddenly clouds of tiny insects appeared, hovering above the waterline in the dusk, and the moon, almost new, gathered light over the sea. As I turned back, a little dog ran toward me along the beach, as though it knew me.

The Greek geographer Strabo, at the beginning of the Christian era, wrote that those who lived on the summit of Mt. Athos saw the sun rise three hours early. Doubtless he did not come to check on his statement: The summit is an uninhabitable steeple of rock. But it may be that his assertion should not be read as the offering of fact that we have come to expect every statement to be, but meant instead "a high place, half legend, on its own terms with morning." Those who live now on the western shore, at the base of the long promontory, are up before the sun, like inhabitants of fishing villages elsewhere. There seems to be no hurry: They shamble through the mist, collars up, shawls over mouths, carrying sacks or empty-handed, as though waiting for something to come or go. Eventually a few figures gather on the cement wharf beside boxes of fish, baskets, oil drums; three or four have knapsacks, there are several black-robed monks with goat-hair bags; last come the fishermen, boatmen, the inevitable policeman. It is not many years since most of the fishing and the coastal traffic were conducted on sailing caïques, and small steamers anchored off the villages fairly regularly, if not often. Since the last war the fishing boats have adopted a less distinctive shape—and motors. The pioneers of the changeover still have tillers and wooden railings with

dowelled banisters. Their replacements are big steel diesels with broad
sterns for trawling or loading, and stertorous engines. Both kinds of
vessel make the run to Daphne, the port of Athos. The boat leaves at
seven. In October the first sunlight has just whitened the east face
of Prosphori Tower and the sea at its foot. The boat noses down the
coast, keeping close in. The monastic state begins a short distance
below the village. The present boundary is a collapsing stone wall,
beyond which the ancient ascetic rule of Athos, instituted, according
to the story by the Virgin herself, obtains.

They say on the mountain that the Virgin and St. John had
sailed from Joppa to visit the resurrected Lazarus, who was then
living on Cyprus. A storm had blown their vessel to the mountain,
where the Virgin went ashore near the site of the present monastery
of Iviron. In that day there was a temple to Poseidon on the spot,
but at the appearance of the Mother of God the idols crumbled to
pieces. She blessed the mountain, said that it would be her garden,
and forbade any other woman to set foot there. For the most part,
the injunction has been strictly kept. In the twelfth century Wal-
lachian shepherds moved into the northern part of the promontory, three hundred families of them, and the women proved fatally
attractive to large numbers of the monks. When the shepherds were
finally expelled, the erring fathers were excommunicated in numbers
that considerably reduced the population of the mountain. At different times the Empress Placidia, and the Serbian prince George
Brankovic's daughter Maria, married to a sultan, are said to have
come to visit Athos. Both of them were benefactors of the monastic
state. But at Vatopediou the ikon now known as the Antiphonitria
of Placidia is said to have spoken to the empress, warning her to go
no farther, "for another queen than you reigns here." Queen Maria,
in the fifteenth century, is reported to have stepped ashore at the
monastery of Agiou Pavlou—St. Paul's—bringing with her gold,
frankincense, and myrrh that the Magi had offered to the Christ
Child, but a voice not of the earth had been heard forbidding her
to take another step, and for the same reason. Village girls from

north of the wall occasionally cross it to pick up olives or fetch goats home, and in 1948 guerrillas, including twenty-five women, occupied Karyes, the capital, briefly. But in general the commandment has been not only observed but extended to include female domestic animals and all "beardless persons," though the ruling on animals varies from monastery to monastery—there are cats about in most of the houses, and hens around some of them—and the ruling on beards, where visitors are concerned, is taken, in practice, to mean simply "old enough to grow one."

As the sun climbs, the misty rays tilt into ravines full of scrub and rocky clefts leading up from the sea. The morning of a place apart. No visible habitation. It looks as though the sound of the boat could not be heard on the shore. Green water over rocks, and around a point a boathouse on the shingle, a walled meadow nearby with a few vines and olive trees. No one in sight. Farther along, another boathouse and a rambling two-story stuccoed building, with a porch along the upper story; a monk out airing bedding on the banister; no one on the jetty. The cliffs rise higher from the sea. Up on tiny ledges, over the water or over narrow gorges, ruins begin to appear. Some of them as large as big farmhouses, with the stone domes of their chapels still intact. They had been *sketes*—the word translates as "cloister": an assembly of monks attached to a monastery but living apart from it under the rule of a prior. Or, if they are smaller, *kelli,* which are settlements housing three or more monks, who work on the land. Or hermitages. The roofs of many of them have fallen in. The sky shows through the walls. Vestiges of garden enclosures and terraces the size of kitchen tables hide in the wild growth, still catching the morning sun. Another point is drawn back, revealing the first of the monasteries on the coast: Dohiariou. Stone boathouse half barn, half fortification; arches and porches, square pilasters and stone chimneys. The monastery rising behind it: high walls, long balconies flung out over nothing, tier above tier of rough masonry, pink and blue painted plaster, wooden struts, rows of windows, russet tiles, cupolas and domes and chimneys all rising to the massive square crenellated keep, at the top, with its back

to olive terraces and the foot of a steep wooded slope. Monks waiting; the boat puts in, a monk gets off, and with him an arrangement
of sacks and boxes. The process is repeated a few miles along the coast
at the next monastery, Xenophontos, which rises straight from the
shingle's edge, another fountain of crenellations, towers, balconies,
domes. And at the third, St. Panteleimon, a Russian monastery and
until the Russian revolution the largest on Athos: enormous, dark,
relatively modern (most of it built late in the nineteenth century), one
whole wing burnt out, never repaired, looking like a mined factory. At
the turn of the century this monastery housed nearly fifteen hundred
monks. There is a harbor where seagoing steamers could dock. In one
of the towers hangs the second largest bell in the world, transported
from Moscow Now there are no more than twenty monks, and there
is scant prospect of others coming from Russia, or of the Greek government allowing them to stay if they did come. Around a point after
St. Panteleimon, Daphne appears: a jetty, a building at the end of it, a
short string of white-stuccoed houses facing the sea.

The traditional uniform for the police of the monastic state
includes a red, gold-trimmed jacket over a white shirt, shoes with
pom-poms, and a hat that manages to combine the shapes of a garrison cap and a beret. Parts of the costume, no doubt, are very old.
For everyday use, almost the only article of this finery that is worn
is the least impressive: the hat. The wearer of one of these, looking
cross, was waiting at the entrance to the customs-shed, at the end of
the jetty, to flag down each visitor, with a handout in four languages:
a brief blurb about the Holy Community of the Holy Mountain of
Athos, leading up to the point of it all in the final paragraph: "You
are consequently requested that, since you intend to visit the Holy
Mountain, your appearance in general, both in regard to clothing as
well as hair, should be appropriately restrained. We shall regret being
obliged to refuse entrance to those who do not comply." Whatever
else it may mean, it means No Hippies, whatever that may mean.
More specifically, and most usually, it equates appropriate restraint
with the canons of the present-day straight, secular, Greek middle

class, and it means No Long Hair—though the monks wear theirs up in a bun, in back. The German boy with blond locks brushing his shoulder blades did not realize it yet, but if he wanted his permit at Karyes, which he would need in order to stay on Athos, he would certainly be led around in back of a building to a barbershop of raw boards, a recent edifice, something between a do-it-yourself privy and a fortune-teller's booth, and there would have his curls appropriately restrained—to above his collar, all around. Two vehicles were waiting in the dust between the customs-shed and the row of shops, in the one street. An ancient bus, with a ladder up the back for luggage, including boxes of fish, and gardenia plants. And a natty gray Landrover, property of the Greek police. I wandered off into a shop to pick up a new map of Athos (there are several available editions, but none is much of a practical guide to the maze of footpaths that wind from ravine to ravine over the ridges) and to look at the hermits' wood carving, and the objects there for sale to the monks and workmen: heavy cloth, thick dishes, lanterns, soap, flashlights, axheads, rope, rice. Everywhere the same and everywhere different. Beyond the third or fourth shop was a pergola, with cafe tables under it. I put down my sack in the shade. At one of the tables was a tall monk with a long gray beard, talking with three men clearly from the outer world, in holiday attire. The conversation was in English, and as I repacked my sack so that the new map would be handy, and put away the no longer needed sweater, I heard the monk, speaking with an American accent, explaining to the visitors, who proved to be Roman Catholic priests, the rules in the different monasteries regarding the wearing of religious vestments other than those of the Orthodox church. They depended largely on the views of the respective abbots. One of the visitors said that he had missed his cassock in the evening, and had felt chilly. The monk spoke apologetically about the severity of some of the houses. The bus beeped, but I let it go rumbling and lurching away over the dirt road. I knew that bus trip: an hour of rattling in the old tin cookie box, up the jeep road and straight over the spine of the peninsula. The backs of monks' heads bobbing sharply in unison. Pinup ikons. No This and No That signs. The road of the flogged engine, and its smell. I was glad I already knew it. This time I would walk.

The road follows the sea for a short distance and then turns sharply to the right and starts up the steep slope. A row of poles for a telephone line between Daphne and the mainland runs parallel to the shore, and drops behind as the road swings up away from the water. Gates into overgrown terraces, in the bright sunlight; mules and horses browsing under olive trees. Sounds of horsebells, finches. The road switches back and forth, climbing, heads up a wide ravine, doubles back to a point above the sea, turns inland. Holly oak, arbutus, bay trees. Bees. Large languid butterflies in the morning stillness. At the top of the first long rise, suddenly a level shady plateau, and off to the right, among big trees, the high walls of a monastery, a small worn bas-relief of a horseman with a spear—St. George?—set into the corner nearest the road, and a fountain with a tin dipper facing it. A peasant stacking firewood under the trees. Xeropotamou: a huge hollow square of stone. Founded in the tenth century on the site of an older village whose name is now disputed. A monastery that survived earthquake and fires and has been rebuilt by several rulers, one of them a sultan, Selim I. He had seen in a vision the Forty Martyrs of Sebaste—Armenians who, in the fourth century, had been set in a lake to freeze to death—and they had instructed him to restore the monastery, which had recently been burned down by pirates. The Martyrs, for their part, would help him fight the Arabs. Long after the sultan's death in 1519, his successors continued to provide oil for the lamps before the ikon of the Forty Martyrs in the Xeropotamou church.

The ascent continues as steeply as before; the monastery, seen from above, dwindles until it looks like a farm on a ledge above the sea. The sun climbs, but the heights grow cooler. The limestone scrub gives way to chestnut woods, mules wandering loose in the sloping shade. The last mists have burned off; the road winds higher and higher. Then, without warning, a sudden presence, off to the right, across a great empty space: the first view of the mountain. Once it has been seen, the sense of it remains wherever one goes on the promontory, whether or not the peak itself is visible. The road clambers on over the ridge, and the eastern sea, the Holy Sea, comes into sight through the chestnut leaves, and down through the woods the roofs of Karyes appear: tile and rusting iron, vineyards' gardens, *sketes*, and *kellis* straggling out from the center, a tilted village turning as the track winds down to become its one street.

Karyes, named for its hazel trees, is the capital of the monastic state of Athos. Except for Koutloumousiou, which is considered to be too close to need one, each of the monasteries has a house in town, known as a *konaki*, for its deputation to the Holy Epistasia, the governing body which meets in the Mansion of the Holy Community, a large, relatively modern building dominating the upper end of the town. The road fans out into a dusty plaza: In the northwest corner, monks and muleteers load and unload the scraggy goat-footed gelded mules and horses that manage to pick their way all their lives over the steep twisting mountain paths, often no more than a series of narrow, rubbly depressions in the rock. The street itself begins with a flight of stairs—with a cobbled path around them: It runs for the distance of a couple of short city blocks, past the few shops, most of which seem to be in the hands of laymen. Windows display the wood carvings and other handwork of the hermits, hardware, dry goods—in one I saw a cartridge belt and a gun case. Cobblers' shops, saddlers. Halfway along, the street crosses the eastern end of the square on which the main church of Karyes, the ancient Protaton, stands, and then turns downhill, toward the woods. There is a rule against riding down the main street, and the monks dismount and lead their horses and mules over the big, worn cobbles. The rule does not seem to apply to the Greek police jeeps—no doubt a jeep is harder to lead. That vehicle had roared past me as I climbed from the sea, driven by a young man ostentatiously in tune with his uniform, his face, and the station in life to which he had risen: the James Bond of Daphne. The jeep was parked on the otherwise empty square of the Protaton, jacked up and wheelless, with a layman on his back under it, and the driver bent over slightly to extend helpful unconcern from his relative height. The police station was still open, and I picked up my passport, but the Mansion, which amounts to the town hall of Karyes, was closed until three, and I would not be able to get my permit until then. Downstairs to the beanery, where the two head men from the police station—the only other customers—were already installed. Some days are fish days, some are squid days. This was neither. Pistachio walls with posters advertising the 21st of April, and a fly-specked photograph of the incumbent caudillo (October 3, 1973) tilting out from on high like a family portrait. In case the decor tempted one to linger, the cook made it clear that he was in a hurry to close: He was late for his siesta. The street was empty. I looked into a tailor's shop, with a tin windowpane to hold a stovepipe, and dusty sewing machines older than anyone on the mountain. A year before I had spent an hour in there, with a thin white-bearded monk, a muleteer, and a French priest in mufti, whom I had met on the Mansion steps, and with whom I had agreed to visit the north of the peninsula; he had wanted to engage a guide and a mule to carry the knapsacks. An hour of delirious bargaining, in a wash of languages, while I tried to see into the crannies in the back of the shop—attics of lives I had thought I had forgotten. I had watched the monk's shoes: black leather boxes, half *sabot* and half slipper, made more for shuffling than for walking, and for standing in through the all-night vigils. The shop was closed; we might never have been there. In the summer, in the middle of the day, Mediterranean Karyes bakes on its hill. But in the autumn, in the shade of the street, a coldness comes out of the stones that is the cold of the mountain towns far higher than those hazel groves, a cold shared with ancient settlements well to the north of Greece, nestled on heights, between limestone and granite. A chill that flows through the empty streets at noon, with the sound of many small streams running down from the chestnut forests and through the sleeping town. I went back to the square, to the west of the Protaton, and sat in the sun, on steps leading up through the late-flowering rosemary and hollyhocks, to wait for something to open. With the knapsack for a pillow, I dozed off to the sound of bees, and a tinkle of horsebells almost overhead woke me: It was the muleteer from the first day of the year before, going up the path, and we wrung each other's hands and exchanged congratulations and pantomime. The church was open. Inside, a young monk was moving a ladder around, replacing beeswax candles in the great brass *corona*, the ring-candelabra suspended in the nave. Strangers are not invariably welcome in every church on the mountain—the French priest had told me of his cold reception at the Protaton on an earlier occasion—and I slipped through the open doorway quietly to look at the murals wall by wall.

The paintings of Athos, indeed those of any of its major churches, demand, and in some cases have received, studies to themselves. The ikons, in building after building, even after centuries of natural disasters, recurrent fires, raids, occupations by alien empires, are still of a bewildering richness. The ordinary lay visitor seldom has a chance to do more than look briefly at a few of them, in each place, perhaps during or just after one of the divine offices. The churches are not museums—yet. Even if he is shown in by a welcoming monk, it is unlikely that he will be allowed to linger as he pleases, and unless he is Orthodox he will seldom be allowed to see anything behind the ikonostasis, where some of the most beautiful of the ikons are hung. Most of the monasteries house one or more ikons that are themselves the subjects of legends: pictures said to have been miraculously painted, or preserved, or transported to their present places, paintings said to have wept or bled or spoken, instruments of divine intervention. Athos, besides, has always maintained schools of ikon painting, and many of the finest ikons are native to the mountain. The murals are another of the great treasures of Athos. They do not represent the historic range of the ikons; most of them were painted between the fourteenth century and the eighteenth. But they are even more obviously integral to the place, its walls, its roofs, its weather, its fate. They were painted where they are; they have suffered damp, smoke, mutilation, and restoration where they are; even if they could be moved, or if the use of their buildings were to change, they would not be the same. Some of the murals are famous, and art historians come to study particular groups, details, progressions. Of the painters whose names have survived, the most celebrated is Emmanuel Panselinos of Thessalonika, an artist of the sixteenth century about whom legends have gathered on the mountain: Monks are to be found who will state positively at what period of his life, and in what order, certain murals were painted. But there is no single mural anywhere on Athos that can be indisputably attributed to him. The murals on Athos vary greatly even on a single wall, and the scholarly purist does not always do justice to the peculiar importance, to the great works, of their settings, including, often, the humbler, cruder patchworks of the tradition around them, and the aging buildings of which they are a part. Anyone who has once seen, high on the two walls under the dome, separated by the arch of the apse, the two balanced protagonists of the Annunciation, the Angel Gabriel on the left, the Virgin with the book signifying the Word, on the right, silently conversing across the dark abyss lit only by a gold crucifix, and has then seen that composition repeated, with greatly differing artistry in church after church on the mountain, is unlikely to think of the separate figures afterwards in isolation from the significance of their placing, and their relation to the whole drama. The thematic arrangements of the murals in each church follows, besides, liturgical and initiatory patterns: It is not by chance, nor for aesthetic reasons, that the entrance to the apse, into the holiest part of the church, should be traversed, above, by the Annunciation, and lead into the place of death, resurrection, and elevation. The ikonography itself, where the art is as rich and as functional as it is on Athos, is sometimes rendered with great vividness by a painting which, taken by itself, would seem neither especially gifted nor forceful. I think, for instance, of some of the images of fish, symbols of Christ, in the frescoes, linking the paintings of the Baptism with those of the Harrowing of Hell. They are crossed in the river Jordan, where Jesus stands on them. The doors of Hell are crossed in the same way and the dead and resurrected Christ is shown standing on them. The crossed doors need only be shown, then, above the west entrance to the church itself, to convey a whole symbology of the body and the spirit, baptism and resurrection. The paintings themselves, as is the case with most genuine symbologies, embody both a conscious and an unconscious tradition, and much of this aspect of them is lost in isolation.

The Protaton at Karyes is the oldest church on the mountain—a basically tenth-century building on the site of a still earlier one, but restored in the sixteenth century. It contains some of the most famous murals on Athos, including some of the ones attributed to Panselinos: contemplative saints, haloed knights and rulers in armor, historic and legendary protectors, along the nave. The paintings above the door have been damaged, and they rise into fresh cement. Even at midday with the doors open, the church smelled of incense and the beeswax of the long candles that the young monk was setting in place for the night's vigil.

Outside, the Mansion was open, and the Athenian policeman, whose manner when dealing with a batch of new visitors at the routine hour had been irritable and forbidding, received me with affable curiosity and served up my permit in the official kitchen, where he and the cook and bottle-washer were passing the afternoon over coffee. It was late to set out for any of the more remote monasteries that day. The shadows of the autumn afternoon were already lengthening. The massive, iron-plated monastery doors that stand open all day are shut and bolted at sunset: a custom that is said to have come from the days of raiding pirates.

Just above Karyes, off the Daphne road, is the *skete* of St. Andrew (Agiou Andreou), a rambling mass of architecture, like a child's cardboard palace that has been left in the rain. It looks Russian, and it was, in fact, one of the buildings that resulted from the great nineteenth-century influx of Russians to Athos. The rank of monastery with the right to a representative in the Holy Assembly is accorded to only twenty monasteries on the mountain, a number that has been maintained despite Russian attempts to change it for nationalistic purposes. Before the Russian revolution the *skete* of St. Andrew housed some eight hundred monks, far outnumbering many of the Greek monasteries, yet in the administration of the mountain it remained a dependency of the monastery of Vatopediou: A lane leads off the road below the *skete* and follows the walls to the main gate. From the windows I could hear boys' voices repeating lessons and singing in unison: Since 1930 part of the *skete* has housed the Athenian School, a seminary run by the Holy Community with the support of the Greek Ministry of Education. The cobbled courtyard, sloping up to another portico and a pair of heavy doors, looked older than some of the structures facing it. The doors of the inner portico were shut, chained, and padlocked. There was a gap between them, and it looked as though a vast abyss full of ruins overgrown with shimmering trees was inside there. Somewhere within the walls of the *skete,* I had been told, was the huge church of St. Andrew, recent, like most of the Russian buildings on Athos: It was finished in 1900. And parts of the *skete* are ruins: A fire, in 1958, raged there for four days, destroying whole sections of it, and many of its manuscripts and other treasures. One of the three or four old monks who are all that remain of the *skete* itself, hatless, long hair hanging loose, venerable shoes that had collapsed into slippers, was sitting out on a stone bench in the sun, chattering with a workman, as I came in. He leaned back against the stone, as I approached the chained and padlocked doors, and asked me about myself, and said that now it was no longer possible for me to go in there. The government, he said, forbade it, and he grew stern as he told me. I tried to find out which government he meant—that of Athos or that of Greece. Yes, yes, he said, the government. The restriction did not seem to make him unhappy but rather to fill him with a vague satisfaction: Things were being properly looked after, mysterious though the process might seem. And the sun was warm, and he was enjoying his conversation and returned to it. The voices of the boys echoed in the courtyard. From a ramp at a lower level, several laymen beckoned to me, and I went and found a small knot of cronies sitting on benches in the sunny end of a long corridor. A single visitor was an object of curiosity, and we found out where we had each come from. Most of them had been peasants from that part of Greece; one of them had traveled, working in a ship's galley. He disappeared and came back with a glass of water and another of *raki* (grape alcohol slightly flavored with anise). He, too, led me to understand that neither the *skete* nor the school, at the moment, were open to visitors. But he insisted that I must be hungry and popped back into the kitchen to fetch me a big tin bowl of cool lentils and onions, a tomato, and a fistful of good heavy sour bread and I obediently consumed the lot while they watched and pressed me to more: There was plenty they insisted, because they had all those students to feed and to prove the point one of them got up and took a large basket full of broken ends of bread out into the courtyard, tipped it into a wooden trough, and led a fat donkey around to the trough to munch at leisure. Another old unkempt monk, tall but bent with rheumatism, came in and sat on the end of the bench—clearly a favorite: a wit and a man of style. It was a lighthearted session, and when I got up to go, the cook popped into the kitchen and came out with more great wads of bread, which he pressed into my hands, to eat on the way.

I went back through Karyes and downhill toward Koutloumousiou: a cobbled path, steep as stairs where it left the town, between walls, and dropped into woods. Hazels overhanging the turns. Little streams running alongside and trickling across. Mud at the foot of banks dotted with cyclamen. More chestnuts. The sea far below, to the left: scattered cypresses, and the tin and stone roofs of small *sketes* and *kellis*. The great east wall of Koutloumousiou was in shadow when I reached it and stopped for a drink at the fountain facing the gate, under the trees. The armored doors stood open; a tunnel the length of a room led into the courtyard, already full of luminous twilight, where a fine grass grew between the stones. As I stood looking in, a white horse ambled past me and in through the blue light of the tunnel, and began to browse in the courtyard. When I followed I saw no one, at first. The hollow square of stone was silent. The center of the courtyard is taken up, in the familiar way, by the church—at Koutloumousiou, the Church of the Transfiguration. Tiers of arcades and balconies face onto it, from the surrounding walls. Cats were running up and down the stairs between the rows of arches, like pieces of shadows. A marble *phiale*—a cupola over a basin for blessing holy water—facing me, was tipped toward the door of the church: The streams running down the mountain and through the courtyard had softened the ground at its base, and over the centuries it had subsided into the grass. Behind it a massive square keep rose high above the rest of the monastery. Empty wine barrels on the grass. Water dripping from pipes by the arches. Tethering rings in the brick columns. Painted plates and jugs set into the brickwork of the arches, and of the church, as ornaments. I heard the sound of wet cloth being shaken, and looked above my head: A monk was hanging out a bit of laundry on a balcony railing. He asked where I was from, and told me that someone would be along to welcome me. An old monk appeared in one of the arcades and started to do some ironing, watching me. After a few minutes a younger monk appeared around the base of the tower, greeted me, and led me up echoing wooden stairs to a broad, recently converted dormitory on the top floor, that looked as though it might be the back room of a country store filled with cots for some annual occasion. A modern tile screen divided the front part from the back and I chose a cot at the back, by a window that overlooked the chestnut woods. But I had to move a little later, when two Greek visitors—middle-aged men with plastic shopping bags—were shown in: Many of the monasteries make a point of lodging the Greeks and the foreign visitors separately. It is customary on the mountain, for guests to be presented, on arrival, with a little tray containing a cup of Turkish coffee, a piece of Turkish delight, a glass of water and a shot glass of *raki* or *ouzo*—to be consumed in whatever order the guest decides upon, but the underlying assumption is that he will knock back the homemade *raki* first, follow it with the candy, and then the water, and finish up sipping the coffee. At Koutloumousiou the ceremony was dispensed with altogether. The monk who had led me up to the dormitory had told me that he would wait for me downstairs, and when I arrived again in front of the church he unlocked it and led me in to see the paintings, including miraculous ikons—many of the features, both of ikons and frescoes, hard to make out in the shadowy building already being overtaken by dusk. The monk indicated a spot at the base of one of the great brass candlesticks where he said money would be gratefully received—the only time such a suggestion was ever made to me on the mountain. The frescoes inside the church, some of them dating from the sixteenth century, are impressive works, but the upper parts are hard to see; those in the church porch get more light. They are cruder, but the themes that are traditional in that part of the building—the Creation and the Apocalypse—lend themselves to naïve treatment, which in turn benefits by the conventions of ikonographic composition. Outside, the monk said I should sign the guest book, and I in turn asked whether I might see the library. It was locked, he said, and hurried off to fetch the book or the key—I was not sure which. He never came back with either. In the dormitory a boy from the States was engaged in stuffing bushels of camping gadgets and clothes into a huge knapsack. He was on his way to the Near East, and had heard of Athos and stopped off to see why anybody would live in such a weird way. He had wandered around the empty corridors, looking for something to eat, and an old monk had given him some apples, and a few figs that were being dried on a balcony. In the dusk, a monk came to lead us both to the dark kitchen, seat us at a table with a kerosene lamp beside us, and serve us each a bowl of eggplants and peppers stewed together, a salad of tomatoes and onions and olive oil, all from the garden, and a pitcher of water from the mountain, while he shuffled around in the shadows beyond the mighty stove. The monasteries, traditional hospitality, instituted in an age of foot travel and pilgrims, has been taxed to breaking in recent years by the swelling current of tourists brought by motors, each summer. As the spate of visitors has increased, the number of monks, and the resources of the monasteries' have been dwindling, The situation—one hears again and again on the mountain—is encouraged by the Greek government, whose tourist office, it is said, is impatient to break the monasteries, round up the remaining monks and get them out of the way, and turn the buildings into museums and hotels. The light drained out of the courtyard. I walked down the corridor and found my way to a balcony hanging over the chestnut woods. The moon was drifting above the ridge, already silvering the eastern slope. The monastery was still. A pair of tawny owls echoed each other in the forest to the south. Beyond them the peak of Athos gleamed in the moonlight and the last pallid emanation of day.

The evening turned cold. A couple of smoky kerosene lamps had been brought into the dormitory. The American boy was still wadding his infinite impedimenta into his finite bag: The loose bits were piled on the surrounding cots and it looked as though the process might go on all night. The Greeks, in the other section, were talking over a table. In a while they began to snore: Deep, determined reverberations. I picked up my sack and some bedding and went out into the arcade to sleep there. The courtyard had filled with moonlight. The domes of the *katholikon,* a few paces away through the air, looked frosted over. Cats slipped along the arcades and fought above the plank ceilings. I was wakened by a grunt: An old monk with a lantern was looking down at me, startled. When I stirred he hurried on, and clattered down the stairs, and the sound was taken up on other stairs and the beat of the semantron suddenly overtook them all.

The semantron is a cousin of the oar. The two arrived by different routes at a kindred form. The semantron looks like an oar blade rising out of its reflection and joined to it by a handle: a double-ended oar, two blades with one handle, made for calling, wakening, warning, announcing. A monk in a black veil carries it on his shoulder and strides around the courtyard, circling the church, turning to the four quarters, striking the forward blade rapidly with a mallet, a toccata rising and falling as the mallet moves up and down the board, faster, slower, pauses, starts again. The echoes leap from the board: dark fireworks. They rebound from the walls of the courtyard and the unlit corridors behind the arches. They rattle the doors. The first of them shatters sleep. The monk pauses at different points in his circuit, and the rapping stops. Then it begins again, urgent, sharp, the insistent wooden syllables forming the name of Adam over and over, the whole summons repeated three times, the calling of Noah to the creation to come into the Ark: first to the things that go upon their bellies, then to the things that go on four feet, and last, to man, who stands up, and knows. Besides the portable semantron there is a larger one in most monasteries, swung from chains in an arcade, or outside the refectory or a church door: a massive beam cut in roundels at the ends. And in some monasteries there is also a huge omega-shape of iron, suspended in a commanding position; on certain occasions these, too, and the bells in the towers, are all sounded together. But the plain semantron, half beaten and half resounding, from a shoulder, each blade in a different part of the same note, announces the hour of most of the services, and of some of the times prescribed for private prayer. The hours themselves are reckoned according to different systems, in different monasteries. In most of them—eighteen of the twenty—time is told according to the ancient Byzantine system, in which sunset is twelve o'clock. Iviron observes the traditional Georgian custom of calling sunrise twelve o'clock. And one monastery Vatopediou, counts its hours according to the custom prevailing in the secular world, with twelve o' clock at noon. The services also vary somewhat from monastery to monastery upon a basic pattern: nones, vespers, and complines in the latter part of the day and on some of the nights vigils lasting through the hours of darkness until daybreak and the opening of the outer doors. In some of the churches the office is read and attended now by only a handful of old monks, nodding, chanting, bowing, in the light of candles, among the glinting of ikons and brass candelabra, and small flames in red glass ikon lamps, and the smoke of incense rising toward the dim faces in the ceiling, to the sound of the worn words.

I was outside the blue doors in time to see the sun appear at the end of a pink, gold, mother-of-pearl path of mist that blurred the sea. The peak was clear, catching the first light, one wisp of cloud trailing from it eastward toward the sunrise. Looking up and back to the walls of the monastery, I saw two old monks out on a high balcony, sitting watching the light before their first meal of the day. They waved me on my way, down the path through the woods, to the southeast. Jays flashed uphill among the trees. The low rays of the sun rebounded from the mist on the sea, and slanted under the chestnut branches. Figs hung out of the woods, over the narrow walled path, with its accompaniment of trickling water: breakfast. Arbutus, the red berries splashed on the ground below the bushes, some of them overripe and broken open in the fall, showing the yellow, mealy, gritty interior: *arbutus unedo,* or *monedo,* as I have seen it written: "arbutus eat one," the name in Latin referring to the effects of the fruit, its property of loosening the bowels, or the notion that it contains an insidious narcotic, or both. But I like the flat dry taste, and as usual did not limit myself to one—and as usual they did no harm. A twist of the path under their foliage. A dry fountain like an empty shrine, set in the mouth of a wooded ravine. Flocks of warblers flying through sunbeams, with silence all around them. Whole banks covered with cyclamen. The smell of pines mingling with that of the mold of chestnut woods and the scent of honey as the undersides of the leaves warmed with the morning. Mysteries farther on: the unmistakable sounds—and the sight—of hens in the woods, from some stone-roofed *skete* or *kelli* on the slope, and at the same time, fox droppings on the cobbled path. The cobbles do not run all the way. They play out, they have washed out, they are abandoned for shortcuts gnawed by the tear-shaped iron shoes of mules, they resume suddenly on a curve skirting a gorge, or at the approach to a stone bridge: On the way down from Koutloumousiou to the south there is a high arch over a rocky torrent, quiet in the autumn. Stone-covered runnels cross the path, the hidden water whispering and splashing like mice. Rags of cloud appeared up on the ridge and vanished over it. Bright sun on the slope to the south. Where the path followed the side of a small valley in sheltered woods, I came on a monk down on all fours, gardening, clearing the weeds from the wall below a long bed of flowers that had been tended with love. His hat was off and it was clear that he had been absorbed in the work since first light, and that his heart was in it. Wild dianthus were blooming along the path a few feet from the nodding yellow heads of campanulas. The soil was black and crumbly and his hands and knees and cassock were covered with it. Just beyond him was a small chapel newly painted reddish-brown and white, with painted tin cans full of basil plants around the door, and rosemary in bloom at the eastern end. Then the path came out into the open, dropped toward bare ground. Cypresses marking far slopes, giving scale. Autumn squills, St. Johnswort with enormous flowers, that late in the year. The green brush gave away to olive trees, each on its separate half-moon of carefully built dry stone terrace, and over the shoulder of the hill came the sound of breakers. I rounded the corner, eastward, and saw below me the huge monastery of Iviron, on its eminence dominating the shore. Gardens, orchards, vineyards around it. One facade with a white-columned neoclassic portal: the main gate, from which a broad cobbled way led down, past roofed fountains and garden walls, to a wharf, and a fortified tower by the sea.

It is there, the legend says, that the Virgin came ashore out of the stormy waves. When she had prayed to her son to be given the mountain, a voice from heaven had granted it to her, to be her garden and paradise, and a place of salvation.

The great ocher walls of the portico lead under a large ikon to a cobbled entrance hall with the gatekeeper's office on one side, and the bright interior at the far end. Fountains, the spouts emerging from slabs of carved marble: bas-reliefs of thistles and birds, angels, suns, crowns. There is a magnificent *phiale* facing the entrance: Even the curtain drawn back between the marble columns is carved in stone. And a cluster of churches in the broad level courtyard, besides the *katholikon* itself, which dates from the eleventh century and contains frescoes of different ages, from the sixteenth century on, some of great vigor and beauty. The chapel of St. John the Baptist, near the church, is said to stand on the site of the original temple of Poseidon, destroyed by the presence of the Virgin, and replaced in the third century by a small monastery named for its founder, St. Clement, Bishop of Jerusalem. The present monastery was built by three Georgian-Iberian (whence the name Iviron) noblemen, late in the tenth century.

Another chapel stands near the site of the old gates, and is dedicated to, and houses, the "Portaitissa," the Virgin-of-the-Gate, the guardian of the monastery: one of the most revered ikons on the mountain, and one of the oldest and richest in legends. Traditionally, it is one of the seventy paintings by the hand of St. Luke, and it is one of several ikons which are said to have been consigned to the sea, to save them from ikonoclasts, and to have been brought by miraculous means to the mountain. The Portaitissa traditionally came from Constantinople, where an imperial messenger had pointed a sword at her and had been frightened off when the picture had begun to bleed. (Another story, about a scar on the painting, says that it marks the place where the sword of an Arab pirate struck the Virgin below the chin, and the wound bled; the sight of the blood converted him, made him a monk, and at last a saint—Saint Barbaras.) The widow who had owned the ikon is said to have taken it down to the sea and watched it sail away, upright, westward. Seventy years later it appeared at the base of a pillar of light, off Iviron, and a voice from heaven named the one monk who would be allowed to carry it ashore.

It was as well that I had been to Iviron before and had a glimpse, at least, of its treasures: Apart from a young monk mending a black garment at the outer gate, who looked at my permit and waved me in, there was no one to be seen, and the church and chapels were locked—except for the porch, with its remarkable frescoes. I crossed the courtyard and climbed the long staircase leading to the rooms for receiving guests, and was met by a layman who insisted on speaking German to me, and urged me to go somewhere else to eat. Iviron is one of the monasteries that has suffered most from the recent influx of tourists: too famous, and too easy to reach, by road directly from Karyes, or by boat, during the summer. It must have been a great relief there when the season was over. I carried my pack down to the church porch again, for another long scrutiny of the murals, and then back out through the main gate. Mules were tethered by a column, and mules and horses by the fountain at the bottom of the cobbled incline, facing the sea. Near the wharf, between the shingle and the wall at the foot of the gardens firewood had been piled shoulder high. More pack

animals were tethered beside it, and an assembly of monks, muleteers, and boatmen were sitting on logs following a heated discussion
between an old monk—obviously in charge of the transaction—and
a boatman. They were both red in the face and beyond concern for
decorum, though not for drama: They danced their indignation back
and forth around one symbolic log on which they visited tokens of
their passions, kicking it, pushing it toward each other, snatching it
back again, putting a foot on it, turning their backs on it, walking
away, and whirling around to deliver a terrible rejoinder. The wind
was off the sea. The argument seemed to have been going on since
sunrise. The audience swayed like the waves, and the mules swished
and stamped. I watched one complete but inconclusive round and
then threaded my way among them, between the walls of firewood,
stepping over the log; I was scarcely noticed, I went on, along the road
that runs parallel to the water, to the end of the wall, and then turns
inland, uphill. Much of it is recent, and raw. Jeep-tracks in the mud.
Mutilated swaths hacked across the slopes for telephone poles, and
bright new wires humming above them. The new divine right. The
road overruns bits of old footpath here and there, climbing. Made for
wheels, and the body can feel it. At the end of a long ascent through
woods, it levels out in sand and granite rubble glinting with mica.
The woods on the north slopes were still green as spring. A few rain
clouds suddenly gathering. The sun hot, the air cool in the shade.
Around a bend, sitting on a lap of vines and gardens at the head of
several small steep valleys, Philotheou rose out of the thinning leaves.

It is not one of the largest monasteries, and its walls, surmounted
by no towers, are plainer than many, though hung with old, windowed
balconies, some of them used now only by pigeons. The road turned
into a cobbled lane that ran along between the garden wall, on the
left, and overgrown vineyards tumbling toward abandoned *kellis* in
the woods, on the right, and it led to a cobbled space surrounded
by grapevines, big trees, benches set along the wall facing the sea, a
fountain under the shade of the vine-arbor, and the doors of the monastery, opening under balconies to the grassy courtyard bright with

the autumn sun. I had sailed, a year and a month before, along this bit of coast, and looked up at the monasteries and *sketes* half hidden on the slopes, silent as paintings, and they had passed from sight, and here I stood. There had been great activity at Philotheou since that first glimpse from the sea. The sound of hammering echoed around the courtyard; a saw joined the music; a young monk hurried past me carrying a board and another saw; a monk balanced on the top of a ladder, painting the stucco window-surrounds of the church dark red. The monk with the board and the one on the ladder both saw me but went on with what they were doing; their lips were moving; they were praying as they worked. An old monk, by a walled flower bed, to the right of the entrance, shuffling under balconies, with a fat cat at his heels, smiled and waved me in toward the dahlias and marigolds, the smell of woodsmoke, the wine barrels lying on the grass with water running into them to swell them; he told me to make myself at home.

A young monk with a hearing aid and a saw and crowbar came from behind me, greeted me with a nod, and wasted no time on his way to join the work on the far side of the church. I put down my sack and stood looking across the courtyard into a wide doorway on the other side, painted cans of basil flanking the door, and inside, a staircase newly painted bright blue, with a red carpet in the middle of the steps, climbing into the darkness. As I looked, two monks (they were all young except the old man with the cat) came from outside the monastery struggling with a huge reluctant sheet of hardboard which kept collapsing in the middle. I grabbed the sagging section despite their polite mumble of protest, and we proceeded across the courtyard to the door I had been considering, and up the blue stairs, and then on up another flight, before we stopped at the entrance to a large empty room. There, while they caught their breath, they asked me about myself, and one of them led me down into the courtyard, while another disappeared to look for somebody and in a moment several monks called me from an upper balcony and I was directed up newly painted stairs, along newly painted corridors, to a pale green room full of light, jutting out into a balcony over a courtyard. A long table down the middle, with a white crocheted tablecloth, and seats on either side, took up the whole room. A shelf of books along the east wall, high up, half of them in English. One monk who looked scarcely old enough to have grown his beard, showed me in, vanished, and returned almost at once with the guest tray, its napkins neatly ironed; he nodded shyly, and left. As he went, another monk entered, greeted me in English, and told me that he was busy at the moment, that he would be back shortly to talk with me—meanwhile I was welcome. His gesture included the shelf of books.

I had opened one of them, but was looking out into the courtyard, listening to the urgent sounds of carpentry and the few words, sharp and abrupt—not a conversation—that broke over them at intervals, when he came back: thin, grave face, fine features; always, in talk, leaning a little forward, as though in the act of bowing, looking up at the last minute, but the eyes never straying from my face. It was obvious that the time for this meeting had been set aside, taken away from something else. He spoke with a constant watchfulness: level, gentle, low-voiced, a slight smile, benevolent, but neither personal nor effusive. His attention was mine, but almost all of his life was elsewhere.

He had learned English as a child, at the American school in Athens. He spoke it softly, carefully, with little hesitation. I remarked on the youth of many of the monks—a sharp contrast to most of the monasteries—and the surge of manual work. He told me that it had been going on only since January. At that time the monastery of Philotheou had dwindled to eight aging monks. He himself was one of a larger group of young monks who had been living farther up the mountain at a *skete* called Provata, and the *kellis* around it; his own had been the *kelli* of Agius Artemius. Their enthusiasm, fired by a remarkable elder, had led growing numbers of new monks to the *skete*, and in a few years it had become crowded. Most of them had been moved, in January, to Philotheou, where the running of the monastery was divided between them and the eight old monks who were there. A similar takeover, he said, was planned for Koutloumousiou, where only five old monks were left, and perhaps for Simonos Petras, across the peninsula. The transition, at Philotheou, had not been without difficulties, for anyone. There was the inevitable friction between the older monks set in their ways and used to having the whole echoing place to themselves, and the sudden overwhelming invasion of youth and ardor. The newcomers, for their part, did not take readily to the life of a monastery. They were solitaries; at their beloved *skete* they had been trying, under the guidance of their elder, to restore what they believed was the all but lost Orthodox mystical tradition of constant prayer, the prayer of the heart, which Athos in particular had nurtured for centuries. In their *kellis* they had been able to devote almost all of their waking hours to private contemplative prayer. In the monastery there were more activities to be undertaken, many of them in common; administrative duties were far more demanding, and more time was devoted to liturgical worship. True solitude was harder to achieve. And the young monks' fervent devotion both to doctrine and to practice also contributed to a current of dissension between them and the older men. He told me that as the monastic calling had waned in numbers, in recent generations the monks had come increasingly from among the less educated parts of the population. Some of them were scarcely literate; very few of them could read the ancient Greek of the early texts. Gradually their understanding of many passages became patchy and distorted. Many things were forgotten altogether, and the process was accompanied by a growing laxity of habits and attitude, and a perfunctory performance of the divine services. My questions about the particular tradition of contemplative prayer to which he referred were met with an inquiry as to whether or not I was Orthodox, why I was interested, and a suggestion that I look carefully into the book that I had open on the table: Kadloubovsky and Palmer's translation of St. Nicodemus of the Holy Mountain's *Unseen Warfare.* "Now," he said, "I will show you to your room." And he led me along the corridor to a green room facing northwest, with a view of chestnut forests climbing the ridge. "I will go and see that you have something to eat," he said. "You will be called." I asked if I could help with the carpentry or, if possible, with the gardens, where

I had seen a layman hoeing rows of cabbages and eggplants. "No," he said, "most of the summer's work is over. We can do it all easily now." I had come a long way, he told me, and what I should do was to rest, and eat, and read the book, which he had urged me to bring with me. I said I would like to have more chance to talk with him, and he told me he would try to find time later in the day. And with a slight bow, which may not have been a bow at all, but simply his way of turning, he left me.

Bare wooden floor. Iron beds painted white. Even the sheet on the bed seemed not to have been used more than once or twice, and here it was, the end of summer. The door opened without a knock. It was a Dutch student, another who was traveling to the East; his knapsack was at the foot of a bed by a window across the room. The sheet on my bed, he told me, had in fact been clean the night before, when he had used it himself; if we swapped sheets we would both be sleeping in luxury. His subject was agriculture, but the methods of its practice at present had disheartened him, and he had decided to see a little of the world while there was time; he hoped to help with some farming in India, where he had friends. India, agriculture—Sir Albert Howard? I asked. But Howard's work on the soil of India, even in the early years of the century, had been at odds with an age in which farming was already becoming an adjunct of the chemical industry, and I was not surprised that his name was not mentioned in the curricula of agricultural schools in the Netherlands. The boy had come to Athos simply because he had heard about it after he had got to Greece, and had been curious. He liked the quiet of the mountain, but could not see what good the monasteries did. Footsteps, at that point, on the flagstones of the corridor, and a light knock on the door. It was Father Mark, the monk with whom I had been speaking, come to tell us that something had been prepared for us to eat.

From the long walls of the refectory, and from the end rounded like an apse, remnants of superb frescoes dominated the room, as though it were the fragment and they were the whole. Faces, haloes, bodies of saints standing, bowing, raised hands, wings, walls painted on walls, boats on the last flakes of seas, among deserts of white plaster. They had survived—as far as is known—for more than four centuries, through periods of poverty, neglect, damp winters, invaders, and a disastrous fire a hundred years ago. Long tables flanked by benches traversed the entire room, leaving the middle empty: The tables were half set, and at two places near the door, bowls of lentils, tomato and onion salad, oil, olives, bread, apples, water, had been placed. Again the bow, and Father Mark disappeared through the green-painted wooden partition that separated the refectory from the kitchen, and we were left to eat in a silence that imposed itself, Sounds of dishwashing came from beyond the partition, and two young monks came and went, continuing to set the tables; others came in, spoke with them briefly, went out again. When they caught our eyes they nodded, and their lips went on with their prayers. The correct greeting of a monk on Athos is "Evlogite"—"Bless me"—and the reply is "O Kyrios"— "The Lord." At Philotheou the exchange is often dispensed with. But one small bright-faced monk, the cook, came to ask whether the food was good, and to tell us to eat more, bustling, permanently amused—he laughed at the very idea of our bringing our plates out to the kitchen, where he was washing the last dishes, a few minutes later, and at our offering to help there. We had scarcely left the refectory when I saw him, clutching a saw, pattering downstairs to join the carpentry, as though it would not wait.

Outside the monastery, one of the old monks was sitting on a bench in the sun, gossiping with a lay workman, their backs to the sea. The gardener was still hoeing the monstrous eggplants and okras, and made it clear that he would have welcomed a bit of willing help, but plainly it would have offended some rule of hospitality or some monastic restriction, if the Dutch student and I had ignored Father Mark's evident unwillingness for us to participate in the work of the monastery. The Dutch boy went off one way exploring, and I another, around to what appeared to be a muleteer's house behind the monastery, a farmhouse with an upper porch, an old whittled banister, pack saddles, horse blankets hanging on wires, tack, old sewing gear, axes, pieces of olive presses, rope—hanging, leaning, waiting in someone's sleep: It was the siesta hour. Around to the newly painted cemetery door, past a storehouse with part of a new floor laid, to some abandoned *kellis* sitting in their arbors of unpruned vines. Up into the woods above a pile of new-sawn lumber stacked to dry. The monastery derives part of its income from the sale of timber. Clearings, up in the woods, healing, full of cyclamen. By the time I got back, the bench was empty and I sat to read, where I could look up and watch the pigeons under the balconies, the shadows moving along the whitewashed garden wall, the sea far below—until I saw a monk in a black veil stride into the monastery with a semantron on his shoulder, and heard it, moments later, sharp and brisk. I got up and went in, but a monk met me in the church door and asked politely whether I was Orthodox. No one who was not was admitted to their services, he told me. I had encountered hostility on Athos before—the feeling of being regarded as a heretic intruding upon holy ground. I had been forbidden to pass behind the ikonostasis, when Orthodox visitors were being shown in to see miraculous ikons kept in the holiest parts of churches; reliquaries had been closed lest I should catch sight of the relics. But such acts had been great exceptions. Never before had I been forbidden to attend a service—and it was done without overt hostility, as though it was perfectly natural and I should have been expecting it. A while later, reading at the window above the chestnut forests, while the shadows darkened on the ridge under the gathering clouds, I heard the service end, and the clatter of feet on wooden stairs, and then the monks chanting in the refectory below. They clattered out. The light knock came on the door. Father Mark, to lead me, in my turn, to the refectory. On the way he said that he would have some time, after I had eaten, to continue our conversation. The Dutch boy was not yet back, but they brought him along when he showed up. A cold light came through the refectory windows. There was no sunset. The merry cook came in to say that his soup (cold on the table) was a triumph (which it was) and should be eaten in quantity along with everything else—chestnuts and okra and olives and bread, in whatever order seemed appropriate. Father Mark was waiting, after the meal, and led me past the guest room, along the corridor, to an old parlor: Yellowed lithographs and photographs of czars and archbishops tilted out from the walls into the early dusk. We sat down at a large round table; the white crocheted tablecloth hung to the floor. In the twilight the table seemed to be growing. There was light enough for some time for me to miss nothing of Father Mark's face: hollow, tilted forward just as it was when he was standing. Watching me out of the tops of his eyes, with their steady burn.

He asked me what progress I had made with the books on the shelf, and what my plans were for the next day. I had originally thought of going on southeast, perhaps to Megistis Lavras, down in the craggy country near the end of the promontory, the first in rank, one of the oldest, largest, and most beautiful monasteries on the mountain. When I had been there, the autumn before, I had seen only a few of its celebrated frescoes and its other treasures. And on the next memorable day I had left at first light to round the steep end of the peninsula, making for the *skete* of St. Anne, on the western coast. It is generally considered to be an arduous trip, along the rubbly edges of precipices, across stretches of scree, up and down over the spines and buttresses that line the south face of the peak. I wanted to have the whole day for it. The footpath ravels into scrub more than once, and is lost. Looking for it, I had pushed through thickets into a high shady meadow ringed with chestnut trees and holly oaks and shining with yellow autumn daffodils; horses without bells, half wild, bolted into the woods at the far end. A little way beyond the meadow an icy spring trickled out and crossed the resurrected path—the place may have been the "Krya Nera," the Cold Waters; snow is said to lie near the place throughout most of the year. And in the woods below, a hermitage not long abandoned, the hearthstone hollow like a shallow sink, the back of the fireplace rounded in the same stone, and the projecting ends of the small stone mantlepiece carved round. The shutters and the cupboard doors were still intact in the one hushed room with horse droppings on its rotting floor. At a farther spring I had mistaken my way and followed the sound of horsebells up the steep slope, thinking that the path led over a shoulder of the mountain. I had climbed through a grove with another spring, far up into clouds and cold winds, the stones wet, the path growing even steeper and less probable, but the horsebells still rang from above me, in the cloud. Until I came in sight of a long low building like a metal tent, on the bleak, foggy, buffeted slope. The horses were loose on the scree above it, and as I came nearer I heard the sound of scraping and the slosh of water. A few monks were establishing themselves there, a bare thousand feet from the summit, where the slopes on both sides drop more than five thousand feet, straight to the sea. They were rebuilding the small chapel of the Panayia, mixing cement in the clammy wind. In one corner of the earth-floored room where they lived and ate, a fire was smoking under a pot. Their ambition included new frescoes. I had left them and clambered down again through the clouds, and the evening woods full of low west light, and at last the miles of steep marble stairs leading to St. Anne's, just above the sea, where they were bringing in the grapes of that year, and the monks and their kittens welcomed me. And from there, in the next days, I had followed the path through the New Skete, to the monasteries crowning the looming rocks of the southwest coast: Agiou Pavlou, Dionysiou, Ossiou Gregoriou, and harder to believe when actually seen than it is in pictures—Simonos Petras, held up, apparently by pure faith, standing on its cliff as though on a wave. And back to Daphne. I had thought this autumn, perhaps, to see Megistis Lavras again, and if the weather permitted, to make my way on to visit the wood-carving and ikon-painting monks at the skete of Kafsokalivia, on the south coast. If the rains broke, I thought I would take the boat back from Megisitis Lavras. But there was no boat from Megistis Lavras now, Father Mark told me. The one going around the end of the peninsula stops running anyway in October, because the sea, which is dangerous even in summer, becomes savage after the equinox. And the fishing boat north to Iviron stops its runs after the first of October for the same reasons that the cafes close in Ouranopolis. The path over the cliffs to Kafsokalivia, and the whole of the end of the peninsula, were not to be recommended if the heavy autumn rains broke, and though the weather on Athos is hard to predict, the clouds on the ridge that evening looked ominous. "Stay if it rains tomorrow" Father Mark said, and he explained that the rule forbidding visitors to stay for more than twenty-four hours was more or less at the discretion of the different monasteries, particularly after the tourist season was over.

It would have been hard to guess his age. A detached authority on the one hand, that was clearly mature, and on the other, a simplicity and candor that seemed distinctly youthful. The features, emerging from the fine beard, left the matter in doubt, though they themselves were sharply drawn and clear, the bones prominent but delicate, the large eyes set deep. Early thirties perhaps. He was twenty-two. He had become a monk five years before. His mother was devout, but his father was opposed to any religious manifestations, and had at first refused to allow his son even to visit Athos. And the boy had gone, during the Easter holidays, to the monasteries of Meteora, looking for a spiritual guide, and there had met an abbot who had urged him to go on to Athos and seek out one monk, the abbot at Provata. His own father's consent had finally been obtained, after some difficulty, and the young man had come and met the brothers, but not the abbot until several visits later. By that time he had decided that he wanted to be a monk at the *skete;* he had asked, and been granted, the abbot's permission to come, and he had gone and said good-bye to his family and come back to take the vow of obedience to the abbot, and be given a monk's name in place of the one he had grown up with.

The abbot, he told me, was a man now in his forties; he too was the son of a devout mother. After she had been left a widow his mother had made part of the house into a chapel, where she and friends met to pray. She had tried to live like a nun, and she had asked her son, who was a priest as well as a monk, to come and consecrate her chapel. While he was there she had asked him to make her a nun; several of her friends had taken the vows at the same time, and they had formed a small convent, with him as their confessor.

The abbot had received his own training, and had been instructed in the sacred teachings, by an elder named Joseph, a holy man secluded somewhere on Athos, who had spent his life trying to rediscover the true hesychast (Hesychasts, "the Silent," from Greek *hesychia*, "silence") tradition, of immeasurable age but certainly going back as far as the Desert Fathers, in the fourth century The practice of hesychasm had involved, from the beginning, a constant inward awareness and invocation of God, a fervent meditative discipline of thoughts, and a corresponding struggle with distraction. It was, and it is, both a way of living and a state of being; it centers on a form of continual inner prayer, the prayer of the heart. Silence, asceticism, self-emptying, all directed toward a more intense focusing: at the dawn of the monastic age the Abbot Bessarion, in the desert, as he was dying, had said, "The monk should become, like the cherubim and seraphim, nothing but an eye." For centuries the monks who had practiced the prayer of the heart had borne witness to it as the way to the kingdom of God that is within. In the thirteenth century Nicephorus the Solitary or the Hesychast, on Athos, had added to the already considerable corpus of writings on the "rule" or "keeping" of the heart, a discussion of the control of breath in prayer, a technique that may well have been an unwritten legacy from much earlier. It was developed in greater detail by later writers; the technique fostered a wave of monastic enthusiasm, and another of reaction. There was heated controversy over its importance, and over the theological value of the inner light that it produced, which some of the method's adherents claimed was indistinguishable from the essence of God, the uncreated light that had shone on Mt. Tabor. The movement had survived the controversy and had suffered from the general decline of monasticism in the centuries that followed. The whole tradition had been revived in the eighteenth century and many of its scattered texts gathered together and published as the *Philokalia* ("Love of Beauty"), a collection that exercised a powerful effect in the following generations, not only in the Greek world, but in Russia. But the ardor had again drained from monasticism, and the tradition had faded in the monasteries for lack of succession and zeal. It had withdrawn to the remote *kellis* and hermitages on the mountain, and it was there, and in the ancient texts, that the elder Joseph—Father Mark assured me— had found it and breathed it back to life. The twilight had gone from the room, and the young monk's eyes were still two points in the shadow. He had not himself told me the story of the tradition, but only of his confidence that it had been found again and resurrected, and that it was the one true way set forth by Christ and the apostles, the unbroken promise. He spoke, he said in his low voice, from experience. When I asked him more about the prayer itself, he said that I was welcome to read about it—more and more of the old texts were being published—but that the reading was only preparation; the learning itself required the guidance of an elder—and of course it assumed the Orthodox faith, the only one that could claim to go back to Christ and the apostles without a lapse. The Roman church, for him, was simply not Christian—a limb amputated, a schism. He spoke of it as hopelessly lost, rather in the way some conservative Roman Catholics speak of Protestantism. The entire contemplative tradition of the West he considered, *a priori,* to have no value whatever. He was also severely critical of a secularizing movement within the Orthodox church itself, which had drawn many of his own generation away from monasticism into a more active life, professing a modern social consciousness; he believed that it had encouraged doctrinal indifference, a hostility to the contemplative tradition, and a disregard for prayer itself.

But it was prayer, the quest for it, that had drawn the young monks to the *skete* of Provata, and its abbot. The night, Father Mark told me, was—at least for beginners—more favorable than the day for silent prayer, and most of the hours of darkness had been given to it. They woke there at sunset (midnight on the Byzantine clock) and spent the next hours, until six on their clock (some time around midnight on ours, depending on the time of year) in silent prayer. Then they had gathered, by candlelight, in their church, for two and a half hours of liturgical worship. After that, they had breakfasted on porridge and at the same time received instruction in the holy texts, and discussed them. Over their meal they had pronounced prayers for the dead. When the meal was over, the lessons and the inquiries into the texts had continued into the daylight, and then they had gone to sleep for three hours before starting the day's work, which occupied them until early afternoon. Then reading, and vespers, followed by the meal of the day, and sleep until sunset. The monastery routine still chafed them, and it was hard not to feel that time was being daily stolen from prayer; the acceptance of the change was an exercise in obedience. At Philotheou they went to bed at sunset, and slept for four and a half hours. The long session of private prayer that followed was two hours shorter than at the *skete,* and the hours of liturgical worship were proportionately longer. An hour or so more was spent in manual labor, instead of reading and solitary meditations. The difference was great enough for a monk such as Father Mark to feel it as a constant yoke. Weaker brothers, he said to me with a slightly ironic smile, are allowed to sleep longer, and urged to eat more. The long services in the church, particularly the vigils, were physically exhausting: the stalls are so built that one leans back onto a shallow shelf, and props up the elbows but remains standing. Some monks develop hernias from remaining from four to six hours at a time in that position.

The rain was falling heavily in the dark chestnut forest. Father Mark had lit a kerosene lamp and we were talking across the flame. The hollows in his face were more pronounced in the unsteady glow. I asked him about his sleep and he dismissed the question at first, saying that there was always time, as long as I was interested. But at last he admitted that he was one of the "weaker brothers" he had spoken of: His health was bad, and the doctors said that he must eat and sleep, because his lungs were not sound. The damp from the woods was bad for him. He shrugged. The Dutch boy came in just then. He had heard our voices and seen the light under the door. He wanted to ask about the life there. What made them come, to be monks on Athos? What made them stay? And his real question, which he asked with diffidence and hesitation: What good were they doing? The young monk asked him what he meant by "good," but it was not an attempt to dodge the question—only to get the boy to consider it for a moment. And the answer, predictably enough, was "good to others": active altruism. "Yes," the monk said, "it is important. But it is not the only good, and we are not even certain that it is always good. How can you know?" The Dutch boy thought for a moment of how one might judge of goodness, and the goodness of works, and he said something about what they did, their effects. "What your works do will never be known to you," Father Mark said. He tried to make it clearer. He spoke of goodness as a cause. He said, "until you have the good inside you, how can you do good; what will it mean?" He said it in several ways, straining his command of English, while the Dutch boy listened skeptically. "It is there," Father Mark said, touching the air as though to wake it, trying to remember something. "How do you say it?" he asked, as though we did "say it"; he was whispering Greek words, groping to bring them into English. "The good man . . . out of his heart . . . out of its good riches . . ." *The good man, out of the good treasure of his heart, bringeth forth good things.* I listened to him making his own translation.

By sunrise the rain was over; the forest was dripping. Father Mark was out in the cold corridor and breakfast was waiting at the foot of a painted saint facing east: heavy bread and apple butter, tea, and a boiled potato. I left my sack and went out through the gate into the morning mist. An old monk tying up a mule—where had he been at that hour?—discoursed to me in Greek and a few words of English, about the path down the slope to Karakallou. Evidently something about me amused him, and so did the thought of all the wrong turnings I might make and where *they* would lead me. The path splits off, without warning, from the new sand road and the swath for the telephone wires, and in a dozen steps leads over a bank out of sight of them, to where the woods seem not to have changed for a thousand years. Trickling sounds in the granite rubble. Flurries of cyclamens, jays diving through the trees with light folded in their wings. A robin, keeping just ahead of me then following just behind me. The sea appearing in patches, far below through the branches and mist. Slate roofs and cypresses on the lower slopes. Mushrooms, smell of chestnut mold in the early morning. Mingled sounds of sea and wind in autumn leaves not yet dry Where the path straightens and starts to drop, a narrow wooden flume, on rickety stilts, keeps it company, dripping all the way. Near one of the biggest leaks, a tin can suspended for drinking from. Rail fences, new rails set into them; sign of young monks in the *sketes*. A gate post, entrance to a *skete*, with a pot of basil in a can wired to it, just watered, still overflowing. Seen from above, the skirts of vines run up from all sides to the roofs of the *sketes* and *kellis*, so that windows, doors, and walls are invisible. The first sight of Karakallou from above: an immense stone tower, wading in the monastery walls. Horsebells in the woods. Sound of wood-chopping, smell of chestnut smoke. The cobbles in the path become more regular, winding down among the trees; the path turns into a lane between outbuildings. In a porch, an old cross-eyed lay-man, splitting wood. To the left of the stone area before the main gate, overlooking the sea, the long vegetable garden, with terrace walls around it. A small cross tied to the top of one of the bean poles. One dry cornstalk standing in the tall eggplants, rustling among their black fruit. Loud sounds of water running: incessant stony bird voice. Gray head, gray coat, bent harvesting red peppers, on the far side of the water sound. Beyond the garden, on the terrace above it, a row of wooden crosses, some painted blue, some green, and a small stone house emanating neither menace nor sadness.

Pink-washed entrance tower, and no one near the open doors. Karakallou is one of the least visited monasteries on Athos. The flag-stones inside continue the outer slope, though less steeply. Bones from a whale over a door, and a racket of carpentry filling the small cold courtyard with echoes. On the tower, facing inward, a blue-washed balcony with a bell, on a level with the tops of the lime trees. Limes glowing in the shade. A huge stone basin near the red church; ancient carved slabs set into walls. Heaps of firewood. An old monk and a layman were putting a new corrugated iron roof onto a flight of steps leading up to a balcony: The racket came from the hammer on the sheet of iron held up on its raw struts, the layman crawling out onto the bending sheet to where the whole tipsy structure was supported by patient divine intervention, and there banging big nails while the old monk approved. Other old monks sorting nuts in the sun, and doing their sewing. The carpenters waved me toward a building that turned out to be the refectory: dark, empty of decoration, spilling out of its farmy kitchen where monks were wandering back and forth. Catching sight of me, they herded me to a table as though I might be wounded, and then dispersed, and in a moment the place in front of me was garnished with bread, lentils, tomatoes, peppers, olives, and a large carved double wooden salt bowl. Monks came and ate in silence. A rounded monk drifted in, selected peppers from wooden trays, slipped them into the folds of his robes, gazed into the kitchen for a while as though into an infinite landscape, and drifted out again. A thin old monk, bent with rheumatism, a delicate open face, came to talk with me. He had been to America, he told me. Working on a ship, fifty years ago. "Now you fly," he said, "don't you?"—with a hint of admiration for the idea, looking at me closely to see what strange effects it might have had I told him that I preferred boats. He shook his head. "You fly now," he said, and showed me how, with his hands. In between talking to me, he talked to himself; his smile changing from the one to the other. He asked me whether I would like to sleep there. I tried to explain that my sack was at Philotheou. "But you're here," he said, and got up to show me the guest room. I followed his thin bent back across the courtyard, watching the neat patches on the holes of his faded woolen socks. His rheumatic walk was clearer than most words: his health, the love of his monastery, the pleasure of being hospitable. With his back to me I thought of his long large slender hands resting on the dark table, flying up and setting again, under the gray eyes, as he talked. Up stone stairs between tumbling bushes of basil and marigolds. He flung open a door off a balcony. It was all mine, he said. The whole place to myself, I had to tell him again about Philotheou.

Karakallou is not as old as Megistis Lavras or Philotheou, but there was an abbot there within a generation of William the Conqueror. The origin of the name has been lost. Monks with the kind of historic perspective one sees in medieval paintings have been happy to credit the Roman emperor Caracalla with the foundation of the monastery, and I was curious to see his portrait, which is somewhere among the eighteenth-century frescoes, but it escaped me. Up on the tower, in the sunlight, a fig tree was growing out from among the stones, above new paint and corrugated iron. The old monk led me back out through the gate, since I was going after all, and stood in the sun describing to me the whole path to Philotheou. I was not to turn off to the *sketes*, uphill or downhill nor to the *kellis*, which he named (there is one nearby where a king and a general, in the sixteenth century, retired as hermits, after building much of the present monastery). His hand wound in the air, taking all the right turns, and then he stood and watched me climb, waving me on, each time I looked back, until I took the right turn, out of sight.

In the afternoon, at Philotheou, I walked up into the valley behind the monastery. The path winds over rocks, along a ledge, following the south side of a gorge, back into the chestnut forests, the far side bright green and gold, the sound of splashing coming up from rocks below. Not far inland, the ravine widens out, the trees are enormous and dark, the water lies in black mirrors at the foot of boulders big as the insides of caverns. A long tenuous bridge of crooked sticks, tacked to looming black trunks, crosses the pools, water striders and chestnut leaves flying over its reflection. On the other side the path climbs again, looks down to where the ravine narrows above the dark glade: rocks set in vast ferns, under chestnut boughs that bend toward the water. In the deep fallen leaves, a small elegant bronze frog watched me climb past, into the sound of a waterfall and a glimpse of the high sunny ridge through openings in the branches. It was still possible, not long ago, to cross over the mountain, on that same path, to Simopetra on the western coast, but Father Mark told me that the forest has blocked the way now. If the young monks move in at Simonos Petras, as they have done at Philotheou, then maybe, he told me, they would be able to open the footpath over the ridge again. They were supposed to be moving in within a few days, he said, but nobody was sure. The government was rumored to be obstructing the change; Simonos Petras is one of the most famous of the monasteries, and the thought of a full complement of young, enthusiastic monks there might not delight the Tourist Office.

Father Mark and I talked together again, at dusk, in the room with the round table. Wagtails were running on the rocks at the edge of the woods, below the monastery walls. I asked him about the wandering monks on Athos, several of whom I had encountered on the mountain. Little is known of them, he said, and nobody knows how many there are. Most of them are not true wanderers but have hermitages or caves somewhere, where they make carvings to sell, like other hermits. Many had left their monasteries in 1924, at the time of the dissent over the adoption of the Gregorian calendar, going as an act of defiance against the patriarch responsible for the change, whom they regarded as a heretic. Some had gone and pretended to be fools, in the ancient way. Some had really become mad. Only when they die, he said, do we find out about them. Then anybody who knew anything about their lives tells it. Some are no good, and some may be saints. There was a Yugoslav who had once worked the garden at Chilandari but had moved away and lived in a hut—a man who spoke five languages and preferred to be thought an unlettered peasant. Nobody knew who he had been, before he came to Athos. He died sitting in his chair, with a bowl of vegetables in his lap. He was thought to have been a man of great spiritual advancement. But there would be no more of the wanderers, so-called, when those now living had died. A man must be admitted to a monastery before he can legally wear a monk's cassock, which means that he must have an abbot's permission to live outside the monastery walls. To obtain permission to live as a hermit is not easy, and to live as a wanderer, attached nowhere—how could permission be granted for that? We talked of the elders and holy men living in remote parts of the mountain, all but unknown, and the tradition of which they are a part. And from them, Father Mark turned the subject to the ancient texts which were now being published at last, a number of them for the first time, and many of them in English. Several of the monks at Philotheou were learning English just so that they could read the translations of these words, since the Greek originals were unavailable. But it was hard getting books from anywhere; hard to know what had been published, to have things sent from abroad and pay for them in foreign currency—it was hard to find enough money of any kind. It seemed particularly ironic that it should be so difficult, when many of the originals had been written on Athos. But I was keeping him from his sleep. The chestnut leaves were beginning to give off moonlight. With my few words of Greek I said that they were beautiful. He echoed the word. "There are so many words for that, in Greek," he said.

In the morning, after a breakfast of chestnuts and tea, I took the back path down to Iviron. Very different from the new jeep road. A narrow, winding footpath, like others on the mountain, cobbled here and there, along old walls. The sound of the sea carries up into sheltered ravines where the sea is out of sight. I came to the monastery from the side facing the ridge, passing its gardens, and horses tethered near a drinking trough, one of them with its bell stuffed with green grass. I went into the courtyard once more, to look at the frescoes in the porch, and the carvings. The German-speaking layman from the kitchen hailed me as I came out—no one else had noticed me. I assured him that I had not come to eat, but that I had had a drink from one of the fountains in the monastery. "Which one?" he asked. I told him. "That's all right," he said. He pointed around a corner to another one. "That's the colic one," he said. And when I asked about that, he explained—what I had already grasped—that its water was apt to produce acute abdominal discomfort and other unpleasant symptoms. And he warmed to his subject and assured me that the two fountains in front of the main gate were the same way: one good, and one colic. "Why do they have a fountain of colic-water?" I asked. He said that the horses could drink it without ill effect, and it flowed into the trough. "And the one inside the monastery?" I asked. He raised his empty hands to indicate that he knew nothing about it, and shrugged, and I walked down to the sea with a new riddle to ponder. The thought that I was not staying to eat had led him to proffer persistent instructions about my route—but I already knew the way.

It led to the sea's edge and then north along the shore. For a half mile or so it followed the road to Karyes, and then a barely visible path dove from the level sand into the shadow between bushes and began to thread its way through dense arbutus thickets, along the cliffs above the sea. It came out onto treeless rocky slopes brilliant with heather, the smell of the sprays of heather in the sun overpowering the sea smell, and the deep hum of bees, in spite of a strong east wind, muffling the sound of the heavy surf. The path dropped to the shore, ran along shingle of white marble. Stones, of different sizes, at intervals of surprising regularity, broken in half, and the broken surfaces, worn slightly round, the shapes of soles of human feet. Climbing past a shuttered house, fisherman's house; a boathouse near it, and beyond, a massive tower commanding the water's edge, empty and doorless. Across the marshy mouths of streams, and up again into heather, over headlands. On one of them the monastery of Stavronikita, built on the end of a long jutting sea-cliff. The path dropped and approached it through rocky pastures; beyond them a garden with a scarecrow in it, dressed as a monk. Horses by a newly painted gate. Young horses, with groomed coats. But from the gate, the sound of a gasoline tractor.

Stavronikita is another monastery that has been turned over recently, at least in some respects, to a group of young monks, but the change has not taken the same form as at Philotheou. The aim, apparently, was different to start with. At Philotheou the manual labor is obviously undertaken with zeal and occupies most of the hours of daylight—all the time I was there, the monk at the top of the ladder was painting the outside of the church with a narrow brush, carefully picking out the window surrounds and the moldings, and as I left in the morning mist another monk was rearranging the slates on the dome; but even while working, both of them were consciously praying, their lips were moving, there was a silence around them. At Stavronikita the fervor of prayer may be as intense, but it is less apparent. The monks there have undertaken to reorganize the agricultural life of Stavronikita—which had long been known for its orchards and gardens—and they have resorted to a modest program of mechanization. At the top of the path, before it turned into an arbor leading to the main gate, a monk was sitting on a small tractor attached to a trailer. His gown was tucked up in his belt, and his beard almost reached the steering wheel. He was talking to a couple of laymen, agricultural workers, one of them sitting near an attachment for a power tool. Above them ran a line of stone arches, an ancient aqueduct, that descended from a spring on the upper slopes. The way to the gate led past the row of stone pillars supporting the end of the aqueduct, square stone cisterns at their feet, surrounded by flower beds. Late grapes still hanging from the dense arbor. From the wall, a view down over the gardens, to the sea.

Someone had been filling the lamp that hung above the main gate: It had been lowered to chest level in the doorway, with no one near it. As I started to walk around it, a middle-aged monk appeared and hustled me aside to a reception room, of recent furbishment. I had sat there the autumn before, in the company of the French priest, once a Benedictine monk who had admired the fresh beige paint of the walls, with the hand-done frieze at the top depicting agricultural activities, and the solid newly made furniture: signs of industry, somebody caring. The monk said that I and my pack must rest, and he left me, for some time. Young monks bustled past the door, in and out, with the abstracted haste that arrives with machinery. A Greek bourgeois entered, sat down; a monk came and greeted him and sat with him. The one who had led me in came back and prepared the traditional guest tray for him. I rose to go, but the monk insisted that I should rest a bit longer, and disappeared again. Quiet talk while the guest tray was consumed, and then a layman, an agricultural laborer, appeared in the door and questioned the monk about the tractor. The guest joined in the answer, the voices changed. They grew urgent, opinionated, jostling each other until all three of the men left together. When the monk who had led me in returned at last, he asked me whether I had hoped to sleep at Stavronikita. I said I thought not. "That's good," he said. "We're very busy here. Have you been to Pantokratoros?" "Yes," I said, "but last year. I think I'll go back." He approved of the idea at once, and said, "Come." He led me briskly into the courtyard and upstairs to the refectory, half filled with sea light, where a place had been set for me at the near end of the one long table: a bowl of boiled eggplant, cucumber and onion salad, even cheese. Up near the farther end of the table, several other places had been set, more elaborately, it seemed, and I noticed wine. I thought of the Greek bourgeois in the reception room, and remembered, on my first visit to the monastery, sitting up at that end of the table, facing the remnants of fine eighteenth-century frescoes on the walls, while a monk and two of the guests discoursed learnedly about the monastery's paintings and the history of the building. When I had finished the meal, this time, and carried my plates to the kitchen, the monk met me again and led me down to the church, to give me a chance to look again at the magnificent sixteenth-century frescoes there. When we came out, the monk pointed up to the massive tower rising above the gate, and told me it dated from the year one 1000 (there was supposedly a tower on the headland in the eleventh century) and had withstood pirates and fire. He was busy as he told me again, and I had seen the library—in the aimless manner of the utter layman who looks obediently at what he is shown, usually without understanding what he has just been told about it—the year before. All at once, as he stood telling me about the history of the buildings, all the libraries I had seen on Athos kaleidoscoped in my head—Megistis Lavras, Iviron, Chiliandriou: the padded doors, the black-curtained windows, heavy smell of mothballs, cloth covers on glass cases. Which illuminated page (the only one that would be seen, lying open under glass) of which water-colored gospel had been where? How far away I had stood from each sample offered to view, and how cursory had been each glimpse of things made to be looked at again and again through whole lives. I thanked the monk and picked up my pack. He must have felt that the welcome at Stavronikita had been somehow wanting, and he told me to wait once more, while he went into the kitchen behind the guest room, where I had been relegated upon arrival, and there he wrapped up several pieces of Turkish Delight in a paper napkin, and handed them to me, with some apples. He walked with me under the arbor, and along the flower beds. Had I no staff? he asked—and thinking I should have one, he selected a bamboo for me from several in a corner. I paused by a flowering bush of rosemary to pick a few leaves to crush and smell on the way and he turned and tore off a whole branch of it for me. When I had said good-bye he stood waving me on to the right path.

Through the thickets and woods along the sea-cliffs again, and up onto small plateaus, past *sketes*, some of them empty but apparently still used at times: glass in the windows, crockery near the fireplaces, patches of overgrown garden. Like Stavronikita, Pantokratoros rises on a stone headland above the sea; its own small harbor is nestled into the rocks at the foot of the promontory, and the approach, from the south, is again, as at Stavronikita, a descent to the level of the shingle to cross a broad streambed that circles around and among the well-kept gardens and orchards below the monastery walls. A cobbled ramp, like a lane in a fishing village, leads up along the south of the main enclosure, behind outbuildings, under the shade of large trees. Hens were exploring among the cobbles as I climbed, and a small pink pig was scratching his side against a stone. At the top of the ramp a wooden gate, open; more pigs and hens and a mule wandering loose on the area in front of the monastery whose domed and columned portico faces the sea. Firewood neatly stacked under an olive tree. On the seaward rim of the open space, a wooden summer house with benches all around it hangs over the harbor and the view of the coast, the cracks between its flagstones neatly bordered with whitewash. A round-faced toothless old monk with a long white braid down his back wandered out through the brilliant blue iron doors and vaguely shooed a nearby pig. I had set down my knapsack under the dome of the portico and the old monk beamed at me and said to come in when I liked; he stood for a while gazing toward the matchless view, and then went back in, himself. I had become interested in the paintings on the vaulted ceiling of the portico, and in the afternoon light on the coast and on the Holy Mountain, and in the intent lives of the pigs. There were swallows nesting in the porch. The paintings clearly were not very old; the monk had not known their age, or else (more probably) he had not understood my Greek; but their symbolism was more than usually abstruse. A central Godhead in a triangular halo. Below the halo, three vertical rows of circles, each of them of three colors, each of them winged, and each bearing inside it a smaller circle, like the pupil of a downcast eye, and in the smaller circle a head, full face, eyes left. Each row of circles flanked by two angels, from a ring of ten; each angel holding a sphere marked with two Greek letters: *omega* over *chi*.

I remembered, from the year before, the huge basil plants in the courtyard, standing in the crisscrossed line of whitewash, under the lemon trees, and the red katholikon at the top of the flagstoned slope. A new varnished banister rail flanked the steps leading to the balconies on the east side of the courtyard. A monk emerged from a doorway and signaled for me to go on up, and up again: The wide corridors of the balconies, too, were flagstoned, and whitewashed, and cool. I sat on a massive bench in the mixed smell of fish, frying, and outhouses. An immense monk with a plastic bag of fish passed me and smiled and told me to take it easy and come to church when they called me, and a few moments later I was hailed by a young monk inviting me down to vespers. He came to me after the service and introduced himself, in English—Father Theodoros—and led me to a kitchen off the corridor where I had been sitting. The room with its huge stove under a hood, and its table covered with oilcloth, opened onto a balcony high above the cliff and the sea. Pantokratoros, like several others on the eastern coast of Athos, is an idiorrhythmic monastery. There are two kinds of rules on the mountain, and each monastery professes one or the other. In the cenobitic rule, all property is held in common; meals are eaten together, and absolute spiritual obedience to the abbot is mandatory Eleven of the twenty monasteries on Athos are cenobitic, and they pride themselves on being better disciplined and more austere than those that follow the idiorrhythmic rule—a later (fifteenth century) development which allows for a more democratic administrative system, and greater individual scope either for asceticism and prayer, as some of its defenders insist, or for laxity and worldly indulgence, as the cenobites scornfully declare. The idiorrhythmic monasteries permit the holding of a limited amount of personal property, and the monks have apartments of two or three rooms, instead of a single cell. Theodoros, speaking to me with a play of grave irony, told me—after a few moments of conversation—to make myself comfortable. He shared the kitchen with another monk, Cyriac, the giant with the plastic bag full of fish, who came in while we were talking, laughed about the fish, laughed about my presence, welcomed me to their hearth, and was gone again. Theodoros led me out onto the wooden balcony and invited me to sit down at the weathered table, where I could look at the sea, while he made some coffee. None for him, he explained: He had a delicate stomach, and it had been troubling him for several days. Fasting, he supposed, was probably indicated, and he had resorted to it, more or less.

The rays of the sun had left the water. The sky was still full of day, but the moon was beginning to gleam, east of Athos. From the balcony the whole coast was visible—headlands and towers, the surf catching the first moonlight, and the abrupt crags clustering at the base of the peak. The sea began to glitter before the stars appeared. An old monk with a bloodshot eye entered the kitchen and came out and sat down, and another, younger monk, behind him, and the coffee-making grew more ambitious. Cyriac came back and we all sat on the balcony watching the evening. We discussed—chiefly with gestures—the old monk's bloodshot eye (the result of bumping into something in the dark)—a theme whose comic possibilities were trotted out for my benefit. Then we discussed Theodoros's stomach and the mysteries of digestion, with Theodoros providing conscientious translation. Cyriac, looking earnest, rolled up his sleeve to present, in the manner of a contribution, a patch of dry skin, which clearly fascinated him, on his huge forearm. Theodoros and I pronounced it an allergy and agreed that his chances of survival were probably fair. It seemed that the young monk should be able to provide a malfunction of some kind for discussion, but he passed; and as for me, I could offer nothing more interesting than a bit of stiffness, contracted by sitting in the shade. We laughed at the orgy of hypochondria; the balcony rattled; the water in the basin where the fish were soaking, on the other table, shimmered with scales of moonlight. The young monk and the old one left; Cyriac went in and began to clatter at the stove, and Theodoros came out and sat down to look at the evening. Supper was halfready, he said, and Cyriac would do the rest. He opened a newspaper—partly to show that he had it. The moonlight was bright enough to read it by, but he gazed at the sea with a deep familiar satisfaction.

I learned that he was in his early thirties. He had been a monk for seven years. He had even lived for a while at Philotheou, but he was not one of those, he said. The place was not for him. He twirled his beard. Too regimented, he explained. His calling, as he had quickly seen, was not the same as theirs. He had become a monk, in the first place, not from an overwhelming desire for the monastic life, but—he began to tell me about life in Greece as he had seen it. He came from near Athens; his father had a restaurant in Piraeus (but not fresh fish like this, he told me). He described the workmen in Piraeus, sitting bored in their cafes, bored in their houses, drinking and centering their lives on their television sets, watching other people kick leather balls around fields: He gave an imitation of his secular contemporaries coming home, ignoring their wives, slumping into armchairs to face the box, as he was facing the Holy Sea. That was not a life he had managed to look forward to, he said. Television, to him, was the symbol and one of the forms of absolute debasement, an abdication of life. "They think cars would be even better," he said. He had not wanted any of that. And then there was politics: Both the right and the left, he had concluded, led naturally and avidly to police states. He did not want to live in a police state—and he believed in God. He had felt that that was a good thing to base a life on, and he was not troubled by the thought of living extremely simply without material ambition. But the fervor of Philotheou had seemed too narrow, and he had not much liked living as a hermit, either: there was a *kelli* up on the sea-cliff where he had stayed from time to time, and which he still could use, when he chose to. We could see it from the balcony up in the moonlit olive trees, above the heather, with its low garden wall around it, and its cypresses—I had passed it that afternoon, and admired it. Too lonely, he said, sleeping up there. He liked to go up and spend the day and look at the wild flowers, but for living he preferred to have his friends around. His frankness was encouraging, and as tactfully as I could I brought the subject around to women—didn't he miss them? That was another matter, he told me. It hadn't been easy especially at first. He liked women. He had almost got married. It wasn't the girl who had changed his mind. It was marriage, as he had seen it in Greece, at any rate. Everything that came with it. For the rest of your life. With some difficulty he had decided against it, but if he had stayed in the world it might have claimed him just the same. And in his view, if he was not going to marry, relations with the opposite sex, as things were at present in Greece, would not have been very satisfactory. "But Cyriac!" he laughed, and nodded toward the big monk padding back and forth, cleaning fish and preparing supper. "He never had a moment's peace." In Crete, he told me, where Cyriac had been born, he had been widely and eagerly sought after and had become terribly—entangled. "What about it?" Theodoros called, and he asked Cyriac to explain how things had been. Cyriac paused in his cooking and, fixing me with his eye, ran the fingers of his right hand lightly up his left arm to the shoulder, raised his eyebrows, ducked, heaved a great sigh, and laughed. Then he picked up the basin of fish guts and heads, and looked over the railing. In the mingled dusk and moonlight, among the shadows at the base of the walls, one could make out hens, pigs, and one kitten, waiting under the balcony for Cyriac's nightly offering. He aimed in front of the kitten, which subsequently disappeared under the scrimmage of pigs and the flapping hens, but reemerged a few moments later. Then he aimed to the side and tried to distract the pigs and catch the kitten away from them. The kitten appeared to be in more danger from trampling than from starvation, but it seemed to be taking care of itself.

"This is one of the best times," Theodoros said. "Beautiful. Autumn. The season's over at last. I never thought, when I came to be a monk, that I'd spend half my summer washing dishes." And the tourists were worse every year. They came in boatloads. Now that there was a road down from Karyes, they came in busloads, too. Two thousand—three thousand—something like that, at Stavronikita and Iviron that summer, and Pantokratoros had not fared much better. "Most of them don't know anything and don't care," he said, "about anything. Do you know why so many come? It's very bad of me to say it, but half, more than half, much more than half, come just because it's cheap." I sympathized. I pointed out that I was prolonging the annual burden. "Oh, that's different," Theodoros said. "You're a guest. In the summer we almost never have guests—there are too many. Even the ones we'd be glad to talk with are usually part of a crowd. You're alone. Make yourself—at home."

How did I feel about eggs? Cyriac inquired. That is, did I *like* them. I said I thought highly of eggs. "Eggs?" Theodoros asked. "I thought we were having fish." An apologetic nod to me, and a hurried consultation between my two hosts. Cyriac had decided that the fish would take too long, and should be kept for the following day. He had prepared a large salad of mixed raw and cooked vegetables, and now was about to complete the meal with some cold scrambled eggs out of a cupboard. There were even some cold noodles. "No, no," Theodoros said, "*I* will do the eggs." And he leaped up and with a practiced hand heated the pan and fried me two eggs, fresh from the hens under the balcony, in oil from the trees on the hill. Cyriac set out the cold scrambled eggs for himself—not all of them: He saved some for a future meal. Theodoros, observing his own medicinal fast, made himself a pot of tea—English tea. He vanished into the corridor and returned in a few moments with lemons from the lemon trees in the courtyard, picked by moonlight, for our greens and his tea. Their cat followed him in and was served a bowl of fish remains, and Theodoros settled in earnest to his steaming cup, which was going to do him good. He moaned a little after each hot swallow and laughed, and after a moment he reached for the transistor, by a pile of gray and black laundry at the end of the table. "The news," he told me. "I try to keep informed. I listen to the BBC when I can." But all that came out of the gadget was a pair of voices selling something, interspersed with snatches of bouzouki music. Theodoros snapped it off. "The usual garbage," he said. "We'll get the news at eight o'clock. It must be too early." But at eight we were talking about other things, and forgot. Theodoros was telling me about the history of the monastery founded in the fourteenth century by two Byzantine noblemen who are now buried in the church. The frescoes were originally sixteenth-century—it is claimed that some of them are, or were, by the great Panselinos; but they were restored in the nineteenth century and, for the most part, ruined. Only here and there patches of the older work remained. I had had a chance to look at them, at vespers and afterwards. The light in the katholikon was better than in many of the churches on the mountain at that hour. I said I was glad to have seen them, restored or not, and to be eating with my hosts, in their kitchen. "Where did you eat at Philotheou?" Theodoros asked, and I told him. "Didn't you eat with them there?" I said that they chanted, during their meals, and probably had not wanted an outsider and a heretic to be present. It seemed consistent with their not wanting a non-Orthodox visitor at their services in the katholikon. But Theodoros was shocked by the whole idea. "Phariseeism," he called it. He strode up and down the kitchen, indignant. "You are *welcome* here," he said. And to prove his point he led me into a dormitory above the surf, the windows overlooking the rocky moonlit coast, and when I had chosen my bed he insisted on making it himself—with clean ironed sheets. The pillow, which he dropped into the ironed pillowcase, was covered in red velvet.

The night's liturgy in the cold church undid whatever good work the tea and fasting might have begun, and the next morning Theodoros had a fever. "Colic," he said mournfully and prescribed a light breakfast, which he ate, green-faced. I went walking that day on the slopes. From the north Pantokratoros appears to be huddled into a crook of cliff, beneath ruins of tall buildings and of an old aqueduct. I passed a fat wagging puppy and a thin one, both tethered with yellow ribbons. Olive trees growing in the lee of crumbling walls, to the exact height of the masonry: pollarded by the sea wind. The path runs along the cliffs through brush, overgrown olive groves, passing under great pines and holly oaks. It splays out into tracks made by mules and horses turned loose to browse on the sparse wiry growth. The soil there appears to be a decayed granite with flakes of mica.

I had come down that way the autumn before, from the monasteries at the northern end of the peninsula: Kastamonitou, first, reached in the twilight after hours of threading wooded ravines and ridges, and winding down through chestnut forests to the shadow of an immense walnut tree in front of the entrance gate, not long before it was closed for the night. Tall forest-circled walls and towers resting on foundations laid in the eleventh century. There an old monk, finding me alone between the evening services, as the glass of the windows was misting over, had fetched a second kerosene lamp to the table by my cot, and hurried off to bring me, volume by volume, his infinite stamp collection, the accretion of a whole lifetime, and had pointed to the empty spaces, as yet unfilled between stamps arrayed in series, had tapped them with his finger and smiled: Those spaces still beckoned to him. The pleasure of having an audience for his collection warmed him. Increasingly he seemed to be sharing a secret, and he grew more and more hurried for fear I might not see—if not all, at least the most interesting, some of the most interesting. At last he had bundled all the volumes under his arm, picked up a lamp with the other hand, signaled with his head for me to follow, and crept out the door down the creaking stairs and along a corridor to his cell, where more volumes were piled precariously on a table no bigger and no sturdier than a hat, and covered with green baize; he had scarcely entered and turned round to welcome me, when a younger monk, whose eyes matched his black beard, arrived in a rage and ordered him to lead me back at once to the guest room. Kostamonitou is a cenobitic monastery: The cells are strictly forbidden to visitors.

And the following morning, I took the path down through woods and gorges to the shore. There, boathouses, heavy towers, porches, balconies, high stone buildings apparently uninhabited, in the early mist; then I climbed over cobbles and along grooved rocks, above twisting ravines, to Zographou, one of the mountain's Slavic monasteries, enormous and silent, at the edge of a steep slope. The big courtyard with its striped churches of red stone and red ocher, empty. Roofs, covered with broad irregular pieces of glittering greenish slate held in place by gravity alone: repairs under way on them, and patches of roof laid bare to the gray boards strange to sunlight, gazing upward again at a particular morning of autumn, slates stacked around them, no one bent over them, for a while. The clocks in the courtyard had stopped at different hours. At last a young monk with a cavernous face came and unlocked the church: the frescoes not ancient but in the great line, and one of two ikons of St. George hung with coins, medals, watches stopped at different times, all clinging to a legend. In the story the three noblemen of Ochrida who are said to have founded the monastery in the tenth century, built the church but then disagreed over its dedication, and to resolve the matter locked a panel of wood inside, while they stayed outside, praying. When they opened the door the panel was covered with a painting of St. George. The name Zographou means "The Painter's." A doubting bishop once touched the ikon, it is recounted, and the little crater beside the nose is all that remains of his fingertip, which had to be cut off. In the thirteenth century when the Eastern church and Rome were rejoined for a while, and the union was widely resisted on Athos, soldiers of the Latinizing emperor burned twenty-six stubborn monks alive in a tower in the courtyard; now there is a stone that claims to mark the place—after seven hundred years.

From there, on over the spine of the promontory to the vast Serbian monastery of Chiliandariou. A peddler with a donkey and a display of mirrors, combs, flashlights, paper ikons looking like candy wrappers—a one-man bazaar, in the shelter of the main portico, tolerated by its frescoes. Who was he expecting, by way of customers? He had gone off to sit on a wall. A monk who had lived in France, a man of learning, opened the church, led the way over its twelfth-century inlaid floors, past frescoes of the fourteenth century—restored, and badly—the great ikon of the Virgin of Three Hands, she and the child gazing out through the incrustation of worked gold, with the third hand, in silver, beneath her right hand which supports the child. Standing in front of the ikon, the monk told the story of John of Damascus, Greek, a saint of the eighth century, who had written against the emperor Leo the Iconoclast, and had been betrayed, in letters forged by the emperor himself, to the caliph, John's protector, so that the protection was withdrawn and John's right hand cut off in punishment, and hung up to rot. It was this ikon, then known as the Virgin of Guidance, to which John had prayed for his hand (though historians declare that the ikon was not painted until six hundred years later). She had rejoined it to his arm and the caliph had been moved to pardon him. Other legends of John and his age arose from that one: stories as conventionally and intricately wrought, and as dark as ikons, most of them on the twined themes of humility and charity.

From Chiliandariou, in the afternoon, a descent along the paths of the east slope of Esphigmenou, seeing it from far above, down on the shore: the massive square of walls set among gardens and vineyards. Arriving at the siesta hour, no one in sight near the entrance with its looming keep. The white limestone giving off a cool light of its own, in the shade of old trees, water trickling through a pond at the foot of the walls, freshness and sweetness in the hushed air, a courtyard full of lemon trees. A young monk, hurrying to the garden, speaking English. And then an older one, portly, stern, and spectacled, inquired as to whether or not I was Orthodox, lectured me severely on the perilous folly of my heretical state, and thrust a publication instructing me on how I should proceed, step by step, to rescue myself from this condition, before he admitted me briefly and with a reluctance born of distaste, to a quick glimpse of the church. The courtyard was more beautiful: the smooth pallor of the stones in the open air.

And from the pool at the gate I had gone on, along the sea-cliffs, taking the rest of the day to reach Vatopedi, a monastery like a medieval city rising and opening out of itself. Sloping courtyards inside the immense gates, stepped like waves on long beaches, dry grass growing in the cracks, in late afternoon light (so that the French priest, who was also there, pursed his lips at the neglect and backwardness of the place: What a difference just a little weed-killer would make to the look of things!) and cats and their long shadows straying through it. Churches open, frescoed; the refectory door ajar for workmen, and the long room elaborately frescoed above the rows of carved marble tables, each set in the embrace of a stone bench the shape of a horseshoe. From my high window overlooking the trees near the gate, and the sea below, I watched a stately monk, his beard still black, trying to catch a stray pullet in the bushes at the foot of the walls, without loss of dignity. The branches took his hat—which involved a separate rescue, and he set the black crown carefully on a ledge, for the duration. Then a twig untucked his hair and a bush caught at his cassock, and both had to be readjusted. When he finally got right into the bush, the pullet, exercising its full genius, dashed out the other side, but was cornered at last, and picked up and smoothed with the same hand that smoothed the cassock, retucked the hair, replaced the hat. Unruffled once more, the monk straightened his shoulders, glanced around at the evening as at an audience, and strode in through the gate, bearing the bird to safety from foxes and the night on the mountain. I had gone down, in the first twilight, to sit in the church porch looking at the frescoes, and an ancient monk with a white beard worthy of the patriarchs in the paintings had come by and beckoned me to follow him—into another courtyard, up flights of stairs, to his room, a cell of white plaster, with only one small window. Dirty; a few clothes, papers, books, strewn here and there. A jug of pink wine in the middle of the floor—Vatopedi is one of the idiorrhythmic monasteries scorned by the stern cenobites—from which we both partook, scarcely conversing (my lack of Greek and his lack of teeth) yet touching on his rheumatism and arthritis, the paintings in the church porch, age—he laughed about them all.

It was from Vatopedi that I had walked, next day along the coast to Pantokratoros, and had come down to the bit of path near the seacliffs that I recognized a year later among the brush and olive trees. The veins worn in the ground by browsing animals disappeared among the bushes. I followed them seaward, over a rise, onto a promontory; the sharp mint smell of pennyroyal crushed by my feet; one wild apple tree; white heather blooming among the purple. I came to a small chapel, the old plaster walls shadowed with age, the apse toward the sea, and a porch almost as large as the chapel, at the door to the west. Stone steps up to the porch, then down inside it again to the stone floor, as though into a pool; a railing around it to the west and south, to keep the horses out, perhaps. And a wall to the north, and benches of stone, rimmed with wood, like mangers, on the four sides. The afternoon light came in under the eaves to the western facade, and filled the cracks in the gray unpainted boards of the door. Empty niches to either side of the doorway, and above it a third niche filled with a dim fresco of St. Nicholas and a head of Christ above him. The door fastened with a hook; inside, another silence with another age. In the center of the dusty blue-painted ikon-screen an eye was carved: a left eye. From the south side of the porch the sea could be heard, but not from the other side. There only the sounds of bees and of the soft wind in the olive leaves came through the sunbeams. The bench faced south over the coast to the blue peak of Athos: a little cloud to the west of it, full of light.

On the way back to the monastery I stuck my head through the doors of the agricultural outbuildings, to look at the garden tools, the storehouses, the olive mill. Outside one of the doors a pile of baskets stained purple from the grape harvest was leaning against the stone wall under the eaves, and through the open doorway I could make out the towering form of Father Cyriac, legs braced wide apart, grasping a thick pole which he was plunging up and down into the grape-filled vat below him. He laughed about the wine he was making—a job that he obviously loved, though he himself drank nothing but water, even with meals. The purple stain was splashed everywhere visible in the dark building, and a gathering of fruit flies hung in the beams of light, swirling in time with Father Cyriac's massive dance. His face was red and shining and he informed me, as though it were a great joke, that *all* of last year's wine had been drunk up a few days before.

Theodoros was ironing his clothes in the kitchen, with the silent transistor among the spilled piles of garments. His stomach was much better, he said, and he was going to Athens to visit his family. We sat on the balcony again, in the evening, above the tongues of mercury slowly licking the coast, and discussed his life. One of the things he loved was wild flowers. In the spring he sometimes went with a few other monks up onto the peak, where we could see the glaciers of moonlight, and camped there for a few days. He had a pup tent, and he took his books—he brought them out to the balcony: botanical guides to the Mediterranean, most of them in English. By candlelight we pored over the photographs of autumn squills and of the three kinds of cyclamen that grow on the mountain and the several yellow flowers that color the sea-cliffs at that season. An owl flicked past in the moonlight. "Athena's bird," Father Theodoros said, and made the sounds of each kind of owl to be found on Athos. "The bird of wisdom," he informed me portentously, "that sees in the dark."

We had our fish at last; Father Cyriac urged me to eat, eat, and Father Theodoros caught the news—the invasion of Israel: war. When the bouzouki music came on again Father Theodoros switched it off and we sat back to discuss the event. Few facts, so far, and when we had run through the first expressions of dismay it began to be clear that Father Theodoros's sympathies were with the Arabs, less because of any inherent sympathy with them than because of a frank anti-

Semitism, a prejudice not vehement but ingrained, obstinate, deaf, and imbued with a familiar obscurantism. There was the old ghost story about an international conspiracy of Jews—financiers, Rothschilds, the veteran figments that sympathized, I found, in a traditional way with freemasons of the old stamp and rotarians of a newer one, for equally hazy reasons. Even the documentations of the concentration camps, and the history of the Final Solution, were doubted and minimized. Father Cyriac echoed the chief prejudices, at Father Theodoros's invitation, and a moment later, when the subject had returned to the evils of war, he told with horror of what he had seen and remembered of the German invasion and occupation of Crete.

I left in the morning as the sun was striking the portico above the sea. Father Cyriac was out in the early light, working under an arbor, with the pigs and hens busy near him, among dry stalks and shadows. The path inland dropped below the monastery walls to the bed of a small stream quietly trickling seaward over rocks and a bed of black and bronze leaves. Both sides of the stream were bright with the new leaf-fall, and the light coming fresh through the trees overhead after the night and the months of summer. Up a lane across the stream, an abandoned *kelli*, a large one, perhaps a mill, and farther along, on a bare rise, another, the door hanging open at the top of a few stone steps; inside, all the rooms open, ruins of beds and a kitchen, ivy creeping in at the windows, a porch facing the sea; one room a chapel full of cobwebs, bran, bits of straw, as in a house that has passed through an old age as a barn. And farther again, a ruin among trees in the gold light, with horses browsing beside it, coming to inspect me as I passed along the wall. The path wound back and forth across the stream and found the old cobbles where it began to climb into the wiry brush of that part of the peninsula. It is not far from Pantokratoros to the big *skete* of the Prophet Elias, as large as some of the monasteries, which is one of its dependencies: The cobbled mule path looped and twisted and led finally between walls of terraces: pastures and vineyards of the *skete*, arbors shading walls, walnut and olive trees in grass with colts running among them, roans and one black one. The path turning among the walls as in a maze; at one turn a ruined windmill at the end of a grape arbor, and a large wooden building faced with sheets of tin once painted white, the rust bleeding through, the edge chattering in the wind. Crows wheeling and racketing around the sinking crown of the windmill, black flashes reflected in the broken window panes.

The arched entrance of the *skete* is on the side away from the sea, shaded in the morning. The inner courtyard capacious, paved. A church, clearly recent, facing the doors. A well with green-painted tin roof, very trim: bucket, rope, spindle. A cement table to the south of the church, with a chair beside it, and newspapers on the table, weighted with rocks, blowing in the wind. No one about but an orange cat on a bench—it sounded as though the bench were purring. The whole *skete* is of recent construction: The first monks who were drawn to the spot were followers of the great Russian monk and elder Paisius Velichkovsky in the mid-eighteenth century, and the *skete* is a Russian dependency of a Greek monastery, just as St. Andrews, near Karyes, is. It was instituted in 1839 but the building and expansion continued through the rest of the century, and the original church was greatly enlarged between 1880 and 1900. Unlike older establishments of its size on the mountain, it is not entirely enclosed by high castle walls: The seaward end of the courtyard looks out across a terrace balustrade, over the lower pastures and orchards and the wild slope of Pantokratoros and the coast. The open end makes the courtyard seem like a spacious flagstoned square, with a church in the middle of it.

Voices to the left. I peered into a windowed gallery like the wall of a greenhouse. Inside it a second row of windows, a darker interior; at one of the inner windows a hand beckoning me in. I found my way through a series of storerooms—wood, fruit, baskets, potatoes, dark jugs—to the kitchen, containing a further glass enclave hung with shellacked prints of saints, and barely large enough for an oilcloth-covered dining room table. In the kitchen an old Russian monk, pale and thin-skinned, in a pointed hat. And the owner of the beckoning hand: a monk of my own age, born in Pennsylvania, not far from where my father had grown up. Blue eyes set in a flat Slavic face:

Father Gabriel's family was of Czechoslovakian origin. His mother had been so strict in her Orthodox observances that she would not cut bread on Sunday—it had had to be sliced on Saturday night, for the following day. He had served in the army during the Korean War, had not minded it, and had gone to an Orthodox seminary afterwards, in eastern Pennsylvania, near a place that I had known as a child. I learned these elements of his life sitting on a bench at the dark kitchen table, under a small window high up in the thick whitewashed wall, where I had been set to consume a bowl of vegetable borscht, a plate of eggplant, potatoes, and peppers, and a salad, all from their garden, and wine and ouzo from their grapes, while Father Gabriel sat facing me and chided me for having failed to become Orthodox—a bad habit, dangerous and inexcusable. He himself had obtained permission to stay on permanently at the *skete,* but it had not been easy with his American citizenship, to acquire the consent of the Greek government, and it would not be easy for anyone else. Talk of Philotheou led him to tell me of the practice of hesychasm at the *skete*—evidently less tightly scheduled than Philotheou. He gave me to understand that they at the *skete* of the Prophet Elias were certainly no less fervent than the monks of Philotheou, though they might not *seem* so obsessed with their prayers. It was obvious at once that the *skete* did not indulge in the free and easy ways of Pantokratoros, where even the monks' title of *patir* had quickly become optional, in addressing them. Father Gabriel informed me, as a rank outsider, that in time one must hope for the silent pronunciation of the Jesus prayer to become a part of one's nature. He might be repeating it to himself at that very moment, while he was talking to me, and I would not know it, child that I was. He implied that his brother monks repeated the prayer without ceasing, as a weapon against the devil—indeed against the devils in the plural, who were presences and creatures of great immediacy for Father Gabriel, and for many of the monks.

The Jesus prayer itself—the simple invocation "Lord Jesus Christ, Son of God, have pity on me, a sinner!"—had evolved out of the long tradition of hesychasm and the prayer of the heart: "pure" wordless prayer. At certain stages of the tradition the repetition of the formula, or simply of the name of Jesus, has been used as introductions and aids to wordless prayer, the "recollection of God." At others it had virtually absorbed the entire practice of silent communion.

The Russian *skete* was a good place to ponder its history. One of the great modern resurgences of the tradition was the wave of enthusiasm that had sent pilgrims, beggars, and fools of God praying over the roads of Russia in the nineteenth century—a movement that had caught the imaginations of both Dostoevsky and Tolstoy. As the surviving writings of those pilgrims make clear, the Jesus prayer was important to the whole movement. The pilgrims came to the tradition through the Slavonic translation of the *Philokalia* by that same Paisius Velichkovsky through whom the *skete* of the Prophet Elias had come to exist. A battered copy of Paisius's translation, and a Bible, had been the only possessions of the most famous of those now anonymous pilgrims. And the first biography of Paisius, written by disciples of his and published in 1847, was another of the works that had inspired the movement.

Paisius was born in 1722, in Poltava, in the eastern Ukraine, the eleventh of twelve children. His father, a priest, died when he was four. His eldest brother, John, also became a priest, and from early childhood Paisius read the available patristic writings and dreamed of becoming a monk. When he was thirteen his elder brother, John, also died, and his mother had taken Paisius to the Archbishop of Kiev to bespeak for him his father's former place in the Poltava church, and Paisius had remained in Kiev to study for the priesthood. But after a falling out with the school prefect he had been severely punished and "his soul had become fired with the love of wandering." He had run away. First to the Holy Monastery of Lyubetz, at Lyubich, on the Dnieper, and then—when a new abbot there frightened him—to the monastery of St. Nicholas, on an island in the river Tyasmin. It was a time of Uniate persecutions of the Orthodox, in that part of Russia, and Paisius had fled, in turn, to a monastery at Kiev, where he had been put to work in a printing shop. There his brother John's widow had found him and told him that his mother, in her anxiety about Paisius, had had a vision, as a result of which she had decided to become a nun. Longing, himself, for a monastic life, Paisius had set out, with two monks, for the *skete* of St. Nicholas the Wonderworker, in Wallachia. From there, in a quest for the lost patristic sources of the Orthodox contemplative tradition, he had gone to Athos, where he had spent three years in solitude, and afterwards had been joined by a single young monk, at first, and then by many others as his reputation as an elder spread. The *skete* of the Prophet Elias was founded and grew to number some five hundred monks before Paisius decided that it was time for him to return to the Slavic world: Wallachia, again, where the governor gave him, and the sixty-four followers who went with him, the Monastery of the Descent, called Dragomira, near the city of Sochava. There he had been formally invested, by another monk, in the Great Habit of the Schema-Monk, a garment which had been shown to an early ascetic in a vision, and denotes particular spiritual advancement and authority. And there he had made the Slavonic translation of the *Philokalia,* which was published in 1793, a year before his death.

It was not, in fact, the first modern edition of the work. Eleven years earlier, the Greek text had been published, in Venice, under the patronage of a mysterious Rumanian prince, John Mavrocordato— nothing else is known about him, for certain. The entire edition had been shipped back from Venice to the East: Until the independence of Greece it was common for Greek works to be printed in the West and reexported. The Greek compilation may have been known to Paisius long before it was published. It was the work of two men younger than he: Bishop Makarius of Corinth (1731–1805) and St. Nicodemus of the Holy Mountain, Nicodemus the Solitary, the Hagiorite (1749–1809), who knew of Paisius early in his own life, and at one time had sailed from Athos to Rumania to see him, but had been driven by a storm to the island of Thasos, had taken it as a sign, and returned to the Holy Mountain, to a cell in the *skete* above Pantokratoros.

Discovery and resurrection were the clear themes of the lives of these men: the unknown in the known, the forgotten in the present, the relic and the breath, dust and freedom, sea light, cave shadow, mountains and islands. Nicodemus was born on Naxos and sent to school at Smyrna. As a young man he met Makarius on the island of Hydra, and at twenty-seven he went to Athos, to the monastery of Dionysiou. It was from there that he had tried to sail to find Paisius, by then a legend on the mountain. After his return to the region of the *skete* of the Prophet Elias, a monk named Arsenius of Peleponnesos came to share his solitude, and taught him mental prayer. Together they sailed to the island of Skyrapoula, 150 miles from Athos, where they lived as hermits for several years; then Nicodemus returned alone to Athos and there moved from place to place, settling at last among the cave-dwelling hermits, called *kollybades* (from *kolleva,* rice eaten in memory of the dead, the ritual mentioned by Father Mark at Philotheou), at the rocky end of the promontory. Makarius came and visited him on the mountain, and persuaded him to help in the compiling of the *Philokalia* and the *Sayings of the Desert Fathers.* They collaborated on a number of other works, and Nicodemus, by himself, became a prolific and important writer, one of the chief heralds of the nineteenth-century revival of Orthodox mysticism. His works did not altogether escape the ironies of history: One of his manuscripts, a study of St. Gregory Palamos, Bishop of Thessalonika and defender of hesychasm, was seized in Vienna, where it had been sent to be printed. The Austrian authorities had taken it to be a subversive work, a (three-volume) proclamation of Greek independence.

Nicodemus's attitude to Western Christianity was not simple. He had translated and adapted the *Spiritual Exercises* of St. Ignatius, and Scupoli's *Spiritual Warfare* into Greek, to make them available to the Orthodox world, but he attacked Thomism as "love of darkness," declared the Roman church to be totally deprived of grace, and inveighed against joining in prayer with the non-Orthodox.

I was shown over the buildings by Father Paul, who had been

invoked during the answers to most of my questions of the morning: "Father Paul will be able to tell you more about that." When I met him, at the main meal of the day, he ignored me, pronounced the long grace to the paper ikon, and carried on the conversation in Russian until the meal was over. Even so, it was clear that he spoke, as he seemed to do everything, with a remarkable mixture of magnetic ardor, authority, severity, and charm. He was only a visitor, he explained to me almost at once when he turned to me after the meal, but he had stayed fourteen months. And as he led me into the courtyard, the *skete* seemed, for the time being, to be his domain. Heretics, outsiders, pagans, were at liberty to join in prayer with the Orthodox—he informed me when I asked, as we entered the church—whether outside or inside Orthodox buildings and ceremonies, but the Orthodox should not join in the ceremonies or prayers of heretics, on pain of becoming, themselves, anathema. The Orthodox should not even pray for pagans, inside the church building, he said, though they were free to do so when they were out in the world. The strictures were set forth with a blunt promptness, courtesy, and a flicker of humor, and added to the impression that Father Paul was, however temporarily, the heir of the place, a feeling that was further enhanced by my seeing it and learning something of its history, and something of his, at the same time.

He had been born in Smolensk thirty-three years—and six days—before. After the war his family had left Russia, and he had been brought up in Austria and in different parts of Europe. In 1951 his family had sailed from Bremen to New York, where they had friends. He had gone as "summer boy" to an Orthodox monastery near Utica, and his mother had encouraged his interest in the place: He had stayed and gone to school there, and when one of the monks had suggested that he join the monastery he had said, "Why not?" This many years later the answer seemed out of character—vague and unformed. But he had been hardly more than a child, and clearly once he had made the decision he had had no regrets. His eyes burned as intensely as Father Mark's but their flame appeared to be fed by a heavier element. Utica, he said, was better than most places he had seen in the States, because of the Catholics there. They were believers, at least, even if they were heretics.

The church building at the *skete* was of little interest, he said (and it was true). The ikons and the architecture both had suffered the unfortunate Italianate influence that had run through Russian Orthodoxy in the eighteenth century. There was one miraculous ikon at the *skete:* the Virgin who wept—and one of the monks saw it—on the eve of the Russo-Turkish War. But almost none of the ikons at the *skete,* in Father Paul's forthright opinion, deserved the name: They were merely pictures, and their real purpose, as one could see, was aesthetic rather than spiritual. He showed me one of the older chapels, set into the building flanking the courtyard, the only one in the *skete* which he said kept the feeling of the old basilicas. It too was recent—compared to the great monasteries of the mountain. A small room, the paint looking almost new, the ikons lacking distinction, but its intention and its simplicity moved him, as the larger church did not.

On an upper story we walked through the long, creaking ceremonial reception rooms painted in the pastels that had pleased the figures in the processions of huge framed photographs and portraits from the last decades of the czars: abbots, bishops, archbishops, and the czars themselves. Black bentwood furniture, black horsehair furniture, tight to the walls. Round tables covered with white embroidered cloths, the fringes touching the floor. On one of them an obese unrecognizable fruit grown in a bottle. To show guests. The silence of the portraits possessing the rooms. Father Paul showed me a picture of the *skete* as it had been in 1880: smaller, simpler, plain, with cypresses in the courtyard. Outside a window of the present reception room a kestrel hovered for a moment around a stone cornice, and then dropped away into the ravine.

One series of rooms—parts of two floors of the west wing—had been used as a hospital in the days when Chekhov was a doctor. Father Paul and I lingered with equal fascination in the dilapidated dispensary and the long paneled pharmacy with its ranks of inscribed jars still full of powders, crumbled leaves, crystals, stacked envelopes with faded labels containing crumbs and dust, drawers where the mice had nested; and in the small consulting room with its horsehair sofa like a burst black doll, its cot for emergency cases and for the dying. The desk of that room was still full of papers, and the cabinets were crammed with tarnished scales and tumbled surgical instruments. A large zinc washstand with a marble back stood in one corner. Piles of rags. And from there Father Paul led me out to a small building on the slope just west of the entrance to the *skete,* and opposite the window of my room. There was no lock or latch: The door was held shut with a string. Inside, the walls were lined with shelves as in a library or the pharmacy behind us, and the shelves were filled with rows of skulls, some of them with names written above the sockets, some of them without. Behind the shelves facing the door was a recess full of bones, all piled together. There were the bones of monks who had died in the *skete* and had been buried in its cemetery and then, in accordance with the tradition of the mountain, had been dug up after three years, to make room for others. Sometimes, he told me, the bones had a sweet smell when they were uncovered after that length of time, and that meant that the life through which they had passed had been holy. Some of the skulls were white, some were tan. Both colors were good. Often the saints were tan, as one could see from the bones in reliquaries. But sometimes the diggers found black bodies that had failed to decompose: the earth had rejected them, and special prayers had to be said over them, and they had to be buried again. Once it had happened three times, and at last the abbot had asked God in prayer what the wretched monk had done, and he had been told the sinner had worshipped with heretics, and was anathema. After the Crusades, Father Paul told me, there had been many black bodies—monks who had been forced or persuaded to pray with the Catholics. And again we turned to that subject. It was forbidden to pray, inside the church building, for the souls that had inhabited the black relics. In fact, one might pray inside the church according to Father Paul, only for the true Orthodox, who represented a very small fraction of those currently professing that faith. The search for the true faith was what had brought him to Athos, he told me, "and even here———." He dropped the theme and led me into the disused wagon sheds and carpenters shops, and around the wine presses. "The Protestants," he informed me, "think that drinking alcohol is of great importance. Like the Mohammedans." The long black robe swept past the empty vats.

Great energy and passion. The circuit of the monastery buildings kept shifting to the foreground of the conversation. Basil is grown by the doorway in the monasteries, he told me, when I asked, because the crucifix is decked with basil at the great feasts of the cross, in particular the seven-day feast of the Elevation of the Cross, in late September.

Father Paul loved clouds, the light in them, and he stood and gazed up at those on the ridge and told me of their conduct on the mountain. Sometimes they would move in, low from the west, emerging over the tree-tops high above the *skete,* and at the same time others, higher still, or a little to the north or south, would be coming from the east, with different light in them. Sometimes they would move landward, to the south, and seaward, to the north, in a great circling current of wind rebounding from the heights; and the whole thing could change in half an hour. (Father Mark had described the same things, as though talking about a distant age.) Father Paul was making a collection of seeds of wild flowers to take back with him when he went: flowers that he liked to find and to smell. He knew none of their names. And he was not yet certain when he would go, but he believed that he had accomplished almost all that he had come for. He felt that there was little more for him to find on Athos, and he had no wish to remain much longer. He had been helped, on the mountain, but not in the way that he had expected. And he felt that what he must look for next was elsewhere—perhaps back at his own monastery. He believed that Athos as a whole was degenerate; that most of the monks, and whole communities (Pantokratoros, for instance) had fallen far from the true faith, and that nothing could be learned from them. I spoke of Philotheou and Provata, but he was skeptical and not interested: Even if the true faith indeed existed there, he himself must move on now. He conceded that there might still be a few holy men, scattered in remote corners of the mountain, but he felt certain of the purity and faith of none except the Zealots, many of whom were living as hermits on the sea-cliffs of Karoulia.

He had come to the mountain looking for an elder, a *staritz*, who might guide him in the pure uncompromised faith, in the light of the original apostolic vision. The Russian *skete* founded by Paisius had been the logical place for him to stay even though it was almost empty (at the moment there were only three other monks living there). He had not, in fact, found an elder, but in answer to his fervent prayers the Virgin herself had helped him, clearing his mind, answering his questions, leading him to the very books he needed. Purity of faith, he explained, implied purity of doctrine, and Father Paul, with the Virgin's guidance, had grown more than ever convinced, on Athos, that the true Orthodox were a dissenting minority within the church. (Part of his guidance had come to him, almost certainly in the form of a periodical, *The Orthodox Word*, published by the St. Herman of Alaska Brotherhood, in Platina, California: the brotherhood holds the *skete* in particular regard, and the *skete* library contains a relatively complete file of back issues.) One of the recent conditions of doctrinal purity was an insistence on retaining the old Julian calendar, instead of the Western, Gregorian one, which had been adopted by the Greek patriarch in 1924. The official acceptance of the Western calendar had been accompanied by the insertion of the patriarch's name in the liturgy: The dissenters refused to include his name in their prayers, regarding him as a heretic. The calendar affected the entire liturgical year, for the Julian calendar had become an organic part of the liturgical cycle of the early church. Father Paul assured me that the Julian calendar provided symmetries and simplicities that were lost in the Gregorian arrangement. The Paschal cycle, for instance, was said to repeat itself exactly every four thousand years in the Julian calendar, and illiterate peasants could calculate the cycle on their fingers. And in the old calendar, Easter always came after the Jewish Passover—in accordance with the Gospel—whereas in the Gregorian calendar it was not always so. But these were minor objections. The real argument against the calendar change was one of principle: an opposition to any alteration of the essentials of Orthodoxy—any change in the church itself. I failed to elicit from Father Paul a clear rule for distinguishing what was essential to Orthodoxy from what are mere accretions, however distinctive. But the essentials, whatever they were, make up the church itself; and the church—so the argument ran—is Christ's body and therefore perfect. There can be only one, and it cannot be changed to accommodate it to other religions, or to anti-religious pressures without implying an imperfection in Christ, hence in God Himself. It was in part their rejection of the calendar reform of 1924, therefore, that had led Father Paul to believe that the true Orthodoxy, on Athos, was virtually restricted to the dissenters there who went by the name of Zealots.

They had taken their names from the Holy Apostle Simon Zelotes, the bridegroom at Cana of Galilee (John 2, I-II) who was converted by the miracle of the changing of the water into wine, and left the feast and his bride to become a disciple of Jesus. (In *The Golden Legend,* de Voragine notes that he was called Simon Zelotes or Simon the Cananean, both names having the same sense, for Cana meant "zeal.") Their leader had been Schema-Hieromonk Theodosius of Karoulia, who had died in 1937. He had studied at the Kazan Theological Academy and had been rector of the Vologda Seminary. In 1901 he had come to Athos in search of spiritual guidance, and after years of searching had found an elder, a Bulgarian named Ignatius—and also a Greek adviser, Callinicus. He had edited works of Paisius Velichkovsky and had translated writings of Nicodemus the Hagiorite into Russian.

Only one monastery on Athos, Esphigmenou (the Tight-Girdled One") had embraced the Zealot position, breaking off communion with the commemorators of the Patriarch of Constantinople who had adopted the Western calendar. But there were Zealots at the *skete* of St. Anne, the New Skete, Kafsokalivia, and the monasteries of Xenophontos and St. Pantaleimon. And there were other contemporary movements of pronounced opposition to the authority of the official church: The Catacomb Church in Russia, the Russian Church in Exile, and the True Orthodox Christians of Greece. It was hard to obtain news of the activities and persecutions: The St. Herman of Alaska Brotherhood, and its publications, were one source. In any case, an undue regard for the mere numbers of the faithful, Father Paul insisted, was the sort of thing that had always typified the West, rather than the true church, which had always cared instead about the fervor of its converts, the quality of their faith. The remnant of the faithful, in the Latter Days, was bound to be small.

We stood in the courtyard as the warmth went out of the daylight. Father Paul pointed out the places where the cypresses had once stood before the church had been built. One thing he would like to see sometime, he told me, was a line of trees he had read about, leading to a church—he had forgotten where it was. In the story, one of St. Luke's portraits of the Virgin had been taken to that church at one time, and all the trees, as it had passed them, had bowed down to the picture and then straightened again, with a bend in their trunks.

It was the hour for him to go and get his veil and semantron, and ring the bells. A Russian belfry; he was a virtuoso. Books and periodicals on subjects that I had asked about had been put on my table, and I read until dusk. Owls back and forth in the trees outside my window. The tinkle of the bells from the service in the church, echoing in the courtyard on the other side. I lit the lamp to follow the stories of the persecutions of the Orthodox in Russia. Among them an essay by Boris Talantov attacking the Metropolitan Sergius of Moscow for collaborating with the Stalinist repression. The legitimacy of Sergius's authority had always been disputed by many Russians who called themselves Orthodox. In 1918, in the blaze of the Revolution, the Russian church had elected its first patriarch since Peter the Great had abolished the office two centuries before. The new patriarch, Tykhon, had been imprisoned in 1922 and had died in prison three years later. A series of *locum tenens* who succeeded him had been arrested, and the

Soviet government forbade the election of another patriarch. Sergius, the *locum tenens* in 1927, in that year came to terms with the Soviet state. He obtained a legal recognition of the church, on the one hand. On the other, he publicly denied that believers were being persecuted by the government, and he declared that there was no essential conflict between Orthodox Christianity and the praxis of Russian socialism—self-sacrifice was the basis of both. "We want the achievements and happiness of the Soviet Union to be our achievements and happinesses," he had written—in what Akhmatova described as a "relatively vegetarian" period, before the great purges of the thirties. He had introduced a prayer for the Soviet government into the liturgy and had forbidden prayers for political prisoners. There had been a wave of opposition to the settlement within the church. Sergius had excommunicated Archbishop Dimitry Gdov, of Petrograd, one of the chief opponents, and in the years that followed, others were executed—among them Metropolitan Joseph of Leningrad, one of the leaders of the opposition. The accounts of the Catacombs martyrs read like echoes of the Final Solution. Talantov's essay accused Sergius and his "adaptation" of reducing the religious activity of the church to external rites, and he listed a series of recent (1960s) governmental restrictions even of those rites—restrictions which he declared had been imposed with the knowledge and support of the official church. The dean of the sole remaining Orthodox church in Kiev, he said, had told him that the local authorities forbade the administering of supreme unction in the homes of believers; as a result, Talantov's own wife died without the last rites, which she had asked for. Talantov himself had been arrested on June 12, 1969, and had died in prison on January 4, 1971.

Outside, the long empty corridor was crossed by rungs of dim reflected moonlight; the roof of the church, the courtyard, and the Holy Sea beyond, ran through shades of silver. I went down to the vigil liturgy, which had begun in the large chapel on the north side of the courtyard. Sound of chanting, more melodious than at Philotheou. Russian. Music was another of Father Paul's interests, and the *skete* contained some manuscripts of ancient music. He and the student from Los Angeles were singing some of the liturgical passages together. The voices filtered out into the moonlit courtyard. A few candle flames, and ikon lamps reflected from gold frames and paintings, shone through the windows; huge shadows wheeled past them. Inside, out of the moonlight, the chapel seemed almost dark. Candles at the lecterns scarcely lit the few monks cowled in their black veils, and the gaunt tiny features of one old Russian in brown tweeds, who read the passages of Scripture, occasionally stumbling over words, without dropping his high monotone. Father Gabriel, with a censer, bowed, swooped, and whirled: The movement of censing became a slow dance before the ikons and into each part of the chapel. The language, the pace, the voices, the undertone of feeling, all different from those of any of the Greek monasteries. I listened without understanding any of the words. When I went out, the shadows had moved around the courtyard, and the night was colder. I went back to the kerosene lamp, and the books. Some of them I would not have a chance to see again: I meant to start early in the morning. But my eyes rebelled at last, and I turned down the wick and blew out the light and watched the moon's shadows on the hill. The owls were silent. A few bright clouds. I heard the vigil end, and the monks come from the chapel, scuffling across the courtyard and up the stairs, and I went to bed.

I hoped to walk across to the other side of the peninsula the next day. It was a long way, and most of the route I planned to take would be unfamiliar. I got up with the first light and went down to the courtyard to see the red sun rise, magnified and elliptical, in the mists over the sea toward Lemnos. A fishing boat appeared, puttering along the coast. In the kitchen, Father Gabriel was up, discussing the day's meals with a workman who was cleaning fish and squid at a dark sink. The squat peasant figure of the gardener, half asleep, in a jacket faded colorless, was wedged into a corner behind the table, by a lighted lamp. No one else was awake. Father Gabriel promised to say good-bye to the others, but he insisted that I stay for breakfast: Turkish coffee and rusks with dark honey from the hillside. A cat and kittens growled over pieces of fish too hot to eat yet, flipping them on the stone floor. News of the war in Israel. The Moroccans said to be sending troops. Father Gabriel stuffed apples and even a piece of cheese into my sack, before I picked it up and went out the gate and up the path along the garden wall.

Cobbles leading up into the scrub. Mushrooms in grass: *marasmius oreades* dried by the sun of the past few days. Some kind of *tricholoma*. The path led out onto a small barren plateau of weathered stone, with a view of Karyes, and the peak far beyond; then it dropped to join the road, the dust leveled for wheels, with canned-beef cans, chocolate, and cigarette papers, toilet paper, cigarette butts, occurring along the edge, contributions of the summer's visitors. Small *sketes* with gardens, along the road, some empty, some inhabited. A plank stile into a pasture full of olive trees, with horses under them. One plank of the stile painted with a stencil: "Return to Monsanto Fawley." A new cement bridge. Sound of a motor: a miniature tractor driven by a young monk, with an old one, white beard flying, and a workman, rattling in the cart behind. Small-flowered knapweed with grayish leaves. Chicory in flower, and the sight of the mountain above its blue.

After an hour or so, Karyes again. The morning cold, and a cold wind swinging between the east and the south. My map showed a path from the *skete* of St. Andrew over the ridge to Xenophontos, and I walked into the courtyard at the *skete* to ask where it began. Nobody seemed to know. A fat layman in a sport shirt, eating tomatoes, with the juice and seeds running down his face, told me that there was no such path: I would have to go to Daphne and take the road along the sea. He appeared to be a surly representation of simple Atrophy: Once the wheels have come the paths cease to be real—retroactively I showed a young monk the map, but he said the path was too complicated. He had never taken it, himself, and I was sure to get lost. I thanked him and walked up the road that leads to Daphne, to a branch at the top of the ridge, which was marked unclearly on my map, but should, I thought, take me eventually to the coast. The mountain, to the south, was pale, and wrinkled with shadow. Dark clouds were racing across the sky. I turned up the side road, following the truck ruts through the chestnut forest that straddles the spine of the peninsula there. Almost at once it began to edge down the western slope, and the other sea appeared, far below. The mud became sandy and the chestnut forest alternated with regions of scrub. The wind turned colder, and the clouds darker. Hours, the road, the woods, empty. Some time in early afternoon, rumble of a motor: An ancient truck overtook me, with two laymen in it, and turned off down a fork that led south again toward a small bay.

The road wound back behind hills, avoiding the tops of ravines, and an upland valley opened before me: the rusted domes of a church, and high monastic buildings of wood and tin. Panes of glass reflecting gray sky. Beyond the building, terraced green meadows with trees, and horses grazing. An old cobbled path dropped away from the road, toward the sea, through heather and marjoram: the link between a small *skete* near the shore, and the rusted church of Sts. Catherine and Barbara, below me. The dome was an octagonal wooden structure, and there was another wooden tower at a corner of the locked main enclosure. The ground among the buildings was marshy, and the grass bright. There is a lake in a hollow of the hills above there, and water trickles into the still valley. The flapping of tin, in the wind. Ravens. The horses were grazing behind a small house tucked into the far slope, under trees; it was almost hidden by its piled firewood. A dog asleep under the eaves, so unused to travelers on the lumber road that it went on sleeping. The wind covered the sound of my feet.

An arm of a steep valley; suddenly on the left, it opened out toward the sea. Groups of *kellis,* tile roofs, a church, all far away on the other side, facing south. The sound of a chain saw in the woods. Abandoned truck tires and oil drums by the road: missionaries. A peasant with sacks and a smile full of gold teeth, riding a white horse, told me where I was, and turned aside into the gate of a *skete,* under big trees. The valley much warmer than the ridge behind me, and the woods. In mid-afternoon the long descent brought me to the coast just above the gardens north of the Russian monastery of St. Pantaleimon, and I turned north on the path that followed the shore, through olive groves. Over one of the terraces above the sea, two kestrels looped around and around each other until the aerial dance carried them over a hill. A large, half-ruined *kelli* in a meadow, the main room used as a stable, full of trodden horse-dung. A broad bat fluttered away from me into a cupboard, and when I went to look, it had disappeared. The chapel, off the main room, was still intact: on the shelf of the ikonostasis, stumps of candles, and a faded paper ikon of St. George.

I approached Xenophontos from behind; it faces the sea. Ruined stables extending back into the trees. Masonry built of boulders: gray russet, black. Lichens. Thickets of henbane, the flowers closed in the dark day. Another outer building, a *skete* or habitation apart from the monastery with a porch along the upper level, and white plaster rooms at either end. Windows broken, doors jammed open, but black garments hanging on the walls. A niche for an ikon above the arched doors under the porch, martins still flying in and out there. A long-tailed wren warning from the bushes on the shore. A stick footbridge across the boulder-lined bed of a wide torrent, dry at that season, to the high woodpiles and sacks of charcoal under the monastery walls. An old monk—long, intelligent face—was sitting among the firewood mending a cassock; he motioned me on, through the open gate under the tower.

The ironshod doors painted bright blue. A circling cobbled ramp led up into the cold. In the first courtyard inside, a bell suspended in a brick arch, above a basin. No one in sight. The northern end of the courtyard flanked by the small church of St. George, locked, but the porch, even in poor light, revealing the remains of great frescoes, including one of several series on the same theme, in the monasteries of that part of the peninsula, depicting St. Jerome and his lion: the human-headed beast wincing as it holds up its paw for the saint to extract the thorn, rubbing its head on his knee, carrying his water-pots, leading his white mule by a long cord held in its lion teeth. In the porch and passage to the inner courtyard, imposing seventeenth-century frescoes of the Apocalypse, half-ruined. It is said that the frescoes inside the old, locked church (not the main *katholikon* of the monastery, which was built in the nineteenth century) were originally painted in the mid-sixteenth century by the great Theophanes of Crete and another painter of exceptional gifts, named Antonios, but the paintings have been damaged and badly restored.

The main courtyard is crossed by a runnel of water; a stone pond is sunk, beside whitewashed arches, in the middle of the open space. The semantron had sounded and the monks were sailing toward the main church, its massive doors older than the building. The black robes were reflected in the water and the white arches. The *katholikon* houses a rich assembly of ikons—two of them said to be miraculous—and two ancient mosaics: St. George and St. Dimitrios.

The stone corridors of the living quarters were empty. Off to one side of a long hall, a chapel no bigger than a cupboard, inside glass doors, with an ikon light burning, and benches outside it. My footsteps were heard, and a young monk, limping, appeared behind me, led me to the guest room, returned a moment later with the tray of coffee and *ouzo,* and left me alone with the two walls of windows, west and south, over the sea, and the photographs of kings and the current dictator of Greece. After the hours of wind, the room sounded like a wooden shell, a steady echo of the shore under the high windows. The building itself was silent. I might have stayed: The monks who had spoken to me in the courtyard had been friendly and the one who had brought me the tray had made me welcome. I was tempted. I would have liked to see the old chapel of St. Dimitrios, which had been there no one knew how long before the monastery was built around it in the tenth century. And the remains of the frescoes locked away in the church of St. George and the chapel of Lazarus. Perhaps even to try to find and converse with the few Zealots living there. But even if I had been shown the paintings, the light of that dark afternoon was already going. I had only one more night on Athos, and I had started that morning hoping to see Dohiariou. Rain was surely on the way. I looked for the monk who had brought me the tray, but he was not to be found. I left him a note, and picked up my pack. Down in the courtyard a layman working with a length of irrigation pipe led me out through a small door in the wall above the sea, and along the terraced vegetable garden—rows of cabbages and tomatoes in sandy dark soil—to the path through the olive groves. It was no great distance to Dohiariou, he told me.

Olive terraces most of the way, the path looping and descending a few times into small wooded gorges made by torrents, full of tree shadows and looming rocks, the foliage greener than the slopes above. Over a shoulder of cliff, Dohiariou appeared suddenly, as beautiful as it is from the sea. Cobbles came to meet the path and climbed among walled gardens, past fountains, under arbors, beside a pavilion that looked out over the water, to the massive iron doors barely ajar, under the tower. The adobe-colored *katholikon* takes up most of the main courtyard, but around it stone stairs, small paved terraces like minute *piazzas* surrounded by raised stone flower boxes, balconies, stone roofs, clamber higher than the main dome: a city in an Easter egg, until one has climbed to the top balconies that look out over it all to the sea, and far beyond, faint on the horizon, the mountains of Chalkidikis. The rain had begun. I sat in a wooden porch near the topmost level, waiting for the guestmaster. Grape vines climbed around the balconies. Geraniums, late marigolds, zinnias. Basil. Yellow lichen on the rounded rough slates of the roofs. Huge pomegranate trees. One of the towers connected to a wing of the monastery by a covered wooden bridge. The wooden doorway off the porch was cut in the shape of a shallow Moorish arch. All at once, soft bouzouki music and the smell of Turkish tobacco drifted out through it together. I coughed, and a round old monk in a gray robe emerged, red-faced, surprised, turned back to put away his cigarette, thought better of it and brought it out with him, to welcome me. His eyes were watering and he was in the pulsing clutches of a terrible cold; affable, and bored. The room where he had been sitting alone was an enormous kitchen, dark only because of the weather, about which he grumbled as he shuffled back and forth making me Turkish coffee, between sneezes. There was a bottle of misty *ouzo* on the table, and he poured me a bit, into a misty glass, with a fat trembling hand and a few words of warning pronounced from the cloudy heights of age and experience.

We tested his French, which was original, but better than my Greek. When he sat at his bench behind the long table, and leaned against the wall, under a crooked calendar (Gregorian) depicting Leonardo's Last Supper with bright improvements, his heavy left hand lay on the curled white back of his cat, and occasionally stroked it. Before I had finished my coffee he had other company, who entered casually and made themselves at home: Evidently my host's kitchen was a meeting place for a wide circle of cronies. The first was a tall slender graying man in a neatly ironed orange sport shirt, with one bloodshot eye, and a trim mustache: a man about some nearby town, with many relatives and his hand on a few slender ropes. He pulled a handful of special coffee beans, wrapped in newspaper, out of his pocket, and unwrapped it slowly on the table, explaining their provenance and virtues. Then from a shelf he brought the monk's old cylindrical brass coffee grinder, poured the beans into it, and began to grind, with majestic satisfaction, while his friend explained about his cold, laughed and shook his head each time he sneezed, and fiddled with the dials of the transistor. The grinding ceased and the mustached visitor took the coffee to the small burner in the corner, by the window, and started to make another brew, with a style born of practice, and long familiarity with that kitchen. A fat workingman in faded farm blues came in and sat down wearily and laughed, and fixed us all with a melancholy smile, and he in his turn learned about the cold, the coffee, and the other's family and then told of his own troubles, which sounded remote but insoluble. The monk opened a tin box on the table: his cigarettes, and a razor blade for cutting them in half. He divided one with his second guest, and then, seized with a thought, got up and left the room, returning a moment later meditatively examining the box containing a jar of Vicks Vap-o-rub. He sat down again between the table and the wall and held it up

in his hand like a crystal he could see into, and he extolled its wonders as though he were thinking of selling it. The coffee came to the
table and was poured, in the middle of his pitch, without interrupt-
ing his enthusiasm, and ignoring it, he opened the jar and gouged
out a generous finger-load of the stuff and worked it well up each
nostril, tears streaming down his face, laughing, and passed the jar
on to his guests, each of whom obediently imitated him, and with
watering eyes pronounced themselves deeply impressed. Until it was
my turn, and I explained with heavy use of gestures that the traumas
of my childhood, in which salves and unguents very like this one had
figured regularly, had deprived me of impartiality—which was not
to say that I did not retain the deepest respect for anything of the
kind. By that time nobody cared. The product was already relieving
the monk, in a way, and it seemed to have suggested to his guests that
they should leave. They were all on their feet. The monk showed me
out, and pointed the way up the stairs to the balcony that I would
have to myself, and the room at the end of it, white and open and
freezing, with a plaster fireplace, and a window looking west over
the whole monastery There was a bench on the balcony and I sat out
watching the rain sheet down, and the clouds sag over the sea. When
I was about to go in and light the lamp, the monk called me down and
asked me whether I had eaten. I answered vaguely, and he told me
that I must eat; it was important; and he invited me to sit at the table
opposite the cat, while he got over a bout of sneezing. I urged him to
take some hot *ouzo* and go to bed, but he had decided to try aspirin,
which he showed me, and he said that his clay's duties were not yet
done. He heated up some old noodles for me until they were tepid
here and there, and watched me conscientiously eat them, accompanying me with aspirin and water.

All night the rain beat on the roofs and ran from the eaves over
the grapevines and the balcony railing, and in the morning it had not
abated. I splashed down the puddled white-washed stairs, avoiding
water-spouts, to the dark churches.

The monastery was founded in the tenth century, nearer to

Daphne, and was moved later to its present site, bought from Xeno-phontos ten years before the Norman Conquest. But the present *katholikon,* dedicated to the Holy Archangels, was built in the mid-sixteenth century. The frescoes, in the Cretan style, attributed to a painter named Zorzi, a master of Panselinos, must be among the most beautiful on the mountain, and ordinarily it is easier to see them than it is to see many of the others: The placing of the dome and windows allows more light to reach the ceiling and walls. But on that dark morning it was hard to make out anything very clearly, and it is a church where the figures form large compositions—a Tree of Jesse, a detailed sequence of the Creation and Fall. The covered passages out-side the *katholikon* are also frescoed; dark maroons and golds glowed against the rain light in the courtyard. In a chapel down a dark fres-coed hall, a litany was being sung. The visitor with the neat mustache was standing in a stall, listening, telling a string of beads, and I stood for a while in another stall and heard the rain stop, and went off to see whatever paintings might be visible. There is a series around the roof of the Well of the Archangels, in the courtyard. Scenes from a legend: a shepherd finding a treasure; monks in league with the devil, trying to drown him. The Archangels had saved him and set him down in the monastery—that was the story.

The rain started again. The guestmaster barked and hailed me feebly as I went past his door to pack. He was not feeling much bet-ter, and the rain and cold did not help. The boat would pass before long on its way to Daphne. I might wait and catch it an hour or so later, on its way back, but he said that if I did so I might miss it: If the sea got much rougher the boat might not put in at all, at the cement wharf. And it was better for foreigners to go through the exit customs at Daphne. I thanked him and said good-bye and went down to the boat shed by the wharf—a tower and squat walls—until the fishing boat appeared, and I hailed it.

The deck empty. As we backed off and turned down the coast again I thought I was the only passenger, until I saw a face at the hatch opening. There were a few others, below there: monks, one bishop, two or three Greek boys on a first visit. Once again I watched the coast to Daphne. The customs-shed steaming, the bags of Greek pilgrims, and my own, searched to make sure that no one was smuggling ikons, relics, manuscripts, the mountain's portable treasures. Even my books and notebooks were opened, leafed through, shaken. The service is said to be in the interest of the monks, but the uniforms, of course, are Greek. And again the boat, back the way I had walked the day before. A scholarly Dutch Orthodox priest and I, sitting out on deck, fell into conversation. He had been cataloguing the libraries of Athos for years—St. Pantaleimon this time. The library there contained wonderful things, he told me; manuscripts of great importance and beauty in a terrible state of disorder and neglect. It was typical, he said to me, cheerfully. He showed me one of his monographs, in Dutch and Greek. With regard to the *information,* he said to me, the situation was rapidly improving: Every year more of the works in the libraries were being microfilmed. From the point of view of scholarship it was becoming simpler to work from films, in Thessalonika. As for the rest——. He got off at the arsenal of Zographou to look at a few manuscripts, and I traveled the rest of the way up the coast in silence.

The mountain itself had been hidden in cloud all morning. The rain stopped. For a moment the clouds separated and a part of the peak could be seen—then the blank clouds closed over it again. I could not tell which part it had been.

Then in time Prosphori Tower came into sight, in the opposite direction. From 1928 until he died in 1954 it had been the home of an Englishman, Sidney Lock, who had spent his later years writing about the mountain with learning, wit, love, and a sharp eye. How changed the place would look to him, after twenty years! I boarded the new bus. The clouds were clearing as we crossed the mountains of Chalkidikis. To Thessalonika. The night train, and Athens in the morning.

The Tree on One Tree Hill

I f you happen to be an expert in some distinct field of learning
such as the order *Physallidae* or cuneiform script, no doubt there
are sections of the British Museum that seem to be not just reposito-
ries but models of human knowledge, reflecting, proving, serving as
emblems of its orderly and progressive nature. The institution origi-
nated, after all, in the middle of the eighteenth century and is still
haunted by the spirit of that age—in Europe—of achievements at
once grand and contained, a time marked there by a faith in symme-
try and an adulation of Reason—a word that those generations used
to describe their peculiar view of what they thought was everything.

But in straying from the familiar exhibits into the surrounding
maze of corridors, even the expert may come to feel that the particular confined area that had seemed to be the mind itself, the orderly
spot to which whole lifetimes of study have been dedicated, is little
more than a makeshift arrangement in a corner of what any child can
see is an attic of empire. While passing the sarcophagi and the glass
cases, the sense of human knowledge may seem neither definite nor
near at hand. In our time, in the greater part of the museum, even the
expert is as ignorant as the rest of us, and much of what has been so
assiduously and ruthlessly acquired and compiled there in the name

of knowledge remains, and is likely to remain, utterly unknown to almost everyone.

The contents of Sir Hans Sloane's original gatherum for which the Old Montagu House was acquired, in 1753, to become the British Museum, were referred to as "curiosities." And where, precisely, as one wanders through the halls, is human knowledge now, that goal of curiosity? We do not even know whether the question is really characteristic of our lifetime or only seems to be because it occurs to us. The museum conceived of as an extended memory has become just as certainly one of the mansions of oblivion.

For almost two centuries, much of what Sydney Parkinson managed to convey of what he knew, from having seen it at first hand, lay in the dark in the museum, along with other relics of Captain James Cook's first circumnavigation of the earth on the bark *Endeavour*, between August 1768 and July 1771. There are certain things that a few of us know now only because Parkinson saw them and drew them, painted them, noted them down. They are among the things we know about Parkinson himself. But they are constant reminders also of the limits of what we can pretend to know about what we are seeing, and about what he saw, and about the young man himself.

By now, at least, this is not so because of neglect. Scholars since the 1950s have been bringing attention to the artists and naturalists who sailed on Cook's voyages. The work of Averil Lysaght in particular helped to put together all that we are likely to find out, in a factual way, about Parkinson's life. In 1983, the Natural History section of the British Museum, in association with the University of Hawai'i Press, published a volume, edited by D. J. Carr, which included essays on Parkinson, on the *Endeavour* voyage as a whole, the successive landfalls and what the English found there and reproductions of more than two hundred drawings and paintings by Parkinson, as well as some finished after his death by other artists working from his drawings and color notations. Two years later, Yale University Press published two sumptuous tomes edited by Rudiger Joppien and Bernard Smith, *The Art of Cook's Voyages*, which contained further discussion of Parkinson's life and work. Alecto Historical Editions is preparing a publication of line engravings made from Parkinson's drawings. A facsimile edition of his sketchbook is in production, and meticulous study of his work is continuing in England and Australia. We are able to catch glimpses now of what Sydney Parkinson saw for the first and last time.

We take it for granted that what we see becomes part of what we know even though we may not remember it. The effect of what we know on what we see is not so easy to distinguish, though it may be just as influential. Parkinson's paintings of birds, his earlier ones in particular, reveal as much about the prevalent contemporary conventions for looking at—or conceiving of—birds as they do about any living creature. Of course, most of his models were not alive at all. They had been shot, as a matter of course, and stuffed, or had their "skins" pickled in alcohol, to be washed out later, dried and propped up for their portraits. For us, come to that. Sometimes it was other portraits that were the models. In either case, any passerine bird was likely to be depicted clutching a chunk of branch, generally inconveniently thick for its grasp, and usually shaped like part of an *s* broken off somewhere, with a sprig and leaves sprouting as though startled from its upper end. The bird often looks as though it had been caught at the moment of trying to recover from paralyzing cramps, except that it is hard to imagine, from the picture, that those appendages could ever move at all. We can notice this even in one of Parkinson's paintings of a bird whose kin he must have seen often, alive, in England: a wheatear *(Oenanthe oenanthe)*, which, perhaps from exhaustion, had made the mistake of alighting near human company off the coast of Spain, on September 4, 1768. The nearside wing (the only one visible) is as stiff as a paper knife and appears to be clamped to the side of the bird, which is evidently just toppling forward from one branch of a generic blasted bush. There is no doubt that what has been set before us is less a bird than a convention that was solid enough to keep well and be brought out when the subject *bird* came up. It was something learned, and so in at least one sense known, and art historians can trace its scant variations from decorative friezes around the Mediterranean Basin, and heraldic symbols and designs on fabrics, through most of two millennia in the West. It was taught. It is possible to guess with some confidence where Parkinson had acquired his own artistic influences, including this one. And there is evidence of his passing the convention on to his thirteen-year-old pupil, Ann Lee, the year before he sailed with Cook. Both his original painting of a yellow bunting *(Emberiza citronella)* and her copy have survived.

The convention is obvious in them both: it is flat, static, and its virtues are primarily decorative. They do not so much reveal life, or a life, as provide something agreeably reminiscent of it, an acceptable abstraction. Something interposed, so that where the convention is the pervasive rule, to the person in whose culture it has become a habit it is what the real thing looks like.

It looks dead. Whatever that is. Rigid, glazed, aware of nothing. Never to stir again. It suggests not life but ornament, usage for human pleasure, and not an original with its own flight and senses. But we look at the convention, too, now, in the light of things that we have come to know, so we see something different from what was apparent to those for whom it may once have seemed, indeed, natural.

It is never entirely possible to separate what we are seeing from what we know or imagine we know. We look at Parkinson's paintings and drawings knowing things about the world and about him that Parkinson did not know when he made them, and we may think we see things in the work that were not visible to Parkinson.

What we think we see there may not be mere fancy. One does not have to know anything about the painter Carol Fabritius, a pupil of Rembrandt's, on entering the room in the Mauritshuis where his painting of a goldfinch on a perch in a plaster wall is hung, to be struck at once by a startling power in that single frame among so many. It flows into the room, dominating it like a musical chord reverberating from an unknown place, touching and commanding everything there. It would be best, in fact, to see that painting for the first time without knowing anything about the painter, so that there could be no doubt that it was simply what one was seeing there on the wall that was having that effect, unmixed with any suggestive knowledge that one might have brought to it. Having seen it then, that watchful imminence and radiant otherness in the form of a goldfinch, it will not be altogether surprising to learn that the painting (which bears a date in the painter's hand) was completed in the same year and within a few months of the date of the painter's sudden death, at thirty-two, in Delft. According to one version, he was killed when a powder magazine blew up, destroying also his studio and many of his paintings. According to another, he was walking home at night with friends, and the explosion killed them all as they passed the door of the magazine. However it happened, it occurred as a blast and a flash of light, and once one knows that one is likely to think one sees it prefigured in the luminous presence that emanates from the painting. One may recall as well the role of the goldfinch in medieval Europe as a symbol of eternal life, and may feel that both forms of knowledge—the symbolic one that certainly figured in Fabritius's intellectual storeroom, and the premonitory one of which he would not have been consciously aware—must have been urgent in the painter's mind and found their way onto the canvas. It looks like a living bird there, perched on the bent rod fixed into the wall above the wooden feedbox, a fine chain keeping it from flying away. But it looks more intense than life, as life usually appears to us. That is how it looked to Fabritius just before it all disappeared.

It requires no indulgence in pathos to note that paintings and drawings are all showing us worlds that have vanished. That is something we know about them that we tend to forget because we want to, and besides, the illusion created by the image in front of us asks us to forget such knowledge for a moment and allow the image itself to be the present. We know, in more ways than may at first occur to us, how much of what Sydney Parkinson saw and drew and painted for us ceased almost at once to be there. His paintings and drawings are all of them testaments of youth, the work of a very young man. He was twenty-two or -three—we cannot be sure—when he sailed with Cook, and he did not live to complete the voyage, but died of malaria after the *Endeavour* left Java, and was buried at sea at the end of January 1771. Knowing that, there is a persistent temptation to foresee it in what he left, in the colors of the flowers he painted, the mouths of the fish, the opened seeds, the bent neck of a girl at work scraping bark as though it must have been visible as he portrayed those things. At the very end, before the fever stopped him, he was drawing boats, the Malay sailing vessels that he had seen in the Sunda Straits and off the coast of Java. *Mayangs,* they were called. The drawings are faint, rather tentative sketches. Many of the boats have large brushes of tassels or radiating discs of fiber at the ends of the booms or fixed in the rigging: spirit antennae, talismans that had been bought from sorcerers for safety and good fortune on the unpredictable way. He was also drawing another kind of sailing vessel, one that he had not set eyes on but had only heard about and imagined. That was the so-called flying proa, of whose speed Western sailors had spoken again and again with amazement. Magellan's chronicler, Pigafetta, in 1521, had been only the first to tell of the proas, and for over two hundred years explorers had marvelled at them. On Spanish maps, the islands where they were built were named "Islas de las Velas" —Islands of the Sails. No doubt Parkinson, having read the accounts, was hoping to see those flying proas. But by the time he was born, the boat builders had been all but exterminated by Europeans, by the Spaniards in particular. Their islands—the Marianas—and what few proas may still have been sailing, lay far from the course of the *Endeavour,* and Parkinson's drawings of their sails and shapes are late guesses at something he would never see.

His own survival among us, though, rests upon his portraits of what he was seeing for the first time and knew he might not, and probably would not, see again. It is the condition of art to see things that way. And his youth and relative lack of sophistication meant that even if he had stayed home, he might have wakened day after day to things that he realized he had never seen before. He was living, besides, at a time when a growing number of people in Europe were becoming aware that the world teemed with things that they had not yet beheld. Parkinson's brief lifetime, and the first two years of the *Endeavour* voyage in particular, were a moment when the sense of that unseen world suddenly became much clearer and more suggestive. When the *Endeavour* sailed from Plymouth, European botanists supposed the flora of the earth to consist, "by fairly safe calculation," Linnaeus said, of something less than ten thousand species. The Linnaean system for cataloguing these was a bright new instrument that filled the natural scientists with hopes of giving every living thing its true name and place in the scheme of things at last. By the time the *Endeavour* had spent a few days anchored off Rio de Janeiro, Parkinson could not keep up with the new material set before him to paint, and the naturalists of the expedition, Daniel Solander (a favorite pupil of Linnaeus and an assistant at the British Museum) and the Finn Hans Sporing, were stretching the system to include biological manifestations that were wholly new to them.

Expeditions long before the *Endeavour* had taken artists with them to bring back records from life. Wilfred Blunt, in one of the essays in D. J. Cart's Parkinson volume, mentions the artistic accounts of Thutmose III's campaign in Syria, in the fifteenth century B.C., and what he describes as "the first known florilegium," which was carved in limestone at Karnak. Later travellers and explorers arranged to be accompanied by artists, or regretted the lack of them, in their own verbal chronicles. But on the *Endeavour* expedition "no people," John Ellis wrote to Linnaeus, "ever went to sea better fitted out for the purpose of Natural History." The complement of naturalists and artists sailing on board was largely due to the interests, originality, and wealth of Joseph—later Sir Joseph—Banks, who was himself just twenty-five at the time of the sailing.

For anyone following the hatching of curiosity in eighteenth-century England, or indeed Europe, Banks is an interesting phenomenon. He was a member of the landed gentry with enough money to do anything he pleased, and his wealth, in the course of his lifetime, continued to increase. "I have a sufficiency," he wrote in Tahiti, as he proceeded, against Cook's wishes, to add a young Tahitian, Tupaia (who also died on the voyage), to those sailing on the crowded *Endeavour,* "and I do not know why I may not keep him as a curiosity as well as some of my neighbors do lions and tygers at a larger expense than he would probably put me to."

Banks was driven by curiosity—it became inseparable from his ambition. As a child, he had been intrigued by Gerard's *Herbal* and had collected bugs and butterflies and shells with an uncommon ardor that led him into a growing fascination with the natural world as a whole or at least the study of it. He went to Harrow and Eton, where the acquisition of the classical European languages was expected of everyone, but his overriding passion continued to be the natural sciences, and above all botany. When he went on to Oxford and found no one there to teach him the subject, he simply went to Cambridge, hired a professor of botany and brought him back. The Latin authors never became his familiar ground, and according to the criteria of the time, he remained a semiliterate man. His own idol was Linnaeus.

When Banks was eighteen, his father died, and he came into an estate that made him completely independent. According to portraits and contemporary accounts, he was good-looking, and everyone agreed that he was charming. He was full of energy, enthusiasm, a passion to know the things he was interested in and those who were engaged in the study of them. He bought a house in London, and instead of travelling on the continent to see the ruins of antiquity, he sailed to Newfoundland to collect insects and botanical specimens. He was still in his early twenties when he was admitted to the Royal Society and it was the Royal Society that proposed to the Admiralty that he, "together with his suite, being seven persons more, that is, eight persons in all, together with their baggage, be received on board of the ship, under the command of Captain Cook." The "persons" (there were more than seven in the suite before the *Endeavour* sailed) included two young servants from Lincolnshire, probably from Banks's estates, two Negro servants, as well as the naturalists, a draftsman named Alexander Buchan and, of course, Sydney Parkinson. There were also Banks's two greyhounds, which may have been considered part of the baggage.

Parkinson had been introduced to Banks the year before by James Lee, a botanist with a vineyard nursery garden at Hammersmith. It is not hard to imagine something of the meeting—its contrast of characters, at least. Lee, a sober, industrious, Scottish businessman, a Quaker, at once reserved and deferential, in conversation with the lively, talkative, self-assured young Oxonian, heir to large estates in Lincolnshire. And Parkinson—we know his face had been marked with smallpox, and we have one, and only one, portrait that is known to be of him (another, said to be a self-portrait, in oils, is oddly amorphous). The one portrait was included as the frontispiece in the posthumous edition of Parkinson's *journal,* published by his elder brother, Stanfield. It shows a very thin, long-faced, earnest young man, wrapped tightly in the clothes of the time, and sitting up stiff and straight at a plain table, holding in his right hand a piece of paper, and gazing beyond it at the grave nature of things. Some plant—perhaps a fern, since the drawing must have been made in Scotland—dug from its life is lying at the edge of the table, as though it were the subject of a drawing in his hand. We have the impression of someone intensely serious, self-effacing, unflagging and yet fragile. Not one for many words, no doubt, nor for idle amusement, but obviously reliable and probably likeable, or at least no trouble to get along with. Banks might not have been surprised to learn that he, too, was a Scot and a Quaker.

It may seem incongruous to us that the Quaker Lee ran a well-known vineyard nursery, but Sydney's father, Joel, embraced a similar combination: He was a Quaker and a brewer. The eighteenth century had not yet been afflicted with Victorian logic. Sydney grew up in or near Edinburgh. We know that he was still very young when his father died, that he was apprenticed to a woollen draper, "but taking a particular delight in drawing flowers, fruit, and other objects of natural history," his brother Stanfield tells us, "he became soon so proficient

in that style of painting, as to attract the notice of the most celebrated
botanists and connoisseurs of that study." There is a good deal of fore-
shortening in this account, obviously, and we have no real details of the
early manifestations of Sydney's passion for drawing the forms of the
natural world, but it seems likely that his family was eager to nurture
his talent and encouraged it, sending him to study with the French
painter William De La Cour, who opened in 1760, in Edinburgh,
the first public art school in Great Britain. One can imagine that the
opening of such a school in Edinburgh might have appealed to serious, modest, middle-class families with some aspiration and a Scottish
regard for education, and that his own family might have been rather
proud to have Sydney enrolled there. Then, when he was nearly twenty,
his mother moved with the boys to London. The Friendly Society
must indeed have befriended the widowed Mrs. Parkinson and helped
to keep the family's means of livelihood from melting away in the
years after the death of Sydney's father, and they may have helped
to make it possible for Sydney and his brother to acquire as much
education as they did. Then, when the Parkinsons moved to London,
a selection of Sydney's flower drawings was exhibited at The Friendly
Society's house there, in 1765 and 1766. Mrs. Parkinson may have
already known her fellow Scot and Quaker, James Lee, before moving
to London. Lee soon engaged Sydney to tutor his gifted thirteen-
year-old daughter, Ann, in painting and drawing.

Banks was sufficiently impressed, by Lee's recommendations and
by the young man's paintings, to employ him to do paintings of some
of the zoological specimens that he had collected the year before on
his expedition to Newfoundland and Labrador, and copies of paintings of tropical birds and mammals that had been made originally
for the former governor of Ceylon. Clearly he was pleased with the
results and with what he saw of Sydney for he went on to enlist him
among his "gentlemen" for the *Endeavour* voyage.

A good deal of what Sydney had done for Banks by then might
be described as painting from death: stuffed animals and birds, skins
and copies. There had been little incentive to go beyond accepted con-

vention. It is not that there were no conceptions of paintings besides those that Sydney had grown up with, but we know little of what he had actually seen when he sailed with Cook. He owned a copy of Hogarth's *Analysis of Beauty*. But painting the natural world from life, to evoke its life—such work as Dürer's, for instance—would he have been aware of it at all? With remarkable exceptions, it was in botanical illustration that representation of the natural world, in Europe, had come closest to a portrayal of it as a living presence, and many painters probably unknown to Parkinson had been important in developing that tradition. Dürer, it is true, had put before us flowers and leaves and plants growing in their lives, and indeed in their social lives, whereas botanical illustration for the most part had set forth the individual plant in isolation from its surroundings, its kin and even from much of the rest of its body: abstracted, projected, held up as a type, in company with the dissected organs that make it typical. It, too, like the portraits of stuffed animals, often presents us with a view of life in the form of death, of life, in a sense, after death. But the botanical subjects were likely to be closer to their lives than were the dried or pickled skins brought back from another continent a year before. There was an urgency in the botanical portrayal of flowering stems and fruit cut off or dug up and brought to the artist's table, a need to try to reproduce the textures of surfaces before they grew dim, the colors before they faded, the grace of leaves and stems and petals before they wilted. For when the painting was done, the subject would finally be lifeless, and there would be only the portrait in its place. For Parkinson, the months on the *Endeavour*—the rest of his life—would be filled with this kind of urgency. It would overwhelm him as the voyage lengthened, and he would not be able to keep up with the growing rush of subjects set before him day after day in the Great Cabin, where the naturalists and Sydney's fellow artists convened to work and confer every morning at eight, stayed at it until two, then returned to it from dinner until twilight. After that, according to one of these colleagues, Sydney "frequently sat up all night drawing for himself or writing in his journal."

In fact, there was more than one journal in which he wrote. After Parkinson's death, his employer, Banks, simply appropriated his effects until the end of the voyage. And thereafter, an unknown number of Parkinson's papers, including notes, drawings of people, landscapes, trees and plants, and a very full personal journal known and admired by his fellow "gentlemen" on the voyage, remained in Banks's keeping and were never seen again. A bitter quarrel arose between Banks and Sydney's surviving elder brother Stanfield over Sydney's effects, a dispute that does small credit to Banks. But he did hand over some of Sydney's "working papers," which Stanfield, against the combined efforts of Banks and Hawkesworth, the official historian of the voyage, proceeded to assemble and publish with his own preface and the portrait of Sydney looking frail and somber. That is what is known as "Parkinson's Journal" and, apart from a few stiff letters and some notes written on paintings and drawings, it is virtually all that remains to us of Sydney's sleepless efforts to put into words the new things he was seeing. We cannot even be certain whether particular comments in the published "Journal" are Sydney's own or were inserted by his brother or by Kenrick, the professional editor, when the material was published. But there was some quality in the account that led the reviewer in *The Cattlemen's Magazine*, in January 1785, to greet the publication of the "Journal" with warm praise, remarking that it represented "a superiority over those contemporary voyagers" who had "departed from the simplicity of Nature." Some of Sydney's notes on light and color, written on drawings as the *Endeavour* sailed among the islands of the South Pacific, indicate how acute and subtle his attention to the visible world had become even while the conventions of "composing" landscape remained with him, and how eager he was to seize what he saw as it slipped past and dissolved before him. They give a hint of what we have lost in his more personal journal, the observations that have not reached us after all.

But the impulse behind his fuller journal was also awake in his drawings and paintings, and though some of them, too, have disappeared, many have survived—very many indeed, in view of the circumstances in which they were produced and the time that has passed since then. Between the *Endeavour*'s sailing from Plymouth in late August 1768 and Sydney's death on the way from Java to Africa two and a half years later, he produced almost a thousand botanical drawings, nearly three hundred of them finished as paintings, and almost three hundred more drawings and paintings of birds, fish, other animals and insects, besides roughly a hundred drawings of people, landscapes and boats—most of these last, in particular, drawn literally from life. And there was an undetermined number of drawings that would be finished, painted or copied by others, and in some cases, ascribed to others altogether.

From the sheer volume of his work, it is clear that he must have been engrossed in an all but constant effort of attention, an attempt to portray forms of the living world that until then had been unknown to him. And he was trying to represent the lives from which most of his subjects had just been deprived. The colors would very soon dim, and in a matter of hours would be gone. The textures would follow, and the shapes. He must have made fervent demands upon his talents and his skill and whatever he knew about painting. He developed an ability to draw very rapidly what was put in front of him, and yet few of his drawings—and virtually none of his botanical illustrations—give the appearance of haste. When he was in too great a hurry, he left the drawings unfinished, supplying the essential shapes and details, painting in crucial areas of color, indicating the rest in careful notes.

He worked in circumstances, furthermore, that required the closest possible concentration on the evanescent objects before him. Most of his work was done at sea in the Great Cabin, with the other "gentlemen" and, no doubt, officers of the *Endeavour* present at the same table, often in bad weather, with the bark pitching and rolling ("seldom was there a storm," Banks wrote, "strong enough to break up our normal study time"); in the midst of almost continuous motion, he was portraying an illusory stillness. When they lay at anchor and he took his easel, pencils and brushes ashore, the conditions were not necessarily much better. In Tahiti, the flies were so thick that they "ate the colours off the paper as fast as they [could] be laid on," Banks recorded, and even when Sydney's chair and table were set up, under a kind of mosquito net, a fly trap had to be put inside it "to attract the vermin from eating the colours."

We know from his figure paintings, his depiction of groups in canoes or on land, that his attention to what he was seeing, and his feeling for it, were growing more direct and intimate in the course of the voyage. Wilfred Blunt finds some of the work "mechanical," but to an amateur's eye, the drawings of native peoples, from this distance, are fresh and poignant glimpses of an irretrievable world, and many of the botanical paintings, including some that were never finished, have a luminous sharpness, an arresting depth, a kind of personal authenticity independent of their scientific accuracy. We know from his writings that Parkinson sympathized with the native peoples they met, that he regretted profoundly the violence that the uninvited Europeans insisted they "had to" visit upon their hosts in order to establish the "peace" and circumstances that would allow them to go about their own purposes. He was interested in the languages encountered on the voyage, compiled word lists and made intelligent deductions about the relationships between the various tongues.

All, needless to say, from the point of view of someone outside, and from outside, coming to the subject and its world from a great distance. At Tolaga Bay in Aotearoa (which Europeans would call New Zealand), he wrote, "the country about the bay is agreeable beyond description," and then, revealing the European, the appropriative itch to tamper, added "and with proper cultivation might be rendered a kind of second Paradise." He saw it perforce, at least consciously, from the viewpoint of an eighteenth-century Englishman, a *ratere*, as the Tahitians said: a stranger. One extreme of the alien approach to all this otherness was put quite succinctly by J. R. Foster, a Prussian botanist, apparently a very disagreeable man and an inferior artist, who sailed on Cook's second voyage. "We were to make it," he wrote, "the object of our special care and attention that . . . nothing would remain unexplored on those shores, and that their natural history should be imparted to the learned world so described and illustrated that no one in future would have any desire to go back again to those regions and examine anything afresh." It was, in effect, an ambition to obliterate whatever was different by recording it, and the South Pacific, when Foster saw it, filled him with a mixture of covetous excitement and a despair at the wealth of the unknown: "everywhere . . . such treasure houses of Nature were laid before my eyes. I therefore saw that all regions to which we were to go would abound in the same riches." Foster was perhaps more candid than he realized about the Europeans' attitude toward the world they had not known to claim. But they would return. The real objective of the *Endeavour* voyage included sounding out possibilities for colonization, and discovering another great southern continent (Australia was not big enough to count), but the expedition's purpose was generally given out to be astronomical study, a project to observe the Transit of Venus from the antipodes in order to determine the earth's distance from the sun. And for their astronomical proceedings, the British built a fort on Tahiti and named it Fort Venus.

(It is worth noting, in that regard, that the fort supposedly was built, at least in part, to protect the foreigners' instruments and other possessions from the natives, whom the English had found to be deficient in respect for ownership of property. A revealing objection, considering that, in the attitude underlying the voyage, in the show of force with which the Europeans landed, in their building forts on land not theirs, claiming territories used by others and in most of their writing about their acquisitive ventures for at least two centuries afterward, the Europeans showed so little respect for the indigenous inhabitants' rights to their very homelands.)

Of course the British were not the first to bring the greed and diseases of Europe to the islands of the South Pacific. The English, preoccupied for almost two hundred years with the investment and reduction of North America, were relative newcomers to this other, vaster region. The Portuguese, the Spaniards and the Dutch had been to many parts of the area long before the British showed up, and in some places, whole European imperial structures had been established and superseded before the British came. It should have been easy for representatives of other European powers to guess the true purpose of the *Endeavour* voyage, but Cook was at pains to see that they found no evidence of it nor of where the vessel had been, when he did eventually put in at the Dutch port of Batavia, on Java.

As it happened, the astronomical instruments on the *Endeavour*, and the timing of the voyage, were important for making imperial claims among the islands of the South Pacific. Other European nations may have known their way around parts of that ocean and laid waste whole cultures and archipelagos, but it was only in the latter eighteenth century that navigational instruments became precise enough to allow accurate maps indicating beyond further doubt the location of small islands among those distances, placing them in a grid at last, bringing them into the net.

The Linnaean system for classifying and naming the natural world was an analogous development, a product of the same urge and the same moment—the moment that Sydney Parkinson was painting. He was observing another transit, in fact, except that the light that disappeared behind the new system of knowledge would not emerge again. The world that the Europeans "discovered" began to vanish as they set eyes on it, and to decompose at their touch. Their words for what they wanted from it even as observers are telling: They must "seize it," "capture it" once and for all, to "take home"—for home was somewhere else, somewhere already known and intrinsically different.

There had been a number of attempts by Europeans to describe the life surrounding and permitting human habitation on some of the islands of the South Pacific before Cook and Banks and their naturalists came to see it. In some ways, the most remarkable of those precursors was the German-born Georg Everard Rump (1628–1702), who came to be known as Rumphius, a resident of Java and then of the island of Ambon from the time he was twenty-eight until his death.

But Rumphius had found words for the world around him in a

manner that would have seemed obsolete, cumbersome and exasperating to the later naturalists on the *Endeavour*, and to others of their generation eagerly following the great pioneer of rational, scientific classification, Carl Linnaeus. Rumphius had had an ordinary middle-class German seventeenth-century education, evidently which would have included the Roman naturalist Pliny and Aristotle, whose procedure of definition and whose view of the structured relations of life as whole would in time become the basis of Linnaeus's system. And Rumphius, in compiling the seven-hundred-odd illustrated chapters of his *Herbal* of Ambon, in twelve books, and his further thesaurus of shells, stones, sea creatures, minerals and other "curiosities," wrote originally in Latin, and provided names in that language, as other European naturalists and botanists had done since the days of Rome. It was by then, for Europeans, the language of "everywhere" and so the tongue of nowhere. It was an articulate abstraction, a dead grammar. Some of the Latin names Rumphius ascribed to flora were known and used by the naturalists on the *Endeavour*, and some are still in use, "grandfathered" in before the present system. But Rumphius was writing and often drawing from life in a sense that was eclipsed in the century that followed him—at least in anything that pretended to be scientific illustration. He described plants and animals in their lives and as they appeared in the human consciousness of which they had become a part. It was an approach that would return to use in the nineteenth century, just as it was beginning to be apparent that life as a whole had become threatened by the human species. And after finishing the first (lost) draft of his *Herbal* in Latin, Rumphius rewrote the entire work in the Dutch that had become his vernacular, and his words convey a sense that he is not standing outside the world he is portraying but is an intimately and endlessly concerned part of it, as it in turn is a part of the ceaselessly attentive motion of his own mind.

"The front of these Wanderers," he writes of hermit crabs, "is shaped like a little Crab, while hindermost they look like a whelk, and they live in the houses of strangers, which is why their origin is uncertain and, likewise, their shape. . . . One of the claws, usually the right one, is always larger than their entire body [and] has been shaped by its house in such a way that it can close the selfsame door with it as if with a shield. . . . These little quarrelsome creatures have caused me much grief, because when I laid out all kinds of handsome whelks to bleach; even on a high bank, they knew how to climb up there at night, and carried the beautiful shells with them, leaving me their old coats to peep at" (E. M. Beekman trans.).

This was not the kind of exactness nor indeed the kind of concern that Linnaeus, his disciples or most of the world they heralded were interested in. There is surely no need to magnify the name of Linnaeus and his system and what they have accomplished. He and his method evolved from a craving of his species to possess a sense of the order of life, to occupy a commanding position in a pattern of existence that they alone understood, and therefore they alone, in the long run, would control. It is no essential detraction from the originality and genius of Linnaeus to suggest that the basic wants of his own kind demanded a system such as the one he provided, and that if he had not developed it, no doubt someone else would have done so. And it is as well to notice that the system is not identical with the lives it codifies, though it ascribes names to them and says where they belong in its scheme of things. It is itself an illusion, and the perfection it aspires and pretends to is bound to life primarily through its source in the unsatisfied nature, the innate imperfection of human desire, ambition and anxiety. Out of that comes its goal and its procedure, which are the same: the deduction of structure and the labor of separation. Separation of role from role, *species* from species, life from life. And abstracted from these abstractions, the isolated human species with its relative knowledge remains the mirror of the unknown.

Within the system of classification and naming that Linnaeus evolved, the first word of the Latin name indicates the genus, the second the species and the third, if any, the variety. The species name in some cases indicates the place where a specimen was found, the place that was believed to be its origin, but what mattered more was its place within the biological hierarchy of the system, and often one or both names commemorated naturalists associated with describing the species, or patrons of the enterprise, far removed from the unchristened lives to which the names were attached. To Linnaeus's immediate heirs, his system must have been without question a part of the pursuit of truth itself, and certainly it is possible to view it as a necessity. But such a view, such a pursuit, indeed, tends sometimes to assume that a perfect and accessible truth can exist in separation from life itself, which is never finished, never in that sense perfect, but arises continuously out of the unknown. Of course, those who are utterly dedicated to such a pursuit can be impatient with such a portrayal of life as Rumphius was attempting, in which the observer is not an abstracted manipulator of a process but a wondering presence whose wholeness is the completeness of existence. They may find it useless and therefore inconsiderable, an embarrassment that they may call romantic.

Still, the difference is relative. Rumphius inevitably had observed from his own distance. Though Ambon became his home as the Pacific never was home to Cook's naturalists, and though he must have conducted much of his life in the tongues of the islands, he described the life around him in the languages of Europe, and he approached it with a mind formed on the other side of the Earth. Which meant that he wrote first of all, and as a matter of course, for the minds of Europeans. He translated what he saw into European terms, insofar as that was possible. He would have been doing something of the kind, though, in any language, since that is the way language works: on the one hand to evoke and identify and on the other to be about something else, to stand in its stead, to take its place and so to interfere. It is a kind of knowledge that at once informs seeing and impairs it. It exists because of a knowledge of separation, and in partially healing the separation, it confirms it, perpetuates it, proves it. It is at once a power and an indication of helplessness, incompleteness, necessity. But between Rumphius and the disciples of Linnaeus and what they represented, as between the artisans of the Renaissance and the producers of the Industrial Revolution, in which the Linnaean outlook would come to be taken for granted, there was a leap, however one may describe it, after which there would, of course, be no going back. The Linnaean system was one of its manifestations, and one way that Sydney Parkinson would have seen it working itself out was in the heated preoccupation with new names.

For it was only the names that were new and not the subjects, which had been there for a long time before there were Europeans to "discover" them. Yet again and again, the novelty of the names was and still is ascribed to the subjects themselves, and so we speak of "new species," meaning forms of life that are our elders but that have only recently entered our awareness. For the purposes of immeasurable memory, the act of naming has always been deeply important, though for a long time there have been some who have noticed that a name at once indicates and obscures its object. But naming is a part of language, of the ceaseless, inevitable ambivalences involved in conversing with the world and about it. Day after day and evening after evening, as Sydney sat drawing, the Great Cabin of the *Endeavour* must have been filled with a revolving discussion of names, Latin syllables that would identify each example that he was portraying and would place it in a hypothetical scheme of existence, without its life. Sydney, sketching and painting the specimens they were talking about, must have heard the names eddying around him, but from what we know of the voyage and of his temperament, it seems unlikely that he said much. After all, he was not a naturalist himself. And the cabin contained, more or less intact, a small section of the behavior of the species *homo sapiens var. Brittanicus* of that period, a hologram of the class structure of England. Banks represented the gentry. Cook was the commander of the expedition, but was Banks's social inferior, and their complicated relationship had been harmoniously established at the start of the voyage. Parkinson was Banks's employee, and though he was one of the "gentlemen," was socially a nobody. This unquestioned order of things extended to the assumed relations of Europeans to the native residents of the places they visited, and no doubt it seemed as immutable and inevitable as the movements of the heavenly bodies that they were recording.

By the time of the *Endeavour* voyage, the Linnaean enterprise of naming the species of the natural world as each was found had become as feverish as the communications of the time allowed, and the process continues today with scarcely abated intensity. Most of the drawings and paintings reproduced in Carr's volume on Parkinson are accompanied by a succession of botanical names that have been ascribed to the species since the late eighteenth century and a brief history of the ascriptions. The principal participants in discussions of nomenclature in the Great Cabin would undoubtedly have been Linnaeus's favorite pupil, Daniel Solander, Banks himself, the impassioned amateur, and his secretary the Finn Hans Sporing, with the ultimate authority resting with Solander. And in view of the volume and unfamiliarity of the material that was set before him, Solander seems to have done remarkably well. The names that he arrived at reveal again and again that he knew what he was looking at, what classification was appropriate to it in the Linnaean system, what its nearest of kin were. Some of the names he ascribed to species are still current, and perhaps more would be if the full results of his labors had been published soon after the *Endeavour* returned to England.

It was not, after all, mere coincidence that Solander and the preoccupation with naming should have formed so central a part of a voyage whose ultimate purpose was colonial occupation. As the history of magic indicates, finding the "real" name of anything is a way of claiming and establishing power over it. In itself it is an act of appropriation, an annexation, and the moment of such naming of the flora and fauna of the South Pacific coincided with the final and most pervasive era of European imperialism, the nineteenth century. And Foster need not have worried about Europeans even having the desire to go back again to the natural world he would see at the end of the eighteenth century. Individual species would survive, but that apparently inexhaustible fabric of flora and fauna, like the world of the flying proas, would not be there to go back to.

At the time, what Cook's crew wanted to go back to was merely England. As the *Endeavour* cleared the northernmost tip of Austra-

lia, Banks said they were "pretty far gone with the longing for home
which the Physicians have gone so far as to esteem a disease under
the name of Nostalgia; indeed I can find hardly anybody in the ship
clear of its effects but the Captn. [,] Dr. Solander and myself, indeed
we three have pretty constant employment for our minds which I
believe to be the best if not the only remedy for it." The quantity of
Parkinson's output would suggest that he, too, had "pretty constant
employment for his mind," but the captain, Dr. Solander and Banks
were evidently immunized as well by their unappeased craving for
what was still unknown to them, unseen, unnamed. The others longed
for a Europe they thought they remembered, in which nothing of the
voyage, nothing that they had "discovered," nothing of the moment
through which they were sailing had been known, or seen, or named.

What Europe—England, Scotland—meant to Sydney Parkin-
son we can scarcely guess. In the published "Journal" he tells almost
nothing of his more private feelings, and it seems unlikely that his
lost, more complete journal would have revealed anything more intimate. For one thing, it appears that the journal, as it was written from
day to day, may have been available to others of the company in the
Great Cabin. And for another, there is Sydney's own shy and reticent
temperament. Of his attachments in England, we know of his mother
and brother and Lee, and of a cousin, Jane Gomeldon, a woman some
years his elder, widowed, to whom he wrote that he had "spared no
pains during the voyage, to pick up everything that is curious for
thee." Besides the leaves and petals fading in front of him.

Other sicknesses besides Nostalgia, rising out of memories of
Europe, lay in wait for them. On the Great Barrier Reef, the *Endeavour*, one quiet night, was badly damaged by a spur of coral. Sea water
soaked part of the carefully stowed herbarium—it was only the beginning of the harm they found, and they were lucky to have survived
at all. They managed to make temporary repairs to the bark by themselves, on the Australian coast, but Cook knew that the hull was in
no condition to brave the crossing of the Indian Ocean and the long
sail northward back to England without a major overhaul. Despite

a distrust of the imperial Dutch, the port of Batavia on Java seemed the best place for the job, and he put in there on October 9, 1770. Five days later, Sydney Parkinson sent off two letters to England on a departing vessel, one to a Quaker friend, Dr. Fothergill, and the other to his cousin, Jane Gomeldon—the first letters from the *Endeavour* to reach England—saying that all was well.

So it was, more or less. They had all narrowly escaped death on the Great Barrier Reef. They had "done great things this voyage," Sydney wrote to Fothergill, "having been very successful in discoveries of Land, in Astronomy & Natural History, having got an amazing number of new subjects that way; our Crew has been very healthy & we have hardly lost any of them yet, but I am sorry to inform you that your faithful servant Richmond is no more, he & another black Servant of Mr. Banks's died at Tierra del Fuego. I felt the loss of him very much." The servants had helped themselves to the entire rum ration of Banks's Tierra del Fuego shore party and had frozen to death. And Sydney's fellow artist, Alexander Buchan, who suffered from epilepsy, had died in Tahiti and had been buried at sea, to the astonishment of the Tahitians. There had been one suicide on the voyage, two drownings, one death from consumption and one from venereal disease—which Cook's crews, like those of other European vessels, spread through the Pacific. But everyone felt they had come through remarkably well: All told, eight of the eighty-five who had left Plymouth had died before the *Endeavour* reached Java, where the Dutch had established themselves by ruthless force almost two hundred years earlier.

Batavia was the seat of Dutch power in the Indies. After they had seized the original port of Jakarta in 1619, they had built their own capital there, laying it out like a Dutch city with a network of canals. The mud along the waterways, Banks wrote, "stinks intolerably, as indeed it must, being chiefly formed from human ordure of which . . . the Canals every morning received their regular quota, and the more filthy recrements of housekeeping." The fetid water and the swamp around the city were full of dysentery and malarial mosquitoes, and one by one the crew of the *Endeavour* came down with one disease or the other until "everyone on shore and many on board were ill," Banks recorded. Solander, and Banks himself sickened; Sydney Parkinson worked on at his botanical drawings and sketches of boats, but already in the letter to Dr. Fothergill in mid-October, he spoke of being "so confused and fluttered about at present that my mind is not settled," referring perhaps to the onset of the "intermittents"—the fevers of malaria.

Not only Banks and Solander but Cook himself fell sick. Some twenty-seven officers and men of the *Endeavour* would die as a result of calling at Batavia. It is impossible to form a clear picture of the life in the ship's company during the months there, though we know that Banks and Solander, at least, could afford to rent houses out of the city in the hills, and hire nurses, and apparently for that reason they survived. Parkinson might have rented a house in the hills and hired a nurse, too, if Banks, before taking off had troubled to pay him the wages that were due him when the *Endeavour* reached Java. Life must have been miserable indeed for most of the crew and officers of the vessel, lying sick and feverish while the bark was overhauled in the foul-smelling harbor, and knowing nothing of the local languages. It appears that there was some cinchona bark—quinine—in the ship's medicine chest, but who used it and to what effect we do not know. At the end of Parkinson's sketchbook there are a few notes about monies paid and monies owed him, and a surprisingly long list of books that, it seems, he had with him on the voyage, including many volumes of poetry: Shakespeare, Virgil, Pope, Dryden, Homer, Ovid, Chaucer and Spenser, La Fontaine, Cervantes. (Joppien and Smith have suggested that he may have compiled the list as he prepared to make his will.) He managed to produce a surprising number of botanical drawings—many of them sketches that were finished later by others—as well as his ethereal outlines of boats, at Batavia, but by the time the *Endeavour* sailed from Java on the day after Christmas, 1770, his work was finished. They sailed west for the coast of Africa. He must have been racked with fevers, growing weaker day by day. The islands of Tahiti and England must have seemed equally evanescent, and all the shores that he had painted.

Among his drawings and paintings, "mechanical" or luminous, stored away there in the patched hull of the veteran collier, there was one of a tree overlooking Matavai Bay on Tahiti, where they had lain at anchor in a happier time. A huge, dark, ancient tree, the One Tree on One Tree Hill. Out on the bay, the vessel floats like a shadow, and on the far shore is the fort that the British had built for the pursuit of knowledge. A young Tahitian woman is poised in the act of walking along the path under the tree, heading toward the bay with a load of breadfruit, probably, suspended from a stick on her shoulder. A man, possibly a sailor, is striding in the same direction, carrying a rolled mat. Two men, evidently Europeans, one with a notebook and staff, have climbed the slope under the tree and are looking up into its branches, towering far above them. Perhaps they are Banks and one of his "gentlemen." And in the shade of the tree, in a tricorne hat, someone is sitting with a pad on his knee. It seems likely that it is Parkinson himself as seen from a little distance, by Parkinson. It is an ancient tree, far older than anything else in the painting, but everything is there in the same time. The Parkinson who drew the tree as we see it has been specific about its botanical identity. It is an *Etoa casuarina equisetifolia:* the first word, in this case, is Polynesian and the second *casuarina,* is a legacy of Rumphius, alluding to the wing of a cassowary.

In England, the tree would be copied from Parkinson's drawing by John James Barralet, who had never seen it. Barralet made the copy for Hawkesworth's official edition of *An Account of Voyages Undertaken by the Order of His Present Majesty,* 1773, a work commissioned by Banks. When Hawkesworth asked Banks whether he should make acknowledgment of those materials of Parkinson's that he was using, Banks replied, "as for Drs. [a reference to Fothergill] intention of saying that Parkinson's materials have been used by you I am strongly of the opinion that that should not be." In Barralet's pencil copy of Parkinson's scene, there is an erasure at the foot of the tree where the seated figure had been.

A month out of Java, at the age of twenty-five or -six, Parkinson joined the subjects he had painted.

Snail Song

The summer morning light through the big trees surrounds the dark branches with a radiance that is never entirely still. The sound of the watercourse on the slope below has been lost in the rustle of leaves and the calls of the few thrushes and finches in the bamboo thickets. There is no path to speak of, up the steep slope, around fallen branches. At the top of the rise the ruin suddenly emerges from among the trunks.

The coral mortar and stucco of the stone facade are not the most usual building materials in Hawai'i, and they have turned gray and green and black with time and the rain, and are daubed with mosses and lichens. Light shines along the surviving shape of the masonry like sunrise gathering behind a mountain. The massive walls have crumbled and have been rounded to the shapes of hills. The tops of bright trees glitter in the clearing behind them in what were once the rooms of a budding.

The lintel is still there over what was the main doorway, though there are roots knotted on the stones and disappearing into the cracks between them. In front of the opening, on a level space that had been a broad verandah, a large stone has been faced with a metal plaque that tells some of the story. The structure was once the summer house—or, as some prefer, the "summer palace"—of King Kamehameha III and his wife, Queen Kalama, in the mid-nineteenth century. It occupies a site in the deep valley of the Nuuanu Stream, in an area called Luakaha, some 800 feet above sea level. There are several waterfalls nearby and the cliffs rise steeply on both sides of the valley. At this height above the South Coast of the island of Oahu, and above Honolulu, the air is cool and softened with frequent mists and showers, and for generations the chiefs and kings of Oahu retired to the upper valley when the weather turned hot down on the plain.

Liliha, the wife of Boki, Kamehameha I's governor, had a house somewhere in this part of the valley and in the summer of 1831 she placed it at the disposal of the German naturalist, Dr. F. J. F. Meyen. Liliha's summer retreat was built, Meyen says, "quite like the Indian huts," which meant a framework of poles lashed together and thatched with the leaves of *pandanus* and with *pili* grass. A decade later, when the present structure was built, views of appropriate architecture had undergone drastic changes. Coral and stucco masonry had appeared in the islands less than 25 years before, with the churches of the missionaries from New England, those purveyors of righteousness who had filled Kamehameha III's childhood and youth with misery.

The choice of the exact site for the royal summer house might have been purely topographical, but Queen Kalama's father is said to have been born nearby which would suggest that the nobility of previous generations had kept summer homes in the area. At some point the place acquired the name of Kaniakapupu, which is generally taken to mean "the sound" or "the song of the land snail."

Hawaiian land snails are small, elegant creatures endemic to the islands. They were once common through the Nuuanu Valley and the upland forests on all the main islands, but now everywhere they are rare and endangered. Meyen, after his brief passage through the region, paid them his own tribute, saying (not quite accurately) that in the Sandwich Islands nature had "placed countless land snails instead of insects on the leaves of the trees." He speaks of their "regular stripes," their "brilliant colors." Some, he says, "are completely grass-green but this color disappears at death."

Meyen also speaks of the dense growth in parts of the valley but by the time of his visit, twelve years after the death of Kamehameha I, the assault on the original forest, particularly at the lower altitudes, was already well advanced. Above the neatly tended taro paddies and gardens and banana plots of the Hawaiians down along the plain he found the trees heavily tangled with vines, which indicated considerable decimation of the older growth. Four decades of European contact, and of supplying vessels and settlers with firewood, among other things, had begun to eat away the delicate fabric of the indigenous forest. The sandalwood trade had dealt a fatal blow to the traditional domestic and agricultural life of the Hawaiians, compelling the men to be away from their farms and families for longer and longer periods. The heavy cutting of sandalwood (most of which was traded to China to the profit of American sea captains) had also led to the destruction or severe disturbance of habitats on the main islands to a degree that now can only be guessed at. By the time Meyen saw the valley the sandalwood had all but disappeared from anywhere accessible to the coast.

There must have been a trail, at least, up the valley of the Nuuanu Stream for a very long time, perhaps since the first period of Polynesian settlement on Oahu. The region, and its winds and rains and the green vanes of the Koʻolau cliffs, like gills of an enormous fish, are alluded to in chants of unknown age. But in the decade or so between Meyen's visit and the building of the summer house at Kaniakapupu, the removal of trees from the valley accelerated. The trail became a wagon road, first for construction and then for the carriages of the nobility and of the state visitors who were entertained there. An edict announcing that "the chief's [or the King's] view must not be impeded" implies that all trees around the site had been felled, at least on the side toward the sea, to allow an unobstructed vista of the lower valley and the coast. There may have been few trees remaining in the neighborhood as the wagons rumbled up the road with tools and stones and coral for mortar. Visitors speak of the seventy-foot waterfall of the Nuuanu Stream as though they had been able to see it from near the house, so the forest of the land snails may have been removed all the way to the cliffs on the sides of the valley, leaving, perhaps, only a grove somewhere to the rear of the house, and a few trees lining the road. At the same time, deforestation was speeding up on all the main islands as American-born speculators acquired land and began to try out different forms of agricultural exploitation.

The house that took shape at Kaniakapupu was spacious but plain, "undistinguished," as one contemporary account put it, "by any architectural beauty." It was roughly sixty feet square, with walls two feet thick, and a wide verandah, raised slightly above the ground that sloped away on three sides. Around the verandah there was a picket fence—a long way from Massachusetts.

The "palace" was in use as a summer retreat in the early 1840s. Its single great moment, the one that came to seem like a play for which the building provided the only possible setting, took place at the beginning of August 1843. The very date varies in different accounts, which may indicate that the event began almost at once to pass into legend. But the occasion for it is beyond question, and it makes the ruin at Kaniakapupu seem like a distant participant in some of the aspirations and passions that resurfaced in 1993, the year in which Hawaiians of a variety of persuasions began to demand restoration of some form and measure of sovereignty. For the legendary royal entertainment at Kaniakapupu in 1843 was a vast celebration of the return of independence after five months spent unwillingly under the British flag.

There are said to have been ten thousand guests. There was a parade up the valley. Three hundred infantry. Officers on horses. The royal standard. Grand marshals. The state carriage drawn by four iron-gray horses. Liveried coachmen and postillions. And the king and queen. Then, five abreast, a thousand women on horses, draped in Spanish ponchos and in leis, and then twenty-five hundred horsemen.

First there was a display of ancient sports on level ground to the east of the house, in particular an exhibition of spear-throwing and catching. Then they all sat down around tables or mats to the consumption of mountains of food: hundreds of hogs and chickens, whole oxen, barrels of salt pork, thousands of fish, turkeys and squid and ducks, pyramids of fruit and coconuts.

The accounts of the original celebration are echoed and magnified and merged into those of commemorative festivities given there, on the anniversary, for several years. Something of the kind no doubt happened in the memories of those who attended them all. The food and the clothes and the dances and the pageantry grew more elaborate as there was more time to prepare them in advance, and the passions of the first occasion, its mingled nostalgia and anxiety, insistence and doubt, denied and echoed the deepening troubles of the kingdom.

And then, by degrees that are not so carefully nor so fondly recorded but which must have kept pace with the declining fortunes of the monarchy, the "palace" at Kaniakapupu fell silent, into disuse, and neglect, and decay. Visitors to the great feasts spoke of a "pleasant grove" of big trees to one side of it. We do not know what the trees were nor where they stood nor what became of them. In the later part of the century much of the upper Nuuanu Valley was described as "savannah." It seems that large areas of the trees remaining at mid-century had been cleared for cattle pasture as ranching spread through the islands.

*   *   *

By the beginning of the twentieth century after the overthrow of the monarchy by American-born or American-minded businessmen, and the takeover of the islands (under cover of the guns of the USS *Boston*), the deforestation of the valleys of Oahu had so reduced the water table that even a city the size of Honolulu as it was then could see trouble ahead. Furthermore, the Hawaiian Sugar Planters Association wanted to be assured of the great quantities of water required for sugar production. A program of "reforestation" was begun, experimenting with fast-growing imported species to replace the vanished Hawaiian forest. Through the 1920s and '30s seeds from other parts of the world were dropped from military airplanes, planted by government agencies, by volunteers, by CCC teams. Albizzias, casuarinas, eucalyptuses, which one sees in the valleys now. Some of the introductions proved to be unpredictably invasive. Some were inhospitable to other growth. In the European fairy tale, the forest that grew up around Sleeping Beauty's palace was presumably original growth returning, but the forest that now envelops Kaniakapupu contains almost no indigenous species of any kind. The largest trees on the lower slopes are eucalypts, and they in turn are being infiltrated, surrounded, choked out by a species of temperate bamboo from China or Japan that is moving rapidly across and up the valley, helping maintain the water table, it is true, and preventing erosion, but dooming every tree it reaches. Up near the ruin the larger trees are mostly camphors, and it is surprising to see a few palms among them, but there the irony continues. The palms are *Pritchardias*, belonging to the genus that includes all palms endemic to Hawai'i, but the trees at Kaniakapupu appear to be members of one of the few non-Hawaiian species, from Fiji, and were planted as ornamentals. The seeds may even have been carried there from gardens by birds.

Only the dense thicket *hau*, the running tree hibiscus *(Hibiscus tiliaceous)*, which begins just outside the west wall of the ruin, is in any sense native. It is not endemic to Hawai'i but it is indigenous, and certainly it had a traditional importance and many uses in the islands. The extremely light wood was used for canoe outriggers and for kite frames; the fiber of the bark was made into ropes, twine, and net bags. The yellow flowers, which on some trees have dark-red centers, change color in the course of the day, deepening to shades of apricot and rust and orange, and fall off before the next morning. They had a place in Hawaiian medicine. In Hawaiian legend one of the sisters of the moon goddess was turned into the *hau*, and on Oahu the tree is said to be the visible form of a wind in a valley parallel to Nuuanu. The *hau* at Kaniakapupu might even be a survivor from before the house was built, or it might have been planted there to be shaped into an arbor. Or again the birds may have brought the seeds.

It must be noted that the few birds that are there now are not native either. Loss of habitat and an avian-malaria-carrying tropical mosquito introduced by a British sea captain (deliberately in a fit of spite) have totally eradicated native birds almost everywhere at lower altitudes in the main islands of the chain. The birds that dart among the bamboo and the camphor trees represent imported species—intentional introductions, or accidental escapes from the zoo or from private houses, some of them quite recent arrivals. Several, such as Asian thrushes and the bulbuls from the Near East, sing gloriously, but the bulbuls have proven extremely destructive in their new habitat, and all are indications of the degree to which the indigenous life of these valleys and of the islands altogether has been disturbed and diminished during the past two centuries.

* * *

And what of the land snails themselves, for whose "song" the place is said to have been named? People who grew up in Honolulu before World War II refer to them fondly and speak of having found the glistening, tentative creatures commonly in gardens and on walks up into the valleys. I might still find a few of the Nuuanu Valley species *Achatinella bellula* left now over along the green cliffs, if I knew where to look and were patient and lucky.

There are four genera in Hawai'i, all of them small and elegant. There were more than forty species of *Achatinella* at the time of European contact, most of which had evolved in and for highly specific habitats. Of the original species only about sixteen are left now, and those are all endangered. Habitat destruction again, of course. Pesticides and pollution of various kinds. And the introduction of other species of snails and of slugs, accidentally or ignorantly, many of them in this century. The giant African snail, of the genus *Achatina*, was introduced in the 1930s as an ornamental, it is said. And then, to control the depredations of the introduced species, several cannibal species, including *Englandina rosea*, were brought in during the 1950s and '60s, and they have probably exterminated entire species of endemic snails, while the African giant and other introductions continue to proliferate. Rats and feral pigs and the collecting of the native snails for their beautiful shells have further reduced their numbers.

And then there are the activities of the military: In Makua Valley, west of Nuuanu, the principal surviving population of *Achatinella mustelina* has been subjected to every sort of weapon, from artillery to bombs to rockets, as the military has used the snails, habitat for target practice and deliberately set fire to the area. The Army has claimed that the scene of its operations is now so contaminated as a result of military use that nobody else could possibly do anything with it, and so continues to blast, burn, and poison the valley while organizing elaborate and expensive dodges to evade the languidly enforced regulations of the Environmental Protection Agency. The once lovely Makua Valley, at the military's withering touch, is becoming a ruin of another sort, louder and more obvious than Kaniakapupu.

Which by now can be seen as a kind of overgrown garden at a late stage, far removed from the original life of the place, and now "natural" largely through abandon. There is a charm to the crumbling walls that the house itself may never have possessed, and the introduced trees and bamboo and birds have composed a shady and retired place, unkempt, suggestive, quiet, with a beauty of its own, even more ephemeral than what was here before it. For the Hawaiian forest, in its evolutions, sustained itself, until it was prevented from doing so, and did it with a constantly increasing biological variety for millennia before the arrival of humans and their commensals. Whereas the present assembly of aliens coexists with little more stability to its relations than that of tenants in an apartment complex, and it would be foolish to hazard a guess as to its future.

This part of the valley is now the setting for a land-use dispute. A neighboring landowner wishes to build two new houses not far from the site. The resulting controversy has elicited a spectrum of attitudes about the place, including proposals to restore the "palace," and others to leave the area exactly as it is, abandoned and all but secret, having at least escaped, until now, the corrosive tides of tourism.

Nobody seems to be sure any longer about why the area came to be called Kaniakapupu. When people once thought they heard the song of the land snails, a biologist told me, they were probably hearing something else. He suggested that perhaps it was crickets. According to legend, when people heard the singing they were hearing spirits. It may be that they were hearing the stillness itself, of course. The silence of the ruin without the snails any longer, and without promises.

The Winter Palace

A few yards away, in the tall fir trees beyond a shallow fold that ran up the mountainside, there were thirty-five million butterflies. The dark boughs of the evergreens were bent under the breathing swarms as though weighed down with the black and gold snow that went on blowing in flurries through the trees, glinting in the afternoon sunlight. Pulsing sleeves of butterflies furred the limbs and parts of the trunks. Clusters hung from the drooping ends of branches like nests of orioles. A sound came from them, rising and falling. A breeze echoing. An exhalation without an end.

In our languages the butterflies were the kind that are called monarchs *(Danaus plexippus)*, a species familiar to most Americans and many Canadians who have walked in the woods in summer. This was January in Mexico, in the northeastern part of the state of Michoacan. We were at an altitude of about ten thousand feet in the Transvolcanic Range, on the southwest slope of the Sierra Chincua, part of an area that Mexico's President Salinas, in July 1987, declared a sanctuary because of its importance as one of the ten known overwintering sites in Mexico used annually by the monarch butterflies. There was a small group of us strung out along the trail. Within sound of the butterflies no one was chattering. I obtained the estimate of the numbers of that winter colony, with its population larger than that of many European nations, and much of the rest of my information about monarchs, later, from Professor Lincoln F. Brower of the Department of Zoology at the University of Florida. He is now the preeminent authority in the world on this species, its behavior and its imitators. Dr. Brower has been studying the monarchs for over forty years and has been president of the Lepidopterists' Society, vice president of the American Society of Naturalists, and is the current director of scientific research of the Monarch Project at the University of Florida. His lectures and papers on his studies have been supplemented by documentary films and a volume of essays that he has edited on the subject of mimicry, an integral theme in his work from the beginning. A few months before our visit to the monarch sanctuary he had been awarded the Linnaean Medal in Zoology by the Linnaean Society of London, which can claim to be the oldest biological society in the world.

Dr. Brower, and the rest of us there on the trail that afternoon in January, had just spent four days together in Morelia at the invitation of El Grupo de Los Cien, the Group of A Hundred, an organization based in Mexico, where it had been conceived and put together during the '80s by the Mexican poet and novelist Homero Aridjis, his American wife Betty Ferber, and a number of other writers, most of them Mexican. The common impulse that brought the original members of the group together was an urge to do something about the intolerable air pollution of Mexico City, a livid presence in all their lives which never left them for a minute. As discussion of the subject progressed among friends, many of whom were writers and teachers, it was obvious from the start that the foul air they were breathing was a phenomenon inseparable from the accelerating degradation of the living world everywhere as a result of human activities. Their subject inevitably embraced what we have come to refer to with nagging discomfort as the environment. Part of the unease that the word touches off is a well-learned response to the facts themselves, the news of which, in our lifetimes, has been consistently and increasingly so ominous that many avoid paying attention to them if they can. But there is also the chronic sense of the word's misleading inadequacy, its suggestion that what we are alluding to all around us, our cause and our effect, is distinct from us. And with that, the realization that we have no other term for it that is not faulty in more or less the same way, and that apparently we did not feel the need of one until recently. It did not take Homero and Betty and the other founders long to recruit a hundred writers and intellectuals throughout Latin America who shared their concerns, and then scientists, writers, and activists from other countries were enlisted as adherents. Funding was acquired from the Rockefeller Foundation, among other sources. A manifesto was prepared and the Group took a full page in *The New York Times* to announce the reasons for its existence.

Some of us standing watching the monarchs had been at the Group's first gathering in Morelia, in September 1991, which had proceeded in the glare of television floodlights and had been broadcast live and virtually complete, like a sports event, throughout Mexico and much of Latin America. Many at that meeting felt that it had few precedents, if any. There were scientists and writers conversing not with glazed politeness but with obvious and undisguised eagerness to cooperate in the face of a common urgency. Together they prepared and signed the Morelia Declaration, a summary of the world situation with regard to population, consumption, pollution, habitat devastation, loss of species, cultural and social erosion, nuclear radiation, militarization, and then a series of recommendations intended for consideration at the Earth Summit in Rio de Janeiro in June 1992, which "the environmental president" George Bush, and his representatives would manage to jam with double talk and evasion.

The second Morelia symposium had met with the intention of reviewing what had happened and failed to happen in the intervening two years. It had been planned as a smaller, quieter, indeed more intimate occasion, less hung with microphones and the exigencies of the media than the first one had been. And so it was, although cameras and interviewers from the Mexican television system, Televisa, met each of the participants at the Mexico City airport, and all the public meetings and press conferences were televised.

And when Lincoln Brower's turn came to present to the gathering, toward the end, a lecture with slides of the monarchs and their wintering sites, the lights for the cameras made it impossible to darken the auditorium at all, so that what appeared on the screen was a series of gray clouds in which Lincoln kept pointing out ghosts invisible to the rest of us. This must have been what the cameras were recording for the future: Lincoln's voice telling later viewers what they cannot see.

Butterflies, like many other insects, have a limited tolerance to extremes of temperature, but different species respond to the cycle of seasons in different ways. The butterfly known in English as the mourning cloak (*Nymphalis antiopa*), for instance, has evolved hibernating behavior that allows it to spend winters in North America without leaving the zones of hard frost. The monarchs, on the other hand, die if the temperature drops much below freezing, and though they journey far into North America during the spring and summer months they retreat annually before the frost, as many birds do, and despite their fragility they have established migratory flight patterns that the whole species retraces every year. The population of monarchs in the western part of the continent seeks destinations that have been known to scientists, more or less, for 120 years and more. In the autumn they cross the Sierras and spend the winter in tall trees, especially Monterey pines and eucalyptus, at some forty known sites near the Pacific. In March they return to their summer range to lay their eggs in the California milkweeds (*Asclepias crinocarpa*, primarily), and then die.

But the wintering habits of the monarchs from the central and eastern parts of the continent, which constitute the main population, were not known until the 1970s. The butterflies' disappearance from eastern North America in the autumn has been one of the marks of the turning season, like the fall of the leaves, and points on their migrating routes have been noted for a long time, but well past the middle of this century observers in the United States could not say what happened to the monarchs after their itineraries converged in Texas. "They slipped over the border," Lincoln said, "and were lost to us."

The monarchs' travels are remarkable even among the plentiful wonders of migratory behavior. They alone, in their subfamily of 157 species have found a way of nourishing themselves on various milkweeds (*Asclepias*)—a plant genus that is widespread in North America, and toxic to most herbivores—while avoiding the North American winter. The achievement is magnified by the fact that a migrant monarch anywhere along the route will be three or more generations removed from its most recent ancestor there. The individual butterfly had never been to the place before and never could have learned the way. It knew it—its knowledge part of a guiding inheritance, along with the aptitude for transforming itself from an egg into a caterpillar, and from a chrysalis into an adult able to fly.

Although individual butterflies do not complete the entire migratory cycle they cover huge distances. From Canada, and the northern United States, some of them, to central Mexico, and then months later, after overwintering, to the southern Gulf states to lay eggs and expire. The evidence of the distance traversed has been found in their tissues in the form of cardenolides, heart poisons derived from the sap of identifiable northern species of milkweed (*Asclepias syriaca*, in particular) occurring neither in the southern states nor in Mexico. The toxins are stored without chemical alteration in the bodies of the monarch caterpillars that hatch on the leaves of the milkweed, and are transferred to the pupae and on to the adult butterflies and retained there—"sequestered" in the language of the professionals—without harming the monarchs at any stage. On the contrary, the sap of the milkweeds has become indispensable to the monarchs not only as food but as protection. For with the heart poison of the *Asclepias* in their bodies the monarchs in turn become poisonous. Their orange and black pattern proclaims that warning to predators, and the message in their highly visible appearance has been important not only to their evolution but to that of other species, and to the study of them.

Contrasting patterns of orange or yellow or white and black often announce that a species is poisonous. Some that are not toxic have evolved patterns resembling poisonous originals as a protection. How that mimicry comes about sheds light on the general process of evolution, and the monarchs and their imitators have become a classic example.

Brower speaks of some of his predecessors in the study of butterflies with a respect that sounds like affection. A pioneer on the subject was an American lepidopterist, William Henry Edwards, whose account of butterfly discoveries in the Amazon basin during the early years of the nineteenth century prompted the great Victorian naturalists Alfred Russell Wallace and Henry Walter Bates to sail from Brazil and the Rio Negro in 1848. It was an historic journey. Wallace's small, succinct survey of the palms of the region remains a classic, and his deductions from the notes he made at the time—a great part of them lost at sea on his return voyage to England—bore such an affinity to Darwin's theory of natural selection that Wallace has been credited by some with having arrived first at the evolutionary hypothesis. And Bates, who spent eleven years in the Amazon and wrote one of the great narratives of exploration, drew from his monumental records of the insects of the Amazon basin a treatise on mimicry whose importance to the theory of natural selection was immediately apparent when he published it in 1862.

Bates concluded that a chance individual of a nonpoisonous species of butterfly at some point bore a degree of resemblance to a poisonous species and as a result was let alone by predators, so that it and those of its progeny that most resembled it had a better chance of survival than the others with no such protection. The hypothesis left many questions unanswered and in 1879 a German naturalist, Fritz Muller, refined and extended it to cover more intricate relations of mimicry, particularly the imitations of "unpalatable" (toxic) species by butterflies of a different group. This process turns out to have, for butterflies, the advantage of extending a single warning pattern so that the number of butterflies that are tasted before predators get the picture clear is greatly reduced.

Mimicry, and specifically the imitations of monarchs, had been important in the studies of Brower's Canadian senior colleague, Fred Urquhart and his wife, N. R. Urquhart, who began tracking the southward migrations of the eastern monarchs in 1941. In the '50s Fred Urquhart questioned some of the conclusions about mimicry and predation that most naturalists by then took for granted as primary illustrations of the workings of evolution. He doubted whether birds really found the toxic butterflies unpalatable in the first place. If they did, he was not convinced that birds could learn by experience to avoid unpalatable models. If they could, he was not sure that they would confuse the mimic with the model. But if, after all, they did, he was uncertain about the point at which the resemblance began to be effective—which is perhaps the most interesting of the questions. Part of Lincoln Brower's and Jane Brower's work in the '50s was directed to finding answers to these challenges.

The research of Jane Brower, in particular, during that decade, established the role of the warning patterns and their imitations more firmly than ever. But the complete migratory path of the main population of the monarchs remained unknown to biologists. It was not until the early '70s that a collaborator of the Urquharts, Ken Brugger, and his wife, Cathy, finally discovered a vast colony of monarchs overwintering in the mountains of south-central Mexico. Fred Urquhart published the news of the find in *National Geographic* and the *Journal of the Lepidopterists' Society* without revealing their locations, and he and his team had the place to themselves for a while. But Brower and his students by then had eliminated the mountains of many other possible regions of Mexico, and there were enough clues in the articles to complete what they already knew. One day the following winter several of them found their way to the Transvolcanic Range of western Michoacan and to one of the sites, and the camp of Dr. Urquhart's surprised researchers.

The people who live in those mountains, not surprisingly, have always known about the butterflies, which had been coming there, as they said, forever. Such pre-Columbian literature as survived the conquest has not, so far, yielded any specific mention of the sites, but the region was border country between the Tarascans and the Aztec Empire, for centuries, and it may have been dangerous and little-known terrain. In the language of the Mazahua Indians, however, in the village of Santiago in the state of Mexico, there is a word that means "the butterfly that passes in October and November," and the Mazahuas, according to tradition, have eaten monarchs for a long time, stripping off the wings and frying the thoraxes on flat *comales,* and they still do it, though nowadays mostly as a show for tourists. I have not heard how they deal with the taste, and the nausea-producing cardenolide toxins. Jane Brower, in the course of her researches, tasted the milky sap of the *Asclepias humistrata,* one of the milkweeds frequented by monarchs and a source of their toxin, and she vouched for its bitterness and for its causing a rush of salivation, and nausea. It is hard to believe that monarchs ever occupied much more than a ceremonial place in the Mazahuas diet but the presence of the monarchs has been part of the local lore for a long time. There is a recurrent belief in the region that they are the souls of the dead returning, which may be related to the fact that their arrival begins some time near November 2, the Day of the Dead in the Christian calendar. Homero Aridjis, who grew up in the state of Michoacan, not far from the sites, learned as a child of the winter butterflies filling the trees in the mountains. (Many of those trees, as he has written, are gone now.)

At the other end of their cycle, Brower, as a child in New Jersey growing up near a kettlehole pond in the woods, saw the summer monarchs come and go with their season, and loved butterflies he says, by the time he was five. He talked about them on the bus crossing Michoacan, heading northwest toward the wintering sites. Lincoln is an amiable, gentle, slightly rotund figure who carries his weight of knowledge lightly. He was wearing a dark tweed suit, in the mountains of Mexico. In a youthful, rather reedy voice he imparts information as a matter of common interest, without pushing it.

Something about him of the grown cherub, clear and benign, kindles his general conversation and shines in his unabashed fondness for his German shepherds, Rosie and her son Uhlrich, whose pictures he carries with him.

As we moved away from urban areas the family resemblance that runs through the mountains of central and southern Mexico became more apparent. The ridges of western Michoacan rise in shapes and contours and qualities of light reminiscent of the highlands of Chiapas, where organized rebellion had begun two weeks before, on New Year's Day. Talk on the bus kept reverting from monarchs to the events in the south—what was known of them. Homero was in daily contact with friends in the Mexican government. One of the participants at the Morelia symposium, Jeffrey Wilkerson, is an anthropologist who has directed the Institute for Cultural Ecology in the Tropics since 1977. His main office was in the country outside Vera Cruz and he had led research expeditions into the Lacandon forest of lowland Chiapas. At Morelia he kept telephoning friends and colleagues in the region, or trying to, and occasionally returning with bulletins.

And in the early '70s I had lived in Chiapas myself, in San Cristóbal de las Casas, one of the principal centers of the Zapatista forces and of the government's build-up in response to them. I had visited that beautiful region within the past few years, and have old friends there. The colonial town set high in its ring of mountains had changed relatively little. The streets were still alive with Indians. Their faces were familiar, and their garments that told what village they were from, what language they spoke, sometimes even who their parents and grandparents were. I heard the sound of their feet half running on the flat stones like a voice I recognized, heard once more the muffled clicks of the Mayan words, the clanging of the thin bells in the towers, the popping of rockets (handmade in Indian villages as a cottage industry) at all hours of the day and night, celebrating that very moment.

I knew the cold of the nights and the sere colors of the winter cornfields on the shoulders of the mountains, and the abiding anxiety about the circumstances of the highland Maya people, their poverty, the way they were treated by officials and townspeople, and the inexorable and accelerating deforestation of the mountains, the awareness of which was like knowledge of a malignancy. Laws against cutting trees seemed to amount to nothing but an occasional pretext for taking something else away from an Indian, since it was the Maya villagers who cut and hauled wood in places where there were no log roads. On winter mornings I would wake at first light to the sound of heavy wood being dragged over cobbles out in the narrow street where the fog still hid the tiled tops of the whitewashed walls, and would listen to the clop of a small horse pulling two raw pine beams, their top ends lashed to their pack-saddle, one on either side, and the lower ends trailing behind. If I opened the low door in the garden wall I would see them pass in the cold cloud, following an Indian in a straw hat and a long woolen *chamarra* who was hurrying ahead. Later in the morning Indian men would weave along the street balancing on their heads tables and rough chairs of raw pine wood still oozing amber pitch, made of trees cut illegally with axes and machetes and shaped into boards with the same tools. They had carried the furniture for hours, in the dark, over the mountain trails, to sell in town. The prices were very low because the furniture was badly made because the wood was illegal, and because they were Indians.

The old buildings in the lovely town had been made of adobe—mud mixed with pine needles and certain half-magic bodily ingredients such as horse manure, milk, and urine. But the new constructions had armatures of iron rebar and cement, and the walls were of bricks made out on the flats in the no-man's land where the dirt streets splayed out. The brick kilns were fired with large quantities of contraband wood brought down from the dwindling forest.

In April the clear air of the mountains began to fill with smoke as the Indians' corn fields were burned over and patches that had been felled to make new fields on the slopes high above the valleys were set alight. Outside the town we could see the thinned and flayed areas spreading upward along the mountains, month by month, season by season. The slash-and-burn agriculture whose damages had been less apparent and more gradual in the level lowlands, with small populations, had brought obvious devastation to the mountains, and as the population grew the wreckage was spreading like a fire. When the trees were felled on the steep gradients the winter rains eroded the topsoil, starting at once, and after a few years when the fields were abandoned the forest could not grow back. Up until then most of the cutting had been done by Indians using only axes and machetes, but huge log trucks also went hurtling along the narrow, twisting cliffside roads. And one spring morning in the early '70s I saw a crowd of Indian men in the broad hats, fringes, and ribbons of Zinacantan and Tenejapa, their machetes on their shoulders, gazing with fascination into the display window of a hardware store, at the center of which, like the infant in a crèche, lay a yellow McCullough chain saw.

Many of my friends there at the time were anthropologists, biologists, ethnobotanists, and after each trip down into the lowlands they came back with woeful news of the Lacandon villages and the rain forest. The first road into that region, built in the early '70s, became at once an avenue for ruthless logging and for nefarious traffic of every kind, and rapidly widening areas of an ecosystem that had evolved over many millennia were wiped out for quick-fix agricultural projects that could not possibly be maintained for more than a few years. The pollution of most of the watercourses was an immediate result, and the plan—which became a perennial growth—to dam the Usumacinta River and flood huge sections of the lowland forest, including major archaeological sites, was under consideration even then. Impoverished and discontented highland Maya from communities near San Cristóbal were transplanted into the lowland rain forest and "given" land to slash and burn and starve on. Such laws as existed relating to indigenous peoples and conservation were ignored, and it was generally taken for granted that the federal police and of course the army were incompetent, corrupt, and distinguished by nothing but their arrogance and brutality. All of that had been in place in Chiapas in the '70s and had been gathering for at least a generation before that, and as we traveled toward the monarch sites we kept trying to guess why it had happened when it did, and not at almost any point during the past few decades.

The deforested ridges of Michoacan were a continuing reminder of the flaying of the mountains of Chiapas, and it was a surprise to find ourselves suddenly passing through the cool shade of a remnant of old fir woods under trees of indeterminate age. Then these vestiges of the life that had covered the slopes there for so long ended abruptly to disclose an ideal image of the magnificent geography of that region. We were high on one side of an enormous valley hazed with distance, whose breadth and depth appeared to be on a scale that one could not grasp even if one knew the numbers, and around it in the colors of smoke rose the shadow of a vast flower of some other time, a ring of sharp summits broken, jagged, receding behind each other as far as we could see. It is not surprising that the place has been called The Valley of the Thousand Peaks.

We had reached the Sierra Transvolcanica, the Transvolcanic Range of western Michoacan, which includes all the mountains to which the major part of the eastern population of monarchs travels so far every autumn without calling them, as we do, Pelon, Acuña, Chivati, Picacho, Campanario, and Chincua. The Sierra Transvolcanica represents a relatively small area of the continent, and it is possible to do no more than deduce from what is known of the monarchs something of how they came to evolve a migratory pattern fixed upon this particular region.

The monarchs belong to a subfamily of butterflies, the *Danainae*, found in the Americas and the eastern hemisphere. They are tropical creatures and because of their inability to survive freezing temperatures at any stage of their life cycle, as egg, caterpillar, chrysalid, or adult, few of the *Danainae* besides the monarchs have been able to extend their range into the temperate zone. Only two other species of *Danainae* are to be found north of Mexico, and they do not go much beyond the southernmost parts of the States. The floral sustenance of the *Danainae*, the milkweeds (*Asclepias*) are also predominantly tropical, but during the last few million years some species of *Asclepias* have adapted to the cold and have spread north, developing 108 new species in North America. In northern and eastern Mexico the months from November to May are dry and the milkweeds, along with many other plants, die back during that season. In the areas where this deprivation occurs, the monarchs, in response to it, evolved a kind of hormonal suppression cycle. In the autumn they produced a generation of butterflies that remained in a state of reproductive dormancy, did not hunt for milkweeds, and aged relatively slowly. It is thought that once they had achieved this method of waiting out the famine they began to extend their range northward each spring to take advantage of the new growth of milkweeds. But as days shortened and temperatures fell with the return of autumn they retreated southward again. The northern and southern movements of the monarchs came to coincide with the autumn and spring equinoxes and apparently the length of days is an important signal for the beginning of their journeys.

The requisites of survival that led the monarchs to overwinter in the western mountains of Mexico include, of course, the improbability of freezing weather. Places that are too hot are not congenial to them at that season either, because high temperatures encourage activity which would exhaust their stored food supply in a season when it is hard for them to replenish it. They need constant access to water, which must not be too far away for the same reason. And they need shelter from winter storms. The fir forests (the tree is the *Abies religiosa,* called *oyamel* in the region) of certain slopes above ten thousand feet, near the summits of the Transvolcanic Range, provide all these. The sites are not unvarying. Wandering bands of monarchs have been found overwintering elsewhere in Mexico, sometimes even to the east of Mexico City, but they have been relatively small assemblies and the sites have not been used regularly.

Large parts of the autumn routes of the eastern monarchs are now known. They narrow into a current crossing the Rio Grande into Mexico, travel south to the Sierra Madre Oriental and then west across the mountains to the Thousand Peaks. The summits of the eastern part of the range average seven thousand feet, with some rising to almost eleven thousand feet. The generation that left in the spring will have multiplied into a large summer population that coalesces into bands of increasing size on the way south. The monarchs fly by day and congregate in trees at nightfall. As they travel they drink the nectar of the autumn composite flowers, asters and goldenrods. In spells of warm weather, if the flowers are abundant, they linger, and when the days turn cloudy, cold, or windy, they move on. The bodily fats that they are building up to see them through the winter are known as lipids, and the nectar sources are important to their survival, for the winter flora in the mountains is sparse and unreliable. In early November the first groups of migrants begin to arrive in the oyamel forests on the peaks. Butterflies that have flown from Maine will have traveled 2,500 miles, at least. Most of those that have been examined were not, as would have been expected, tattered and exhausted, but appeared to be in perfect condition, as though they had just left the chrysalis. The egg from which each of them had grown had been laid singly on a milkweed leaf, and the caterpillar that emerged had immediately explored the rest of the leaf looking for other monarch eggs there, to eat them in order to make sure that there would be enough food for one caterpillar, at least. But as adults, and great travelers, there are advantages to being part of a large assembly and the first groups that settle into the oyamel firs obviously welcome still larger congregations: They have been seen above their trees in spiraling columns a thousand feet high signaling to other groups, "Here is the place."

Our own approach, some two months later in the season, was directed toward the Sierra Chincua, the most accessible of the sites to human visitors. Part of the peak is designated as a monarch butterfly sanctuary named El Campanario, the only such reservation that is open to the public. The site itself has been intensively studied by Lincoln and his colleagues.

The road descended along the side of a valley through a scattering of firs standing near the road like people waiting on a station platform. The oyamels bear a resemblance to other *Abies* occurring in the ranges of the western part of the continent. The trees we passed through were a park at the outskirts of the town of Angangueo. Houses at the edge of the municipality appeared in pistachio greens, cranberry pinks, and butcher blues. The bus nosed around corners under balconies overflowing with potted petunias and geraniums, ferns and aloes, daisies and roses. There was an Alpine aspect to some of the buildings in the pitch of the roof, the eaves and balconies and windows. Some of the roses in tubs, and some that were tumbling from untended hedges looked like varieties from the last century or earlier, and I was reminded of the old French roses with trunks like trees, in gardens in San Cristóbal in Chiapas, which must have been taken there by Napoleon's representatives during the administration of the hapless Maximilian. The bus stopped under a balcony from which an Alaskan husky barked at us through a row of flower pots. The road beyond Angangueo is too steep, rough, and mean-spirited for a self-respecting bus, and we climbed out and into the backs of small rugged open trucks that would shake and jolt us to the end of the line, at the monarch sanctuary The trucks represented one form of human employment that the butterflies have recently brought to the region.

Across the street on the hillside was a complex of mine buildings—scaffolds, conveyors, trestles, metal towers, all painted yellow, and all silent, climbing the slope like the escarpments of a tin castle. The glimpse of prosperity current or remembered, in what we saw of Angangueo, is a legacy of what has been one of the major silver mines in Mexico. The mine had finally closed, very recently. The shafts had been dug back into the mountain for a considerable distance, but eventually the lode was worked to the point at which the ore no longer repaid the cost of extracting it. As the trucks spun their wheels and wound up the dirt road that climbed out of the end of the street, we passed the piled guts of the mountain: long, vast yellow mounds layered like pyramids, cracking and eroding along the side of the road until the road wrenched away from them at a hairpin turn. A man and a dog walked slowly and without evident purpose along one ridge of tailings over whose parched contours the first sparse grasses and scrub were struggling to start from scratch. The story of the mine— the discovery of the lode, the displacement of the indigenous inhabitants, the excavation and development, the wealth, generosity, and injustice of the owners, the legends and accidents—were the local lore and identity of the town for generations. Foreign investments were important in the mine's history, and silver out of that mountain had become part of the fortune that endowed the Guggenheim Foundation. Through the whole age of the mine the butterflies had come every autumn to the forest on the summit. In the history of the monarchs and their migration the anecdote of the mine amounts to only a page, though it may prove to be one of the last.

The mine had increased the population around Angangueo, and its closing inevitably reduced the opportunities for making a living in the region. We saw log trucks parked in the back lanes and beside the mounds of mine tailings. As the trucks that were our own transportation rocked and reared over the ridges we could see that the slopes had been denuded far up toward the summits and in some places all the way to the top. Homero told us, and we heard from other sources, that in Michoacan, as in Chiapas, the logging continues with little or no regard for legality and such ordinances as may exist are not enforced. Illegal sawmills operate openly and in great numbers, and officials tolerate them for reasons not hard to guess. An oyamel fir tree can fetch $500 on the black market, and some of the small communities run their own lumber mills. We passed small cornfields, with the dry winter stalks standing in them, hens scratching in the roadside bushes, slat and adobe houses scattered on the mountainside. No bustling activity. Homero said that when he had asked people living out near the mountain what they lived on they had said without exception or hesitation, "the forest." Most of the households have many children—ten, fifteen, even twenty—and take it for granted that they will have many more. "What will they all live on?" he had asked, and again they had said at once, "the forest." At the foot of the mountain a nursery under the auspices of the government employs a sizeable work force growing seedlings to put back into the forest. Near it another sawmill is cutting up trees that have been growing for the better part of a century at least. The arguments in favor of logging are the usual ones based on the assumption that of all the species on earth only one has a right to exist.

The forest that remained reached to the top of the ridge and to the peak ahead of us, and a sweep of bared valley fell away to our right. Lincoln raised a hand and said, "There they are." The truck stopped to let us look where he was pointing, at several big trees near the top, whose color, instead of being the dark green shadowed with black of the rest of the forest, was dimmed with a suggestion of old gilding. The trucks lurched on to where the road narrowed, and stopped. A series of stands like oversized packing crates, made of very recently sawn rough boards, lined the downhill side of the road, nothing on their shelves but a few bottles of soft drinks. Down across the shallow upland hollow with its rustling cornfields a line of slate roofs, like a stopped freight train, covered benches and tables, and charcoal stoves for feeding the visitors who come now during the winter months, mostly on weekends, to visit the sanctuary and see the monarchs. We were there on a weekday when no one was expected. Several small boys appeared from between the stands to beg in a halfhearted way. The meandering settlement is called El Rosario.

From there on we walked. The ruts curved between cornfields and dusty bushes. School girls appeared in twos and threes with articles to sell—glass lapel pins in the shape of butterflies, resting in plastic foam inside elaborate clear plastic cases, all turned out in some factory far away. One child has diminutive napkins, not entirely clean, each of them embroidered with a small orange and black butterfly in cross-stitch. She told me she made them herself when she got home from school. How many did she make in a day? "Maybe one," she said. She asked less than a dollar apiece for them.

A trickle of water crossed the path and I looked down to see a cluster of monarchs trembling on the damp earth beside it. I could see that some of them seemed to be sipping at the water's edge, but others, perhaps because the day was cool, had been too weak to keep from falling in and drowning. The small watercourse was no broader than a hand, and the sticks and dead leaves along it were adorned for several yards with the orange and black wings of dead monarchs.

The path came to an intersection and a few more stalls offering cross-stitched embroidery and T-shirts hanging on clotheslines, and a sign announced the sanctuary of El Campanario. A number of men, none of whom looked unquestionably official, materialized to make sure we paid to enter the preserve. The transaction was carried out in a dark building like a trading post, according to an apparently impromptu procedure. A dusty footpath led up from the building along a section of chain-link fence that appeared to be more symbolic than effective. From there on up the mountain we were accompanied at every step by an assorted contingent of men whose job it was, they said, to keep an eye on us, to make sure we did not leave the path and stray into the forest. Some of these escorts came and went, some hung around in groups talking, at bends in the trail.

From a distance, and from below, the forest on the upper slopes and the summit looked dark and dense, broken here and there by openings that looked like part of the natural order. The steep, powdery path above the fence led up into what was indeed a forest, but a much disturbed and damaged one. The scuffed tracks across worn roots told of the passage of many feet. The trees had obviously been thinned. Clearings showed up as we climbed, and there were few young firs in the open spaces. Trunks had been cut and, for some reason, left where they had fallen. If one stepped a few feet from the path one found stumps in the undergrowth, which had grown dense in the sunlight. Placards commanded pedestrians to stay on the path and urged them not to step on butterflies. As we walked the wings were everywhere in the dust, and under the bushes to either side. Some of the wings were fluttering feebly, some were still, some flew up and floated away. The butterflies' energy depends partly upon temperature, and those that fly out of their trees after basking in the sunlight, and glide down to water, may be caught in tree shadows, cloud shadows, or cold drafts, and not have the strength to get back before they die on the way.

I was wondering about the understory flora of the forest that I could see along the path: various labiates, senecios, and geraniums, many of them no doubt endemic, some looking like widespread introductions. I asked one of our escorts what he called one small flowering bush. "Maria Antonia," he said. My luck was different with another of the men and another flower. "I call that a green plant," he said. But several of the men turned out to be biology students from Mexican universities, who were interested in these nectar sources. Studies have identified many of the flowers—*Alchemilla procumbens*, *Senecio anguilifolius*, *Eupatorium mairetianum*, and a number of *Salvias* prominent among them.

To our left, as we went up, was a shallow side valley, sunk into the mountainside. We turned a corner of the path and looked across the long hollow, and a clearing, to the tall trees. Again Lincoln pointed, and we stopped to watch the nearest of the oyamel firs dripping with butterflies, the flurries of sparks swirling in the sunbeams and up over the forest, down toward the main valley, and back up toward us.

As we watched them a cloud passed overhead. We saw its shadow cover the trees, and felt the warmth drop out of the air, and as it did a great cloud of butterflies rose out of the firs and spiraled high above them, circling around and around. Lincoln told us that a sudden chill was a danger signal to them, a warning that they must not remain away from the colony, weakened by cold. If the air temperature drops below a measurable "flight threshold" the butterflies cannot take off at all. They respond to a cloud shadow by flying up to hurry home— even if they are home already. The apparently inappropriate maneuver allows the butterflies to resettle into the trees in groups arranged not for exposure to sunlight but for insulation.

We were not yet close enough to hear them, and as we stood there watching them return to the trees Lincoln told us something about their poison. Many butterfly species have evolved ways of using plants that are toxic to most herbivorous forms in order to nour-ish and protect themselves. There are species that feed and lay eggs on various kinds of Solanaceae fatally poisonous to almost all herbi-vores that might make the mistake of ingesting them, and the South American *Heliconiinae* butterflies feed on *Passiflora* species, the leaves of which release hydrogen cyanide when digested. The monarchs' tol-erance of milkweed poisons allows them to use the sap for nourish-ment and to sequester the plants' defensive toxins. The toxic plants' evolution of their own defenses, in the first place, is an earlier chapter in the story. Those butterflies that have managed to incorporate the plants' defenses need to signal to predators that it would be unwise to taste them, and the bright colors and contrasting patterns perform that warning. The easily recognizable appearance reduces the risk of being eaten, but does not eliminate it, for the birds' knowledge of such matters is not instinctive but learned, and a bird may taste a bright butterfly, or more than one, before being certain that it is not a good idea. The distinctive appearances of many poisonous species of but-terflies which have led, in turn, to imitations by butterflies without such defenses have also produced complicated variations. A primary example in research into butterfly mimicry is the viceroy butterfly, *Limenitis archippus,* which has developed a close resemblance to the monarch where their ranges overlap. But in southern Florida, where monarchs are rare most of the year, the viceroys have come to resem-ble a different member of the *Danainae,* the Florida queen, *Danaus gilippus berenice,* which is not orange but a dark-shaded walnut color with white spots. And in southern Texas, where the prevailing mem-ber of the *Danainae* is the paler birch-hued *Danaus gilippus striposa,* the viceroy becomes as pale as its model while retaining the black wing-veining reminiscent of the monarch. But only in the adults does mimicry appear. Whereas the caterpillars of the poisonous species are banded in bright colors and unmistakable, the earlier phases of the mimic species are camouflaged to disappear into the bark and foliage around them. Some of the mimic species, including viceroys, appear to be developing toxic arguments of their own. And the actual toxicity of the poisonous species varies depending upon the time of year, the region in which the butterflies have hatched and grown, the members of the milkweed family on which they have been nourished, and the age of individuals. Alfonso Alonso, one of Lincoln's students, has discovered that monarchs lose their stored cardiac glycoside toxins as they grow older, so that if a bird were to fail to recognize their warning appearance, after a certain age they would turn out to be digestible after all.

The delicate temperature balance that the monarchs need to survive the winter and set out on their spring migration has been provided with some certainty by the forests near the summits—though a sudden exceptionally cold spell in the winter of 1991–92 destroyed more than half of the butterflies at some sites. But another evolutionary development on the history of their poison and its uses has overtaken them at the winter sites. Two kinds of birds that prey upon butterflies have found ways of dealing with the monarchs' toxic defenses. It is something that may have happened fairly recently, as agricultural practices in the monarchs' northern range, in the U.S. and Canada, have led to the proliferation of milkweed species with low toxicities on which the butterflies feed in the early stages of their lives.

It was afternoon when we stood watching the outskirts of the colony at El Campanario. At sunrise, Lincoln said, when it is too cool for the monarchs to fly, flocks of black-backed orioles (*Icterus abeillei*) and black-headed grosbeaks (*Pheucticus melanocephalus*) arrive from the valley and fall upon the immobilized butterflies clustered densely in the trees. They tear into the monarchs, devouring them into a storm of wings, killing some fifteen thousand a day in one colony. In a single winter, Lincoln said, they may destroy close to a million butterflies. By the late 1970s they were known to be wiping out over half the population in some places. Bird predation upon monarchs on such a scale has never been observed anywhere except in Mexico. Monarchs in Massachusetts, at the other end of their cycle, averaged a very much higher level of toxicity than was found in those in Mexico.

The grosbeaks, furthermore, have developed a tolerance of the milkweed-derived poisons that amounts to effective immunity. The orioles have learned to determine by taste which of the butterflies are less poisonous than others. And besides tearing off the wings, they strip out the thoracic muscle and the abdominal contents where the stored poisons are concentrated, and eat only the internal tissues. As the monarchs' bodily poisons diminish in the course of the winter the predation increases. Some research suggests that the butterflies have begun to evolve a different kind of poison, or several kinds of poison such as pyrrolizidine alkaloids, but so far the evidence is not consistent or substantial.

In contrast, the western population of monarchs that overwinters in California feeds at all stages on milkweed species with a dependably high cardenolide content. Some butterflies average more than four times the toxicity of the ones overwintering in Mexico, and the birds know it and leave them alone.

Besides the dwindling effectiveness of their toxic defenses, the monarchs at the wintering grounds in Mexico are threatened by the steady depletion and destruction of the oyamel forests, which provide the very conditions for which they have evolved their migratory cycle. The mitigating facts of the forests on extremes of heat and cold have been studied in detail, and so have the consequences of thinning and clear cutting. If the reduction of the forest continues, the larger eastern population of the monarch species, at the end of its vast migrations, will be edged out of existence.

Up until now the Mexican government's administrative flourishes establishing sanctuaries and preserves and regulations of the overwintering area have amounted to little more than environmental rhetoric to convey the illusion that something has been done, while allowing business to proceed as usual, a phenomenon that has become familiar on both sides of the border.

Brower is convinced that the principal danger to the survival of the eastern monarchs is not bird predation nor climatic uncertainties but the destruction of the sites by human population pressures and the logging industry whose appetites and mores are everywhere the same. He has argued for preservation of the forests at the monarchs' wintering sites not only in order to save the eastern monarchs themselves but in order to allow the migratory phenomenon that they have evolved, this extraordinary natural achievement with a value beyond our estimation, to survive. He and others see a possible approach in the outright acquisition of the wintering sites and their administration along the lines of national—or international—parks. Mexican officials invoke laws that would make such ideas difficult or impossible, and they claim to be legally and financially helpless.

"What good are butterflies?" ask those inhabitants of the region who are impatient to cut the trees until none are left. Certainly alternate employment must be found for the local people, something besides whatever they can take out of the forest, and means must be found to limit the geometrical multiplication of their numbers.

The monarchs' cycle is not confined to Mexico, and perhaps the other two nations through which it passes without regard for human boundaries can provide the Mexican government with help and influence to safeguard the treasure they do not own but share. A conservation group in Mexico, Monarca A.C., under the leadership of Rodolfo Ogarrio, is working with governmental departments to try to save the sites. The World Wildlife Fund has been supporting conservation efforts connected with them. Before the second Morelia conference was over, writers and scientists from the three countries the monarchs pass through formed the Monarch Alliance, dedicated to trying to elicit international support for the butterflies.

We stood in the afternoon sunlight in the sound of them, a sound of words before words, a whisper of one syllable older than language, continuing like a pulse. In the updraft from the valley the monarchs fluttered toward us, lighted on us. At one moment there were fifteen of them on me, trembling on their way. The fragility was not only theirs.

The Winter Palace Revisited

Since it is during the months from November to March that the monarch butterflies occupy their winter palace in the mountains of Michoacan, in Mexico, visits to them there are winter journeys. Six winters after my first sight of those mountains in which their southern migration ends, and the *oyamel* fir trees hung with curtains of monarchs, I was invited back again. The occasion for the first visit had been an environmental conference of writers and scientists, convened in Moreha by the Mexican poet Homero Aridjis and his wife, Betty, in 1994. This return invitation reached me as part of the Orion Society's plans for presenting its John Hay Award for the year 2000 to Homero Aridjis himself.

In the years between the visits, the news from Mexico, in the papers and in letters from friends, had not been heartening. Public assassinations, skillfully orchestrated kidnappings, violence of many kinds, major fraud in high places, economic quicksands, deepening environmental devastation all seemed to be part of the daily round in that unhappy country. Homero and Betty had received repeated death threats and had at least one attempt made upon their lives. The Mexico City airport had acquired a reputation as a scene of menace

and ambush, and I was glad that arrangements had been made for me
to be met there when I arrived.

The flight south from Los Angeles was cloudless, above the vast,
hazy beige splendors of the west coast of Mexico and the Sea of Cor-
tez. I had a clearer view of the immense tumbled arrugations of the
mountains of Durango than I had ever had before, for whenever I
had flown over them they had been hidden by clouds or I had been
flying at night. And with the sight of them I felt the old love of that
torn and gifted country—which for me has always been set in its
mountains—stir again.

The Mexico City airport was quite recognizable: a vast swirl, at
once polished and dingy, even more crowded, rushed, loud and apparently erratic than I remembered, and its light, I realized, which might
have been filtered through a bandage, was obviously a function of the
perpetually masked sky over that city. I had flown across the Pacific,
without sleeping, the night before, and was quite ready to be guided
to the new airport Marriott, where I seemed to enter a framed picture
of a hotel lobby anywhere, and then a room looking out onto airport
roofs, to catch a few hours of sleep, at last, between worlds.

There had been trouble with the car rental agency. The vans which
representatives of the Orion Society had reserved far in advance had
turned out not to be available when those same representatives arrived
in Mexico City. They were told that at least one of them had been stolen. After some time and shuffling they were provided with a different
number of vans, not of the same size they had planned for. Then there
had been trouble with the airlines. Several of the guests invited to
the gathering in Michoacan had been delayed between flights routed
through Texas. When I was wakened and it was explained to me it
seemed that I had heard it all before. I was told that we were going to
go on ahead and drive to Michoacan, and the other guests would follow us in another van, the next day. And we set out across the smoky
labyrinth of the largest city in the world, managing to find Homero
and Betty's house on the way, and take them along with us.

The city seemed never to leave us, though the light of the afternoon brightened and gradually filled with the yellows and hennas of the latter part of the day. The highway signs slipped past, sometimes eclipsed by trucks, or undecipherable with the westering light in our eyes. The scarred and crumpled pavement led vaguely west between painted facades of poured cement, one-story buildings with clustered growths of rebar ravelling up out of them against the glowing sky. Their silhouettes and the furnace exhaust from the capital accompanied us uphill and down, hour after hour. In Tolucca, a sprawl of unrelieved drabness, ugliness and desiccation, we got lost repeatedly and asked our way of one wonderfully cheerful and courteous taxidriver after another, each of whom explained at once the simplicity of the route that was eluding us. At one U-turn we edged past a dark open truck from which we watched a succession of adolescents, all dressed in dark unidentifiable uniforms, climb down with automatic rifles in their hands. The trip to Zitacuaro was supposed to take three hours or so, but it was five hours before we reached it, and it was dark as we drove beyond it to the lovely hotel converted from the adobe buildings of a ranch of indeterminate age.

That was the preamble to the visits to the monarch sanctuaries—the first of them—after the other guests arrived, the next morning. My eyes had been uncomfortable ever since I had arrived despite repeated applications of protective ointment. I had expected the irritation to subside as we got farther from the acrid air of the capital, but instead it got worse. When we set out for the Chincua sanctuary, still a couple of hours' drive away, it seemed to me that there was far more traffic on the roads than I remembered six years earlier. And it had been an unusually dry winter. The dust was constant, everywhere. The town of Anguengueo looked drier, dustier, more crowded than my recollection of it, and as though the upper edge of the municipality had been pushed and piled up against the disused metal buildings of the old silver mine sprawling up the hillside. In the little church square fringed with souvenir stalls there were wooden models of lumber trucks loaded with logs, for sale. I was assured that they had been made of wood from the first of the mountains. From the old trees, "which would only have fallen anyway."

The long road from Anguengueo to the Chincua sanctuary was like a dry river bed, twisting, climbing, dropping, at moments all but invisible under clouds of dust. Six years earlier we had ridden the last hour or so from Anguengueo to El Rosario in the back of an open truck, holding on as it lurched and bounded. There had been few other vehicles then. This year it would have been a miserable ride. The traffic of cars, trucks and buses was constant, and the dust was a moiling cloud the whole way. It lay deep on the pitted, rocky, narrow road and on the leaves of the bushes and trees beside it.

The Chincua sanctuary had not been open to the public at the time of my earlier visit. What we arrived at—after a sinuous approach through mountains on which we could see the straw-pale cornfields and bare pastures displacing the fir forests far up the slopes and in some places clear to the tops of the ridges—was a large denuded stretch of valley side, stripped of trees and of almost any vegetation. It was, in fact, a huge parking lot in several sections, with a keyboard of buses, and straggling ranks of parked cars on both sides of the end of the line. And up to the left, on the side toward the mountain, were trestle tables and booths offering food, souvenirs, soft drinks, for sale. And picket lines of horses, perhaps a hundred of them, attached to waiting "guides" of all ages.

At the Rosario sanctuary, six years before, the purchase of a ticket had brought with it the company of a guard who had made certain that one did not stray from the path, or damage the undergrowth, or take anything away. At the Chincua sanctuary this year there seemed to be no supervision at all, and in the intervening years the crowds of visitors had multiplied explosively. The buses must all have been full, and the cars too.

I cannot say how far it is from the stalls and the parking wasteland at the foot of the mountain to the monarchs' last hope of refuge in the big firs high on the ridges, but it must be at least four or five steep and tortuous miles. And it is not a path any more. The main route is broader than a cart track in late February after a dry winter. It was everywhere many inches—at least a hand's breadth—deep in powdery, gray volcanic dust. On either side of it loops and swags of alternate tracks, often as wide as the main route, have been beaten through the dust-laden understory. The flowers of the surviving bushes are often the same color as the gray leaves, and the butterflies dying on the ground turn gray before they stop fluttering. At the foot of the trail ambulant vendors of postcards and butterfly souvenirs also purvey what look like green surgical masks, as protection against the dust. They seem to do a fair business in them, but many of the masks are abandoned on the way up and discarded along the trail, for they interfere with breathing on the steep incline, at that altitude (around ten thousand feet).

All the way up, the trail was crowded with people and horses and occasionally open trucks, coming and going. Foreign visitors were heavily outnumbered by Mexicans of all ages coming to see the now-famous *mariposas,* some of them after travelling considerable distances, in what is clearly a spirit of pilgrimage, with something of the indefinite aspiration that might have led them on an arduous trek to the distant shrine of some popular saint. There were staffs for rent too, at the stalls at the foot of the way up, and I saw old people, cripples, couples carrying tiny children, men and women heaving such ponderous bodies that I would have thought it difficult for them to get up a flight of stairs. And as far as I could see it was not the oldest or most cumbersome who seemed to clamber into the trucks halfway up, or allow themselves to be hoisted onto horses that were being led back, riderless, from the trip uphill. How many turned back partway up I cannot tell. An ambulance ground its way up, through the unbroken dust cloud.

The first of the monarchs' wintering trees are on the far side of the ridge. This year, Lincoln Brower told me, the size covers roughly four and a half hectares of forest, which means that there are, or have been at some time in the season, about forty-five million butterflies there. With the continuous flow of people passing and talking, the ghostly breathing sound of the clouds of butterflies was less distinct this year than it had been on my first visit to El Rosario. And the butterflies too were clearly suffering from the dust. Lincoln Brower said that the respiratory systems of the monarchs near the trail were surely so clogged with dust that they could not possibly fly very far when they started on the northward migration. There were signs in their behavior, he said, that some of them were already preparing to begin that migration this year, in late February, almost a month early, perhaps because of the shortage of water this winter, perhaps because of disturbances to the site, or both.

The understory growth, the salvias and other flowers on the sides of the trail, has been mauled and trampled almost to the foot of the monarchs' trees. Their flowers, Lincoln said, actually provide little nourishment for the wintering monarchs, which have to have stored up enough fat—or lipids—in their tissues, on the way south, to last them through the turn of the year and into the start of the spring migration. Those who seek nectar in the winter growth are probably already in trouble, using up more lipids than they can replace, and the dust and the cold caused by deforestation, and the drought, all contribute to their worsening situation. I lay looking up into the trees full of monarchs as the temperature dropped, at the end of the afternoon. Many were settled for the night in long draped clusters; others were still sailing among the trees, lighting on pilgrims and horses. Some had dropped to the ground and, as the chill of the shadow touched them, perhaps would not be able to rise again. Monarchs may court in the air, but they mate, surprisingly enough, in the missionary position, on a surface, often the ground, and after mating the male carries the female up into a tree again. As I looked up, as far from the crowd and as close to the monarchs as possible without getting too near the trees, I saw one such post-nuptial flight, and then another. The female, I understand, can mate with a succession of males, and her body can not only use the sperm to fertilize her eggs, but can digest it as protein. And I am told that the females tend to survive longer on the spring migration than the males do.

On the way down the mountain, the crowd was thinning. People had been going home, hoping to start back in daylight. The edge of the cold was creeping across the mountain. The cloud of dust was somewhat thinner, and I noticed the size of clearings among the trees even high on the slope and well within the "sanctuary" (it seemed to me increasingly appropriate to use the word with quotation marks). In the clearing some of the stumps were recent and there were marks of logs having been dragged out. A number of big trees had been felled near the path. One lay with an end at the edge of the dust track, waiting to be taken away. As I came on down the mountain I noticed signs of cattle in the trampled undergrowth. The so-called buffer zone of mixed agricultural and forest land that surrounds, and theoretically protects, the "sanctuary" is rapidly taking over the mountain. It was an ill-defined category and hard to maintain, from the beginning, and is fast becoming meaningless. At the edge of the parking area I saw small flocks of sheep being herded from the trees across the open ground.

On the road from the foot of the mountain the cloud of dust followed us out between the slopes, with the last rays of the sunlight hanging in it like beams in murky water. With the first torrential rains of the Mexican summer all that dust will, of course, erode and wash away in a slurry of mud. I had been watching the monarchs' forest being turned into a desert, a process that cannot take more than a very few years.

We went out to El Rosario on the following day. The same clouds of dust around us, and at the foot of the mountain the row of stalls and eating sheds of six years ago, had grown into what was already the principal street of a village dependent on tourism. The stalls had become open-fronted shops, and the upper dirt lane had been cemented over. It all had the air of having passed into a later age of establishment. Behind the shops along the ridge the cornfields and scuffed pastures fell away to narrow, rocky stream beds, with debris littering the slopes and the channels.

El Rosario is better organized than Chincua. There are still men of various ages taking the role of guards, but they do so now in a perfunctory absent-minded way, making no pretense of accompany-

ing the crowds of visitors very far up the mountain. The central path
has been better marked and contained than at Chincua, and has not
straggled out into loops and short cuts. But at El Rosario too there
are now horses for hire, and the path in places is ankle-deep in dust.
The monarchs' trees are not so far up the mountain as at Chincua—
two or three miles, perhaps—but they are almost a mile farther up
than they were *six* years ago. Farther away from the invaders? That
familiar, but apparently vain, hope. One must climb, as at Chincua, to
the top of the ridge, and down the far side, and then partway up the
next ridge, to catch sight of the edge of their part of the forest. As
I stood watching the trees the last sunlight was going and the cold
was arriving with the shadow, like the touch of rising water. I saw the
colors leave the flowing bolts of monarchs in the trees, and the pale
undersides of their wings darken. Those that were on the ground then,
or even near it, would probably not fly again. I had felt their presence,
years before, lighting on me, on the mountain, and that evening I felt
the chill that was overtaking them.

The friends who were at the gathering had been talking all morning about what can be done, but we really do not know. What makes
the monarch migration unique in evolution, as far as we can fathom
it, is something that we understand very inadequately, for all we have
learned about it, but what we do understand of it is a great wonder, a
measureless splendor of life which we have not even begun to value.
Perhaps that is something that we will never be able to do. Our own
gifts, in the end, may render it impossible. The return visit did not leave
me feeling optimistic about the survival of the "sanctuaries," even if the
Mexican government delineates and declares, on paper, a whole string
of them. They would have to be consistently maintained and preserved,
the ruthless and powerful logging interests permanently excluded, the
horses and cattle and sheep kept out, the people living near the forests
given other means, and more attractive means, of livelihood. And the
monarchs are threatened at the other end of their migration by genetic
modification in the agribusiness of the North American prairie states,
which is eradicating or impairing several species of *Asclepias* (milk-

weed) essential to the monarchs' survival. Our own survival does not bode well for that of this beautiful butterfly with its dazzling gift for life. Our apparent inability to alter our own aims and behavior enough to safeguard so marvellous and mysterious a fellow creature does not promise much for our own future.

Name in the Sand

In the early 1960s I was living in a village in southwest France, overlooking the river Dordogne, for most or all of the year. I explored the countryside on foot, and eventually I bought, from an acquaintance who was leaving the region, a Vespa, a wonderfully quiet model on which I could go putt-putting along back lanes too far away for me to walk in an afternoon. There was far less traffic in those days than there is now and before I had had the *moto* for long I took to fastening a bedroll and a few essentials onto the rack over the rear wheel and taking off to wander for a few days at a time, discovering the country to the southeast, southwest, always to the south. I wound my way along the Aveyron and across the Causse Noir. I slept in empty barns or in woods or in small village hotels. The country, as I remember it, was still magically unself-conscious, as one hopes discoveries will be. It still had years to go before the touch of tourism reached it. I am not sure now how many times, on those trips, I crossed the river Tarn and went up the hill along the river into the main square of Albi beside the huge brick block of the cathedral.

In college, a few years earlier, I had read what Cyril Connolly had written about Albi, a favorite city of his. He considered it one of the key points of what he called the magic triangle, the heart of what he loved in southern France, and in Europe. I had never seen Europe when I read him, and I had tried to imagine the Albi he wrote about, where he, in turn, looking out across the river from a window of the old Bishop's Palace—a kind of fortress that had been turned into a museum—had tried to imagine the Albi of roughly half a century earlier, when it had been Toulouse-Lautrec's city before the painter went off to Paris. I had not known then, when I read about Toulouse-Lautrec, just how long the echo of those two names, Toulouse and Lautrec, had resounded in the antiquity of the region. I had read almost nothing about the city's earlier history. My knowledge of what came to be called the Albigensian Crusade—named for the city of course, although Albi was not one of those that suffered most—was sparse and scattered.

Connolly had written of his admiration for the massive red cathedral and for its looming, grisly altar piece with the figures of the damned reaching vainly out of a sea of damnation, for the world they have lost, and I stared at it trying to recognize what he had seen in it, since I knew little about the place or the painting except what I could remember of his writing, and the details in the few brochures in the church porch. I had not heard then of a French explorer named Jean-Francois Galaup de La Pérouse, who had been born in that city, and it would be twenty years and more before the La Pérouse museum would be opened there, across the river. I went slowly through the quiet art museum, roamed for a while in the square and the streets around it, and then set off again on the Vespa into the countryside along the valley of the Tarn.

* * *

Some fifteen years later I first visited Maui. I would, in fact, come to live on the island, though I did not know it at first as I drove past the few hotels (then) and the handful of houses along the southwest-facing coast to a dry unpopulated lava flow and a crescent of sand and shingle that has come to be known as La Pérouse Bay. When I asked, I was told that the name was that of a French explorer who had first—in fact, I am not quite sure what I was told that he had done. Until late in the twentieth century those who wrote or spoke European languages thought nothing of saying that someone had "discovered" some part of the world that may have been inhabited by non-Europeans for millennia. La Pérouse of course did not "discover" Maui. He was perhaps not even the first European to see the island. It is possible that Spaniards knew of the Hawaiian islands in the sixteenth and seventeenth centuries. Spanish vessels may have been shipwrecked there, and others may have stopped on Pacific crossings. Bits of Spanish metal from that period, iron daggers and other objects, have turned up in the islands, and there are legends, but there are no records, and the maps that have survived are unclear—in some cases perhaps deliberately so, in order to mislead strangers into whose hands they might fall. One Spanish chart of the Pacific, dated 1555, shows a group of islands that might represent the Hawaiian archipelago.

Captain James Cook was the first European to make a recorded landing in Hawai'i. He visited Kaua'i and Hawai'i, and he saw Maui in 1778, on his second voyage, and anchored offshore in several places to trade, but he did not land there.

When La Pérouse with his two frigates, the *Astrolabe* and the *Boussole,* approached the island from the south at the end of May 1786, Cook had been dead for seven years, killed by inhabitants of the island of Hawai'i under circumstances that remain unclear, since the written eyewitness accounts, inevitably, were left only by Europeans. La Pérouse knew those narratives well, as he knew everything available about Cook, and he had had some hesitation about stopping in Hawai'i at all.

* * *

His two frigates had sailed from Brest on August 1, 1785, on what was intended to be a voyage of circumnavigation and exploration that would take several years. The enterprise had been meticulously planned, from its benign purpose (which was to add to the general sum of scientific and geographical knowledge) to the itinerary and the equipment, and even to the appropriate attitude. In the early days, when hopes were high, La Pérouse had written that he wanted this to be a voyage of circumnavigation that would shed not a drop of blood and would not give the native peoples they met any cause to regret the Europeans coming.

They had crossed the Atlantic to Brazil—a hundred days to the island of Santa Caterina—and then to Cape Horn, slipping through the Straits of Magellan more easily than they had dared to hope. Then in early February they had sailed north along the coast of Chile to Concepcion, where they stayed three weeks, resting up, replenishing stores, making repairs to the vessels. They loved the place. La Pérouse pronounced it delightful but backward (his, after all, was the age of the Enlightenment). The women dressed up, he said, in "that old cloth woven with gold and silver thread that used to be manufactured in Lyon."

The original plans for his itinerary, approved by the Minister of Maritime Affairs and the King, called for the vessels to sail due west from Chile, across the South Pacific to Tahiti, but La Pérouse had been given liberty to alter the plans according to the circumstances of the voyage, and since it was so early in the year, he decided to sail northwest instead. He landed on Easter Island on April 9, 1786, nine months and a week out of Brest.

The islanders were the first indigenous people whom they had visited on the voyage. In France Rousseau's fantasy of the Noble Savage was in vogue. La Pérouse had a view of the subject that was respectful but skeptical. He had read not only Rousseau but descriptions of violent encounters with native peoples in the accounts of earlier voyagers, besides Cook's. He was aware that the ignorance and aggressiveness of the Europeans probably had helped to cause some of the incidents, but he saw no reason to assume that the motives of native peoples were very different from those of his own men, and he remained tolerant but watchful. And the instructions for the voyage, signed by the King, Louis XVI, were explicit about any shore party being well armed and never losing contact with the frigates. He directed his men to use "all possible kindness and humanity" toward the inhabitants, so that the visit would not be a misfortune to them, but "a means of supplying them with advantages of which they have been deprived."

They stayed on the island for a matter of hours, giving the inhabitants goats, sheep and pigs (no blessing, in the long run, any of them, but the French did not know that) and seeds of orange trees, lemon trees, maize, and "every species that might do well on their island." They walked up from the shore and Jean-Nicolas Collignon, the young man chosen to be the gardening expert for the expedition by the King's gardener who had also supplied the seeds, sowed cabbage, carrot, pumpkin, corn, beets and fruit tree seeds in places where he thought they might grow well. Meanwhile the friendly inhabitants stole the hats off their heads and the handkerchiefs out of their pockets and ran off with them, and the women offered their favors to anyone who gave them presents. La Pérouse laughed at the thefts, and to prevent trouble over them, promised to replace whatever was stolen.

They left that same night and sailed on northward, passing the northeast coast of the island of Hawai'i on the morning of May 28, 1776, and on across the 'Alenuihaha (Big Crashing Billows) Channel toward the south coast of Maui, along the island to the 'Alalakeiki (Crying Baby) Channel at the southwest corner, looking up the vast mountainside of Haleakala (House of the Sun) toward its upper slopes hidden in cloud, a single mountain so enormous that it appeared to be an entire range.

The sight of Maui, La Pérouse wrote, was "ravishing." "We saw the water cascading down from the heights to the sea, irrigating the house plots of the Indians on the way. There are so many of those that a single village seems to run for three or four leagues (about ten miles) with all the houses built along the edge of the sea, and the mountains are so close to the shore that the habitable land appears to be less than half a league wide. One would have to be a sailor, and reduced, as we were, in that burning climate, to one bottle of water a day, to have any idea of what we felt at the sight. The trees that crowned the mountains, the verdure, the banana trees around the dwellings looked inexpressibly delightful to us. But the sea broke on that coast with terrible force, and like Tantalus in our time we were reduced to desiring and devouring with our eyes what we could not reach."

They edged along the south coast, watching one green, deep valley after another slip past with its distant waterfall, but finding no bay or safe anchorage, and the shore grew drier and stonier as they sailed until, instead of the dense rain forest colors and shadows that they had first seen, they were looking up across black lava flows and arid slopes to a landscape of dry forest shimmering in the sun.

They stood offshore all night and in the morning rounded the southwest corner of Maui, and as they came in closer to the coast the vessels were surrounded by Hawaiians in canoes, trying to keep up with them. When they turned the corner of the island they found a bay, with a village around it, and there they anchored. In a moment the deck of the *Astrolabe*, commanded by an old friend of La Pérouse, Paul-Antoine Fleuriot de Langle, was a mass of "these Indians," but "they were so docile, so anxious not to offend us, that there was no trouble at all in getting them to go back into their canoes. They were wildly excited by pieces of our old barrel hoops, and they were quite adept at bargaining for them." In exchange for them, they offered pigs and fruits. La Pérouse had come well provided with nails of different sizes, iron tools and metal fishhooks. In the barter there on shipboard, and later, on shore, the officers acquired for the expedition a cloak, a red helmet, tapa cloths and mats, a canoe, small objects made of feathers and shells, and more than a hundred pigs, bananas, and an immense quantity of fruit. Two chiefs had come aboard the *Boussole* and given La Pérouse pigs as presents, and La Pérouse, in return, gave them medals, and axes, and assorted pieces of metal.

La Pérouse and de Langle put together a shore party, guarded by forty soldiers, and they were received on shore with the same warmth and eager welcome. It was a tiny village, ten or fifteen huts covered with grass. They were the same shape, La Pérouse noted, as the thatched cottages in some parts of France. "The roofs are pitched on both sides, and the doorway at the gable end is only about three feet high so that one has to bend down to enter. The houses are furnished with mats, used like carpets. They cover the floor neatly, and the inhabitants use them to sleep on. Their only cooking pots are painted gourds " Everywhere he was met by the same gentle behavior and the same generosity from the chiefs. When he came to write about them, upon reflection he said that he could not help comparing them to the people of Easter Island. The Sandwich Islanders (as they were then called by Europeans) were superior in every respect, "even though I was wholly prejudiced against them on account of the death of Captain Cook. It is more natural for navigators to regret so great a man than to examine coolly whether some incautious action on his part might not, in some way, have forced the inhabitants . . . to resort to justified self-defense."

But he wrote that some time after he had left Maui, and Hawai'i. As long as he was there, an image of Cook's fate must have stood beside him, redoubling his caution, for he did not hand out presents of hoofed animals and of seeds as he had done on Easter Island, nor give the botanists and other scientists permission to conduct observations of the flora and fauna of the bay and the volcanic shore. The current in the channel, the uncertainty of the anchorage, the weather, may also have prompted him to be on his way. He stayed there the rest of that day, filling the water barrels, noticing the marks of skin eruptions on the inhabitants, most of them, presumably, venereal disease which Cook's crew is thought to have introduced to other islands in the chain. His own men had a chance to mingle with the island women, and no doubt contributed to the contagion, or picked it up to pass on.

And though he was the first European to set foot on Maui, despite the example of earlier explorers (Bougainville had not hesitated to lay claim to the Society Islands for France), he did not claim the entire island for his own country "in the cool fashion of the time," as Mark Twain had said of La Salle, a century earlier, formally proclaiming the whole Mississippi basin French. La Pérouse had not been sent on a voyage of imperial aggrandizement, and he did not think much of such easy arrogation. "The philosophers must groan," he wrote, "to see men, merely because they have cannons and bayonettes, count as nothing sixty thousand members of their own kind whose sacred rights they dismiss, and whose land, which they have watered with their sweat for centuries, and which is the tomb of their ancestors, they take to be an object of conquest."

He did not want to linger in Hawai'i for whatever reason, and in the evening he weighed anchor and sailed west and north between the islands, toward the cold. His journal of the visit would survive, but he himself would not see Hawai'i (or France) again.

The name of the bay and of the cluster of houses around it, was— and in Hawaiian still is—Keone 'o'io, (Bonefish Sand). When La Pérouse had forgotten it completely it would be named after him.

The village disappeared long ago. Within a decade the English captain George Vancouver tried to find the place, using the La Pérouse journal account of the visit, but what he found seemed so different from the description that he believed there must have been a lava flow between the date when La Pérouse had been there, and his own arrival. That was the generally accepted view until recently when carbon dating showed that the last lava flow to the shoreline there took place much earlier. One of the aims of the La Pérouse expedition had been to contribute to the cartography of the Pacific, and the maps that were made in the course of it were remarkably accurate for their time. It would be strange if Keone 'o'io had been an exception, carelessly or hastily recorded. In any event, what La Pérouse saw there has disappeared with him, and it would be years after I first saw the bay before I began to piece together bits of his story. with the assistance of friends, and eventually of Retired Admiral Pierre Bérard of the La Pérouse Museum in Albi, the biographical research of John Dunmore, Yves Jacob, and Jean Guillou, the undersea and archaeological explorations organized since the 1980s by Alain Conan, of New Caledonia, and his colleagues, among other sources, to all of whom I am indebted.

* * *

La Pérouse would have one more brush with Hawai'i, and when considered in retrospect it has the appearance of something more than a warning—an omen. Five months after he sailed from Maui in May, as he was crossing the Pacific from Monterey in California to the coast of Asia, early in November they were sailing far to the northwest of the known islands of Hawai'i when they saw birds all around them, gannets and terns which, as he noted, are seldom far from land. At several points on their Pacific voyaging they had looked carefully for islands that had been described in earlier accounts or that appeared on old charts, but whose real existence was unverified. More than one navigator had recorded a mirage, and La Pérouse had eliminated several "nonexistent islands" in the course of that year. When he sailed from California he searched for the island of Nostra Señora de la Gorta, but he passed the place where it was supposed to be, and recorded that there was no such island. But where the birds were circling, northwest of Hawai'i, there was nothing on the chart, and they proceeded cautiously under reduced sails at night. On the evening of the 4th of November they sighted land ten or fifteen miles to the west. Barely a speck, but it seemed likely that there might be others. They tacked back and forth all night and the next morning moved in closer and found a bare rock some thousand yards long and a hundred high, without a single tree, but grassy near the summit, and white with the droppings of birds, the sides sheer as a wall, with the sea breaking against them. There was nowhere to land and he sailed on.

At night the sea, he wrote, was so quiet that they scarcely heard the sound of breakers until they were almost upon them. They were not a hundred yards away when both vessels became aware of them at once and veered sharply. Then they learned just how close they had come to disaster. La Pérouse praised the quickness and calm of his crew in saving them. Hoping to avert danger for others there in the future he returned at daybreak and saw a small atoll or jagged rock not more than fifty fathoms in diameter and twenty or twenty-five fathoms in elevation at its highest point, but there were also sand bars stretching away to the southeast of it, on one of which they had nearly been wrecked, and there was a ring of rocks just breaking the surface, "like a circle of diamonds around a medallion," on which the surf was crashing. Neither the rock island with its birds, nor the atoll marking the site of its ancient summit, nor the barrier reef like a ring of diamonds, nor the sand bars had been on any chart. He named the inaccessible rock table Necker Island (for the French Minister of Finance) and the ring of reefs French Frigate Shoals "because it very nearly put an end to our voyage." The highest rock in the middle of it, the final remnant of the original volcanic mountain, was named, years later, La Pérouse Pinnacle.

* * *

In the legend that still hovers above the wake of the expedition, we are told that Louis XVI, shortly before he mounted the steps of the guillotine, asked those who were close to him, "Have we any word about M. de La Pérouse?"

It may have happened. Louis XVI, if we except a passion for the hunt, was one of the most amiable and decent human beings to wear the crown of France. He grew up with an amateur collector's curiosity about various kinds of instruments, from locks to barometers, thermometers, chronometers, all sorts of navigational equipment, and he loved to draw maps. There is still one of them, in the archives of the Bibliothèque Nationale, of Versailles and the surrounding area, with blanks marked "Unknown Places," like the "Unknown Regions" on old navigators' charts. He followed the scientific developments and explorations of his time with passionate interest, and when he became king he encouraged them in France. He espoused, or at least repeated, many of the humanitarian ideals of the contemporary encyclopedists.

It is not possible to be certain now exactly what his role had been, during the winter of 1784, in planning the great voyage of circumnavigation which La Pérouse was to command. The Marquis Charles de Castries, who was the Maritime Minister, and an older friend and mentor of La Pérouse, worked out many of the practical arrangements, but up until well after the expedition sailed there were obvious advantages to presenting the expedition as the King's idea, and stating that the directions for it were "by order of the King," who certainly signed them. Ten years later, when the time came to edit and publish the surviving journals of La Pérouse, the terror of the guillotine loomed over France, and Baron Milet de Mureau, the army general whom the National Assembly chose for the task, thought it prudent to reduce his own name to plain (relatively) Milet-Mureau, and he went to considerable lengths to remove from the journal references to the King and to the aristocratic assumptions that had prevailed when the expedition had been conceived and had sailed. In recent years the texts and records have been re-examined, by Paul and Pierette Girault de Coursac and others, with a view to establishing the King's part in planning the expedition.

As a king, Louis XVI was not distinguished by decisiveness or strength of character, and his vacillations finally were his undoing, but after his coronation in 1774, France, despite several painful defeats in the continuous imperial struggle with England, was enjoying a brief surge of national confidence. The star of the time, the great explorer of the age, was England's James Cook (1728-1779), whose journals, by 1784, were part of contemporary European culture. The French hoped to assemble an expedition that would complement Cook's explorations and stand comparison with them, and the original idea for the voyage may have come from Charles de Castries or Claret de Fleurieu at the Maritime Ministry. Fleurieu too was a friend of La Pérouse, who was then just forty. De Castries may have divulged something about the plans to La Pérouse as early as the spring of 1784, when La Pérouse wrote to him about the prospect of "leaving his own country for five or six years." But nine months later La Pérouse wrote to his wife that he was still uncertain about the plans and his part in them.

They were shrouded in secrecy, probably in a rather ineffectual effort to keep the English from finding out about the expedition and its proposed itinerary for as long as possible. But the rumor spread, and with it gossip about the King's part in the project. In the French Musée de la Marine there is an often-reproduced painting, by N. A. Monsiau, showing *Louis XVI Discussing the Plan of the Voyage with La Pérouse*. The King is sitting at a table on which a great map, partly unrolled, spills toward the floor. There is a globe behind him, and the King's posture is reminiscent of Cook's in a famous portrait, but perhaps the arrangement of legs, breeches, and white stockings in seated positions was limited by conventions at the time. The royal finger is on a point of the map, the other side of which is in the right hand of La Pérouse, who is standing over it. Behind the King stands a figure who must be de Castries. The picture was painted, it should be remembered, in 1817, years after the expedition was lost and had become a continuing topic of speculation.

As late as the end of March 1785, two months before the expedition was supposed to sail, La Pérouse was under the impression that the design of the project, its goals and plan, were the work of de Castries, though he realized, as he said in a letter, that the enterprise was "before the eyes of the King." He knew by that time that "the plan for this voyage, I dare say, is vaster than any before. . . . If we accomplish what the minister has envisaged, this voyage is certain to be mentioned by posterity, and our names will float in space along with those of Cook and Magellan."

He had been fretting about the continuing insistence on secrecy. How could such a thing be kept secret, he asked his friend Fleurieu, when the shipyards outfitting the expedition had already received their orders? In April he wrote that he had received ten letters, all of them referring to the coming expedition. He had even been told specifically, he said, that he was to command a 36-gun vessel, and a frigate, and that the King was paying for the ships out of his private funds, and the whole idea had come from the King. He sounded doubtful. "One can expect to see a hundred absurdities hatch with regard to this voyage but there's no harm in that."

On June 28, that summer, he had an audience with the King, a meeting of which de Castries reminded him in July, shortly before he sailed, when he gave La Pérouse the detailed written sailing instructions which had been annotated, and perhaps in part drawn up by the King himself. The King had gone over some of the main points with La Pérouse in person. In the opening pages of his journal of the voyage, La Pérouse summarized the instructions. The plans worked out by de Castries and Fleurieu, he said, had been endorsed by the King "who, more than anyone in his kingdom, had appreciated the merit, talents, and character of Captain Cook." The principal purpose of the circumnavigation was described as scientific, and the approach to native peoples was to be as tolerant and humane as possible. Fleurieu supervised the preparation of the maps, of which the King had duplicate copies, and he provided La Pérouse with a tome full of scientific notes, and discussions of earlier voyages since Columbus.

In the careful choosing of the officers, aristocratic title was still of importance, but talent and experience were more pertinent. In 1954 a passage of the notebooks of Alexandre-Jean des Mazis was published, recalling his years at the École Militaire as a fellow student of the young Napoleon Bonaparte. At an earlier school that trained students for the navy as well as for the army, Napoleon had been one of the naval cadets, and the school report stated that he was "highly suitable to be a naval officer." His mother, however, considered that the army offered more ambitious possibilities, and had told the school that she wanted to hear no more about his naval prospects. Mazis remembered being in the mathematics class with Bonaparte, and two of their teachers, Dagelet and Monge, both well-known in their field, applying for posts as astronomers on the La Pérouse expedition and

being accepted. "Bonaparte would have liked this chance to show his
energy in so splendid an enterprise," Mazis wrote, "but Darbaud was
the only one [of the students] selected. They could not take any more
pupils." And so Europe was not spared Napoleon.

* * *

Whatever finally happened to the ships and crews of the expedition—
and we have learned many things that neither Louis XVI nor anyone
in his generation ever found out—we can be sure of a few images
that must have returned to the mind of La Pérouse, and to his mind
alone on those two vessels, until his last conscious moments. One of
them is the dour facade of the building sometimes referred to as the
manoir, sometimes as the château, of Go (from the Occitan word *guo*,
meaning "ford") across the river from Albi, which in the middle of
the eighteenth century was a town of 10,000. It was inside that plain,
looming structure that La Pérouse was born, to be christened Jean-
Francois de Galaup, on August 23, 1741. There he spent the summers,
at least, of his childhood. The Galaup family had two houses in town,
but in the warm months lived out at Go, where their lands extended
to the Tarn river flowing in a great loop around them on three sides.

The present structure was built, at some time after the Middle
Ages, to dominate a now long-disused road to the ford. Something of
the centuries of menace and fright, repression and resistance that had
marked that beautiful region had found expression in the unadorned
building at which Jean-Francois would have gazed up as an infant,
and which he would have beheld in dreams, and have left with a tan-
gle of anguish frustration—who knows what else?— and would have
recalled with longing in moments of inexpressible homesickness. Two
massive brick sections, nearly symmetrical, each with a single window
above and a smaller iron-grilled aperture below, are thrust forward,
with a wall half their height joining them, and the arched entrance in
the center leads in to a small square courtyard, with the house rising
around it on three sides.

As a child he would have remembered like an image from a dream the family arms on the coach door—the rearing horse *âu galop*—of his father's family, and he would have memorized the sight and sound of the river, and could never have forgotten the towering brick cathedral built like a fortress to represent the might of the Church and of the Inquisition after the suppression of "heresy" in the Albigensian Crusade. Images of it and of its altar piece would have recurred to him long after he had been attracted, as a young man, to the philosophers of the Enlightenment.

One of his associations with the dour facade at Go must have been the face of his father, Victor-Joseph, the stern features expressing his determined social ambition and his conviction that Jean-Francois, his eldest son, was its predestined instrument. Members of the Galaup family had held posts in the municipal government since the fifteenth century, and in the sixteenth the family's prosperity had allowed them to buy from the Cardinal of Clermont an estate near Albi which brought with it a title of nobility, so that Jean Galaup became Jean de Galaup. Eleven years later the Ordonnance de Blois decreed that the purchase of a piece of property that was a fief did not automatically elevate the buyer to the nobility, but members of the bourgeoisie who bought old fiefs adopted the attached titles when they could. The de Galaups had got in just under the wire, and their new estate at Orban brought Jean de Galaup the title of Seigneur et Baron de Brens et de Saint-Félix. The house at Go had been bought later. By the eighteenth century the de Galaups were established in the provincial aristocracy but in fiscal matters were still members of the bourgeoisie. Jean-Francois' father, Victor-Joseph, had the expensive honor of being one of the most highly taxed citizens of Albi. If his son were to enter the King's service as an officer in the army or navy, the tax burden would be cut to little or nothing. This appears to have been Victor-Joseph's plan from the moment Jean-Francois was born, compounding the anxieties of his infancy and early childhood, when it looked as though his parents' firstborn might not live. For the child's health was not robust, and infant mortality rates were not encouraging. His mother had a baby almost every year until she had given birth to ten in all, and only three of them reached adulthood.

She had been born Marguerite de Resseguier, daughter of a colonel of a famous regiment, and through her subsequent pregnancies she undertook the beginnings of Jean-Francois' education. He went on to a nearby school on the Rue de L'École Mage, and at nine he entered the Jesuit College where he was taught for six years. One of his schoolmates, an exact contemporary, would grow up to be an admiral. That was Pascal de Rochegude, whose claim to nobility was more impressive than that of Jean-Francois, and whose title certainly sounded better than "Galaup de Go." There was another piece of property in the Galaup estate, a small tenant farm near Albi called the Métairie de La Pérouse. It may have been in the family for some time, or Victor-Joseph may have bought it for the express purpose of putting it, as he did, in Jean-Francois' name, so that he could be called Jean-Francois de La Pérouse (the name itself had a history that led back to the Crusades). None of this, to his father's abiding disappointment, was of much interest to Jean-Francois. Already his passions were navigation, ships, the sea.

That craving for somewhere far away is one of the few images we have of his childhood. He had never seen the sea at all, and the fascination with it, for a boy from Albi, land-locked except for the Tarn river which was too shallow there for anything but river traffic, seems surprising at first. But the careers suitable to a boy in Jean-Francois' circumstances narrowed down to the army or navy and the navy was cheaper. That might be said to provide a practical basis for his, or his father's choosing the navy. The passion came from somewhere else.

Two relatives of the family were already prominent in the navy, commanders with distinguished military records. Jean-Francois no doubt admired them as a boy, and boasted about them and made them his heroes. One of them, Clement Taffanel de la Jonquière, stayed with the de Galaups briefly when Jean-Francois was eight, and again, in the company of another naval officer, the Chevalier de Ternay, four years later, and both men undertook to become Jean-Francois' sponsors and protectors in a naval career. La Jonquière would take charge of the boy's finances, including, presumably, the income from the La Pérouse property.

He would also, as it turned out, provide Jean-Francois with a helpful example in a later argument with his father. La Jonquière had married a Creole woman from a wealthy family on the Ile de France in the Indian Ocean, and brought her back to his chateâu near Albi without causing the slightest social disturbance. However, the tension between Jean-Francois and his father was embedded in their lifelong relation with each other, and the disagreement on this particular subject lay some years in the future when, in the winter of 1756, Jean-Francois, who had just turned fifteen, started north for a life in the navy.

* * *

Toward the end of that year, under cold skies, he first saw, and then heard the sea, as he approached Brest. He saw the forest of masts in the harbor, the crowded channel, the ribs of vessels being built in the shipyards, warships at anchor, quays being extended, a navy being assembled. The perennial rival, the enemy in view, was England.

Brest would be his home port for the rest of his life. He began as one of the *gardes de la Marine*, cadets from the aristocracy training to be officers. They lived in an old house on a residential street, not far from the middle of town, and applied themselves with particular rigor to mathematics (for which Jean-Francois had a gift), astronomy and navigation. The studies alternated with drills and shipboard training in the harbor.

He got into several rows in the town soon after he got there, and La Jonquière, keeping account of his money, recorded that on the 24th of December (on Christmas Eve) he had given Jean-Francois a sum of money "to have two of his suits and a waistcoat and breeches repaired, and on the 20th another sum to Oudart the tailor for his repairs to the suits, waistcoat and breeches, and on Jan. 25th repaid money lent for a broken glass and his sword." There was a further payment for "the prison inn" and the repair of his sword. The fifteen-year-old cadet had spent a couple of his first weeks in Brest in jail.

His studies had scarcely got under way when war broke out. La Jonquière was getting his vessel, Le Célèbre, ready for action, and Jean-Francois, in the middle of February 1757, was called aboard with him, and put to sea for the first time, the beginning of a naval career that would continue for thirty-two years.

It was, obviously his first war, too: the one that would be known, on the other side of the Atlantic, as the French and Indian War, provoked by a long series of hostile encounters in eastern North America. Most of the aggressions had come from the English, who had begun seizing French ships at sea long before war was declared. That was the same piratical activity on the part of the English that would lead, twenty-five years later, to the War of 1812 with the fledgling United States. The English were anxious about the build-up of the French navy, and the French challenge to them on the seas of the world.

Le Célèbre, a vessel of sixty-four guns, sailed from Brest on May 3, 1757, in a squadron of ten ships, which crossed the Atlantic to Louisburg, Cape Breton Island, Nova Scotia, taking supplies to the French garrison there. For Jean-Francois the voyage was a continuation of his training. He sailed back to Brest, and then out again on a smaller vessel, the frigate Pomone, under the command of his other patron, the Chevalier de Ternay. Then another voyage with Ternay on the frigate Zephire, in another squadron to reinforce Louisburg. The British navy outnumbered the French. Louisburg was doomed. The Zephire was sent back alone, narrowly avoiding the British fleet blockading the Newfoundland coast.

In the next few years Jean-Francois gained broad naval experience, which included serving briefly, in 1759, on a ship of the line, the Formidable, that was to lead an invasion of England. The expedition did not have the wild luck of William the Conqueror. Instead, bad timing and treacherous weather led to the French being caught between two English fleets and defeated, with heavy losses. The Formidable had taken the fire of fifteen English ships, had lost her captain, over three hundred men killed, more than a hundred and fifty wounded, an unknown number drowned, and finally the ship was captured. Jean-Francois, who had been wounded in the stomach and in one arm, was exchanged for a British prisoner. He was seventeen.

* * *

In 1763 the war ended in a defeat for France, and Jean-Francois had a chance to go home to Albi for a visit. His father raised the question of marriage, but did not pursue it. It was nearly seven years before he was home again, after a series of routine duties at sea, and this time his father was feeling his age and wanted to get his son's marriage settled, but none of the suggested arrangements interested Jean-Francois.

He sailed to Martinique and witnessed slavery and the slave trade, against which the writers of the Enlightenment, whom he read, had written with passionate eloquence. In 1772 he was sent to the Indian Ocean, to the Ile de France (now Reunion Island) in the Mascarene Islands, a developing colony.

The islands were already severely deforested, veiled constantly in wood smoke, with an already unsuccessful economy based on slave labor. Slaves outnumbered European colonists by more than three to one. The harbor town of Port Louis was shabby and filthy, but much of the island outside it was still very beautiful. There were the intricate tensions and schemes of the social world of a small remote colony. La Pérouse had arrived under the command of de Ternay, who was to be the new governor of the colony. After years of duty in the gray North Atlantic, and the rare trips home to Albi where his father had become increasingly persistent about him getting married, for the sake of the family, into a life that must have grown increasingly unreal to him, the tropics, the Ile de France (as described by Bernardin in *Paul el Virginie)* marked a turning point. He was just over thirty, and up until that point he had done just what his father wanted him to do.

The former manager of the French India Company, Pierre Poivre, had built a country place five miles outside town, and called it Mon Plaisir: a house with a long verandah, some two hundred acres, a lake, and an extensive aviary. Poivre had tried to encourage the agricultural development of the islands, and his ardent interest in botany had not only played a part in that enterprise but had led him to plan the formal gardens around the house, where he grew many kinds of plants that he had introduced to the island. They included spice plants, tea, coffee, cherry trees, mangos, the breadfruit trees which, thirty years later, would lead to the mutiny on the *Bounty,* and the species of roses that had recently been brought back from China. On the neighboring Ile de Bourbon damask roses, the old *Rose des Quatre Saisons,* were grown in hedges around some of the colonists' gardens, and the recently imported species from China, when crossed with them, produced the first of what later would be called Bourbon roses.

The opulence of Poivre's gardens was due in part to the supervision of Philibert Commerson, a distinguished botanist who had crossed the Pacific with the great explorer Louis-Antoine de Bougainville, in 1768. Commerson had arrived at the Ile de France only four years before La Pérouse did, and was then forty-five, in poor health, and famous.

Bougainville's voyage around the world, from 1766 to 1769, is not as well known to the English-speaking world as Cook's achievements, but it was a generously conceived undertaking, drawing upon the talents of some of the finest botanists and other scientists of the age, and it made a major contribution to human knowledge of geography, botany, and other natural sciences. Bougainville's own account of it was widely read in England as well as in France, and it certainly was familiar a decade or so later when de Castries and Louis XVI were planning another voyage of circumnavigation and exploration.

In 1772, when La Pérouse arrived at the Ile de France, Philibert Commerson, besides his international celebrity as a botanist, had a reputation for being testy, and he was also said to be a libertine, a view that may have grown from gossip after the revelation that his valet on his voyage with Bougainville had been a woman disguised as a man. Her name was Jeanne Baré, and she was still there with him four years later. Commerson had a house and garden of his own on the west coast of the island, and there were others on the Ile de France who had sailed with Bougainville, one of them Charles de Romainville, a fine cartographer. In the small society on the Ile de France La Pérouse would have come to know them all before long, and there must have been opportunities to talk with them about Bougainville and his voyage, the written journals, the unwritten details, and about other voyages of exploration in the southern seas, successful and unsuccessful. When La Pérouse got there they were all discussing the "discovery" by Yves de Kerguelen of a new southern continent.

Kerguelen had sailed, several months earlier, in October 1771, on the *Fortune,* in company with another vessel, the *Gros Ventre,* commanded by Francois de St. Allouarn. The two ships had become separated, and each independently had sighted land. The captains had agreed to sail on to Australia, if they lost contact with each other, and meet there, but Kerguelen had sailed back to the Ile de France instead, to report that he had seen what appeared to be an inhabited and cultivated country and that he had discovered a new world for France. Then he had sailed on to France with the news, several months before Ternay and La Pérouse arrived in Port Louis, on the Ile de France.

The other captain, St. Allouarn, had taken a better look than Kerguelen. He had not seen any southern continent, "inhabited and cultivated," but an icy, fog-bound island, all sea-cliffs, with the surf crashing onto them so that landing had been impossible. St. Allouarn abandoned the dangerous venture and sailed on to Australia to wait for Kerguelen. When no one showed up he took on fresh supplies, and then, terminally ill himself, sailed back to Port Louis and died there at the age of thirty-five. In the meantime a number of other vessels had sailed to look for the new "continent," and Kerguelen returned from France in command of another expedition to explore the Island of St. John of Lisbon, as he had named the ice-bound, wave-lashed rock which is now called Kerguelen's Island—an outpost of what we now know as Antarctica.

Before long La Pérouse, to judge from his letters, began to feel a liking for the tropics and the Ile de France The vast difference between the place—its light, its fragrance and beauty, its very distance from northern seas and from his father's unmoving expectations—would have figured among its attractions. There almost at once he seemed to enter upon a new maturity, a measure of independence, a sense of having some say in his own life. Within a year he sailed out of Port Louis and back in command of his own vessel. And there, on the Ile de France, he fell in love.

He probably met Louise-Eléonore Broudou soon after he arrived there. Her father, Abraham Broudou, had brought his family to Port Louis four years earlier, in 1768, from Nantes, where Eléonore had been born. When La Pérouse arrived she was seventeen.

Her father was the manager of naval storage in Port Louis, and supervisor of the hospital: a government employee. His family occupied a respected position on the island, and would have formed part of the small circle that Jean-Francois frequented.

La Pérouse and another naval officer, a friend and former classmate named Mengaud de la Hage, were usually invited together to the Broudou house, since there were two daughters, and the two men, before long, bought a house not far from the Broudous. How that came about we can only guess, but the whole sequence speaks of the rapid awakening of an aspect of Jean-Francois, nature that had not been apparent before. Mengaud was Jean-Francois' confidant about his feelings and about the problems they presented.

Jean-Francois was quite aware that Mlle. Eléonore Broudou would not be acceptable to his father's plans for him. Even though her father was a government employee at the time, he occupied only a minor post, and he had been in trade before. Besides, he had no money. Her family could never have provided a dowry that was remotely appropriate. Yet it was not long before he knew that Eléonore was the woman he wanted to marry.

* * *

But for all his new life on the island, his naval career continued its claims on him. In May 1773, after his first nine months on the Ile de France, which when he looked back upon them may have seemed like an enchanted age, he sailed from Port Louis in command of *La Seine,* a *flute* or cargo vessel, north to the Seychelles, to complete the existing charts of those islands and reorganize the twenty-odd settlers who had been there for five years trying to establish a French colony. He did what he could, and then sailed on to India, to the French-controlled port of Pondicherry and other outposts of what remained of French power in India. He was gone for ten months, then back on the Ile de France for five.

He was in his thirties. He could see no immediate prospect of promotion, and his distance from France, in a remote, unprofitable colony in the Indian Ocean, offered little hope of advancement. Letters from his family, waiting for him when he returned from India, urged him to come back to France, of course, and his father's anxiety to have him properly and advantageously married was growing more persistent. It was eighteen years since he had set out for Brest and a career in the navy, and now, in Victor-Joseph's mind it was time for him to come home and take up the family concerns that he had been born for. But ten months away in command of his own vessel and of unfamiliar situations had not dimmed Eléonore's presence in his mind and feelings. Seeing her again, in his days and evenings on the island, deepened his attachment, though a recurrent strain of guilt may have troubled his new sense of self-determination, his love of the island and of Eléonore.

He was in no doubt that it was Eléonore he loved. He asked her to marry him and she accepted his proposal. Though it was said locally that she had first refused him and when he persisted she had said that her elder sister, Elizabeth, was in love with him, and that she could not hurt her sister by taking away from her the man she loved most. According to that story, Jean-Francois went at once to call on Elizabeth, who, when she realized how deeply he loved her sister, withdrew. Jean-Francois then approached Eléonore's father, Abraham Broudou, who accepted the idea at once and Jean-Francois and Eléonore were engaged.

Then he was sent on another voyage to India. When he came back to Port Louis and Eléonore he was thirty-four and things had happened in the world that would change his life. Louis XV had died, and Louis XVI had been crowned at the age of twenty. And at Lexington, in the American colonies, the shot had been fired that was heard round the world. He was certain about his feelings for Eléonore, and though he wrote nothing about them to his father, in a letter to his sister (which his father was sure to see) he confessed "I am a little in love with a young person from this island, and this could well end in a marriage, but nothing has been decided yet."

In the following year he was sent to Madagascar as part of an expedition to shore up a failing attempt at French colonization there, an enterprise that had been undertaken by an adventurous character of Hungarian birth named Maurice-Auguste-Aladar, Baron Benyowski, son of an Austrian general. Benyowski had a wild, and finally hapless history, and so did the colony. The old vessel on which La Pérouse had sailed there, the *Iphigénie,* was in such disrepair, leaked so badly and sailed so slowly that her proposed date of return to Port Louis passed and receded, and she was given up for lost before she finally made it back. There, La Pérouse learned that his patron and superior, Ternay, was planning to resign as governor and return to France. Within a week, Jean-Francois had to pack up his belongings and board Ternay's vessel. His marriage plans too had run into serious trouble by then. His sister had let his mother know what he had said in his letter, and the news had reached Victor-Joseph who had reacted immediately, writing to Ternay to appoint him Jean-Francois' official guardian and asserting his objection to any marriage that might be considered inappropriate for a naval officer. He gave Ternay no more choice than Jean-Francois himself.

But Jean-Francois and Eléonore did not give up hope. Eléonore's mother had gone back to Nantes, and two weeks after La Pérouse sailed with Ternay, Eléonore too sailed for France. They both hoped, apparently, that Jean-Francois' words and Eléonore's charms would be able to win Victor-Joseph around if he was confronted with them face to face.

As soon as La Pérouse and Ternay reached France they set out for Paris to report. La Pérouse was at once promoted to lieutenant and made a Knight of the Order of St. Louis, and when his letter of acknowledgment bluntly pointed out how long it had taken for these distinctions to reach him, he was awarded a pay raise of three hundred livres a year in recognition of his services in Indian waters.

He was eager to travel to Albi and enlist his mother's and his sisters' efforts in bringing his father to agree to his marrying Eléonore, but he was kept at Versailles for the time being, where the French talked happily about the troubles the English were having in America. Benjamin Franklin was in Paris acting as the American ambassador. There was warm sympathy for the American cause. Beaumarchais and others arranged to send supplies to the colonists, and Lafayette, cheered on by most of the court, had sailed for America to join Washington.

La Pérouse had been in France for three months, with Eléonore waiting at her mother's house in Nantes, before Ternay gave him leave to go to Albi. It had been five years since he had last seen the house at Go. His father was in his seventies, and had gone blind, and he felt the end of his life approaching, while his son still had not followed his wishes to assure the future of the family, by marrying someone of Victor-Joseph's choosing. The tensions between him and Jean-Francois must have been present from the start, and probably no time was lost before bringing up the subject of marriage. Jean-Francois knew that Eléonore, besides the long wait and the uncertainty after her voyage to France, had not been well for a while, and he may have been in no mood to have her situation dismissed. And his father had already written to him to say what he thought of Jean-Francois' idea of the person he wanted to marry.

"You make me tremble, my son," he had said. "You are cold-bloodedly contemplating the consequences of a marriage that would disgrace you in the eyes of the Minister and cause you to lose the protection of powerful friends! You display contempt for the opinions of your friends; you will lose, along with the rewards of twenty years' work, the esteem that you have gained, and would seem to have deserved through the elevation of your feelings. We had felt proud of that, but by lowering yourself you would bring humiliation on your entire family and those related to you. You are laying up nothing but regrets for us. You are sacrificing your fortune and the responsibility of your condition to the frivolous beauty and so-called attractions which may exist only in your imagination."

And where, he asked, would this woman live? In what house? In what carriage would she be driven? Besides, the Broudous would not be able to provide a dowry. It was all very well for Jean-Francois to argue that M. de la Jonquière and others of the nobility had married Creoles, "but what those may have lacked with regard to their birth was made up for by their fortune. Without this to redress the balance they would not have demeaned themselves by marrying them. . . . The laws of honor and probity do not oblige you to hold to ill-considered engagements which you may have made with this person or her parents. Do you not know, or do they not know, that you are subject to me, that you are not free, and that whatever you may have promised is not binding?" Victor-Joseph suggested other women whom he considered acceptable. While he was in Albi Jean-Francois made it plain that he was not interested, and he went back to Paris.

Once again France was on the verge of a war with England. Washington had defeated Burgoyne at Saratoga, and England was startled to realize that she had a new and redoubtable enemy. Lafayette had been wounded at Brandywine and wrote letters to France from his bed, where he was nursed by Mrs. Beckel and her pretty daughter. He urged his friends to come to the assistance of the Americans. He even wrote to the Minister of State, Maurepas, proposing that the French join the Americans to fight the English "under the American flag."

La Pérouse was sent back to Brest to prepare for war in the Atlantic. The English planned to fight mostly at sea. Their main objective was to defeat France. They intended to use troops merely to maintain footholds on the American coast. They underestimated, even at that point, the determination of Washington and the Americans, and their concern with the French distracted them from the colonial Revolution. In 1778 France recognized the new American government.

La Pérouse, who still had not seen Eléonore since he sailed from the Ile de France, was given command of a small, wretched corvette with fourteen guns, the *Serin,* and a crew so poorly trained that none of the sailors had ever handled a gun. He sailed off the French coast for three weeks, reporting that "I cannot sight an English frigate from my top-mast without being sure that I will be taken unless I am very close to a port."

Then he was allowed a month's leave and a chance, finally, to go to Nantes to see Eléonore. He was recalled to St. Malo and given command of a new frigate, the *Amazone,* still being outfitted. When she was ready he sailed into the North Sea with two other French warships, and they captured a dozen English vessels in one short cruise. Next he sailed with a convoy to the West Indies, under Toussaint-Guillaume de La Motte-Picquet, one of the finest veteran commanders in the French navy. La Pérouse was present when the French defeated Admiral Byron off Grenada on July 6, 1779, which crucially diverted the English blockade off the American coast. In August, sailing north from the Caribbean in a battle fleet, the *Amazone* engaged in a fight with a British frigate and captured it, and then sailed back across the Atlantic to Cadiz, then to France to report to Ternay, and on to Versailles to give an account of the war in the Caribbean. He was allowed a brief visit with Eléonore, in Nantes, on his way back to Brest.

After that he was off once more, his vessel part of the escort of a large French convoy sailing to join Washington's army. They landed in Newport and La Pérouse was sent back to France to request reinforcements. He was back again, off the coast of Canada, when the

English general Corvallis, surrounded at Yorktown by a French fleet and cut off on land by Washington, surrendered, and the American part of the war was over.

The French, however, were still fighting the English, and La Pérouse was sent to join the fleet of Admiral de Grasse in the Caribbean, and was there at the Battle of the Saints, on April 12, 1782, when a trick of the wind led to a decisive defeat of the French and gave the English naval superiority in the Atlantic.

At that point, La Pérouse was given charge of a kind of end-run expedition that had long been planned: a midsummer raid of the English outposts in Hudson Bay. For the expedition he commanded a fine vessel, the *Sceptre*. The English, however, had managed to keep all charts and navigational details of the region to themselves, and when the raid was over La Pérouse wrote to his mother, "I must tell you that I had neither a chart nor a pilot. No French person in the last hundred years has been within a thousand miles of that bay . . . and today when I have almost made it back from there, I can swear that they were justified in thinking that no one would come so far to find them."

He sailed to the bay with two companion vessels, one of them, the *Astrée*, commanded by his friend Fleuriot de Langle, who would accompany him in the same capacity on his great voyage of circumnavigation a few years later.

The need for secrecy and the danger of spies tipping off the English that they were being equipped for cold weather kept the French from being issued winter clothes, and as they sailed north they began to feel the need of them. In June, off Labrador, they ran into banks of fog. There were icebergs on all sides of them and as they approached Baffin Island the ice pack closed around them. They disembarked on the ice and met Eskimos who sold them fur clothing in which they climbed the rigging "looking like bears."

They sailed across the bay, received the surrender of the Prince of Wales Fort and made friends with the fort's commander, whom they allowed to sail back to England. They seized the furs, and blew up the fort. Then they went on to take Fort York, the other English outpost. At the end of August an English pilot from there guided them out of the bay. But sickness overtook the crews. Seventy men died on the way back to Europe and another four hundred were seriously ill.

The war was virtually over. The French did not do well in the peace negotiations. They lost Canada, but they gained an ally in the new American nation.

*   *   *

Eléonore was still living in Nantes with her mother part of the time, and part of the time with an aunt in Brest. La Pérouse had not dared to marry her in defiance of his father's angry reaction. Faced with that, he had not taken Eléonore to Alibi.

When he got back to Europe, Eléonore had been waiting six years, and La Pérouse learned that his father had picked out someone else for him to marry. Feeling helpless and guilty, Jean-Francois tried to submit dutifully to his father's demands. The young woman was Mlle. de Vésian, almost twenty-five years younger than he was, a daughter of a family of distinguished nobility in Albi. Victor-Joseph had arranged the preliminaries, and had bought a house for the couple to live in (next door to the house where Toulouse-Lautrec would be born). Obediently, Jean-Francois wrote to the girl's family saying that he was willing to marry the young woman his father had chosen, but pointing out that he scarcely knew her, insisting that he would marry her only if that was what she herself wanted, and declaring openly that he had been in love with someone else. He authorized his own mother to tell the de Vésian family of his "former loves." "I was only thirty," he said. "My heart has always been a novel . . . and I hope that I shall soon be free." Evidently he was trying to persuade himself that he could go through with it, while giving the family every chance to call it off. To his sister he wrote, "I have a deep sorrow."

He travelled to Paris. Eléonore was living there too, then, as a boarder in a convent. His mother wrote from Albi in her husband's name (since he was blind) asking Jean-Francois not to see Eléonore, and he agreed, at least for the moment. He wrote again to the de Vésians, listing more reasons why they, or their daughter, might find the proposed marriage less than ideal. For one thing, he said, the young woman would have to spend a great deal of time at the Galaup house, since he would probably be away for long periods. He was squirming. But he wrote to Eléonore asking her to free him from his promise to marry her, and offering her twenty thousand livres—an enormous sum for a person in his position—to provide her with a dowry.

She answered that she did not want any money from him, and that if he did not any longer want to marry her she would not hold him to his promise but would enter a convent. She did not want any other man in her life.

With that, she had won. He hurried to her. After so long without having seen each other, all the old feeling welled up in them. He wrote to his mother the next day, "I had spent twenty days in Paris, and kept my promise to you not to go and see her. . . . I received a tear-stained letter without a single reproach but filled with deep suffering. . . . At once the veil was torn away . . . my situation filled me with horror. I was a liar, not worthy of Mlle. de Vésian to whom I was bringing a heart gnawed with remorse and worn by a passion that nothing could extinguish, and unworthy of Mlle. Broudou, whom I have been weak enough to want to abandon. My excuse, dear Mother, is the deep desire I have always had to please you; it was for you alone, and for my father, that I wished to marry Mlle. de Vésian. . . . I can only belong to Eléonore. I hope you will give your consent."

Ternay, his guardian, who conceivably might still have stood in his way, was dead. On July 8, 1783, La Pérouse married Eléonore in the church of Ste Marguerite in Paris, not with a great family ceremony but with the requisite number of witnesses. In the following month he took Eléonore to Albi, and the family put on a great show of celebration, including a nuptial Mass in the cathedral. They had to make it seem as though they welcomed her, and in the end she herself was so modest and gentle that she seems to have charmed them. The women may never have been a problem. And Victor-Joseph—who knows?

His father had predicted the disgrace that such a marriage would bring upon Jean-Francois and the family, and indeed La Pérouse still lacked the permission of his superior at the Ministry, de Castries, for his marriage. He wrote to de Castries from Go, "The great kindness you have shown me requires me to make a confession which I address, not to the King's minister but to the Marshal de Castries: I am married and have taken my wife to the Languedoc. My story is a novel which I beg you to be so good as to read. . . . Eight years ago on the Ile de France I fell madly in love with a very beautiful and charming girl. I wanted to marry her. She had no money. The Chevalier de Ternay objected . . ." and he told about bowing to his father's wishes, love receding, his parents arranging for him to marry someone else, his moves to break with Eléonore, the outcome, with love conquering at last.

The reply from Castries was not all the kind of thing his father had predicted. The Marshal answered at once, "I will always feel more favorable toward this kind of union than to one that our customs allow to be dictated by self interest. Enjoy the happiness of making someone else happy, and the tokens of honor and distinction you have received from your fellow citizens. You have deserved them, and as a former citizen of Albi, I join in them with all my heart."

And yet, after all those years, his father's stamp on Jean-Francois' sense of what he could decide for himself could not be shaken off so easily. When he wrote to de Castries with his news, the habit of being his father's son may have had something to do with his saying, "I have brought my wife to my elderly mother. . . . But I have agreed with her to make amends in the Service, and I am ready, My Lord, to go around the world for six years if you order it." To *make amends?* The idea may have come from talks he had had in Paris with his friend at the Ministry, Claret de Fleurieu. The idea for the voyage of circumnavigation may already have been in the air. La Pérouse may have been anxious not to risk the chance of losing a major part in it. Yet the unnecessary compensatory reference to it during that brief moment of hard-won happiness has a fateful ring. It is as though he could not believe that he would ever be able to earn his father's blessing and the right to be happy.

His offer to Castries seems even more needless if (as John Dunmore suggests in his biography of La Pérouse, *Pacific Explorer)* the Ministry had known of his marriage before it took place, and had approved, and the exchange of letters had been largely or entirely for the benefit of old Victor-Joseph. The proposed long voyage may already have been discussed in Paris too, so that Jean-Francois was simply referring to something already agreed upon. Absence, the looming approach of having to leave what he loved, must have hung over Jean-Francois whenever he was at Go, ever since his preparations to go off into the navy when he was fourteen. The sense of it must have ached more painfully and deeply this time than ever, since he was leaving Eléonore there as well. He went back to active service in October, after three months of marriage.

* * *

He spent the fall and winter in Lorient and at the Ministry in Paris, while Eléonore waited again, in Albi now, with his family He wanted her to be with him—and indeed, why was she not? There were exciting things going on in Paris, which they might have watched together— the Montgolfier brothers, hot air balloons, the first performance of Beaumarchais' *Le Marriage de Figaro.* Jean-Francois travelled to Albi when he had a chance to, and Eléonore seemed happy there.

In Paris the plans for the great French voyage of circumnavigation were taking shape, but La Pérouse complained, in a letter to a friend, about not being able to spend time in Albi. "It is not natural," he wrote, "for a married man to leave his own country for five or six years without having a few months to put his affairs in order." But the actual plans dragged on, and in February 1785 he wrote to Eléonore, "Nothing is decided . . . and I am wasting time and money far from what I love."

By the end of that month he was certain of the nature and scope of the plans and of his own place in them, and he wrote to tell Eléonore. The ships were being fitted out, with Cook's example in mind in their choice and preparations. Two store ships were sheathed in copper, re-commissioned as frigates, and given new names: the *Boussole* (or Compass), which would be the vessel on which La Pérouse would sail, and the *Astrolabe*, which would be commanded by his friend Paul-Antoine Fleuriot de Langle, who had commanded a companion ship in his raid into Hudson Bay.

The proposed itinerary was laid out, giving La Pérouse freedom to alter it as he went, as circumstances arose. It was based on a consideration of how much of the geography of the Pacific still remained unknown to the European world, and the route that seemed appropriate for exploring it. On June 28 he had his audience with the King, at which the itinerary and general intent of the expedition were discussed. On the following day he was taken to meet Marie-Antoinette. And on the first of July his orders sent him to Brest, with no arrangements made and no time allotted for him to see Eléonore to say good-bye.

At one point that summer she thought she was pregnant, but that turned out not to be so.

She would not see him again.

The elaborate outfitting of the vessels continued all summer. They were provided with every foreseeable need, and their cargo included seeds, trees, and shrubs to be given to the populations they expected to visit. They had with them a supply of gifts of other kinds, from medals with the King's profile on them to a thousand pairs of scissors. The ships were so tightly loaded that a hundred sacks of flour and many crates of biscuits were finally left behind. The main deck was crowded with animals: five cows were tied to the mainmast, thirty sheep were penned in the longboat, two hundred hens in cages aft. Fish hung in nets from the rigging, drying. As the moment for departure drew near, La Pérouse wrote to a friend, Mme. de St. Géry, about "the sacrifices of the heart." But he said, "I will do whatever I can to make sure that the inhabitants of the islands whom we may meet will never regret having received us."

The vessels were towed out into the channel on July 11 to sit for two weeks waiting for the wind. At last on August 1 they put to sea, shouting "Long Live the King!"

* * *

Among the many things we do not know at all about the expedition, and about La Pérouse himself, is what was in his mind at that moment, besides the attention to the immediate details of the departure. He was aware that he would not see Eléonore for four years (if he ever saw her again) and that the old ogre, his father, and his long-suffering mother might not be alive by the time of his projected return. The great ambition underlying the venture in which he was the leading actor had claimed him entirely and he had welcomed it, apparently without a moment's hesitation, as though he had no other life, and no choice, and perhaps indeed he had none. As he sailed, just the same, it may have occurred to him with an instant of shock—immediately suppressed as unseamanlike, or ascribed to the excitement of being under way—how completely the enterprise, and his life now, were dedicated to the unknown. Maybe no flicker of doubt entered his mind.

The portraits depicting him in those months before the expedition sailed look slightly ridiculous. A plump figure, short, slightly pompous in the fashion of the time, decent and ordinary. There is little evidence in the paintings of the determined, patient strength of character, the sound judgment and steady command of himself and others that we find in his writings and his achievements—in the things we do seem to know about him.

* * *

Two weeks after they left Brest they dropped anchor at Madeira, then at Tenerife in the Canaries, and then continued across the Atlantic and down the coast of South America, through the last of the summer, and the autumn, to the Falkland Islands (where Bougainville had tried to set up a colony for French refugees from Arcadia whom the English had deported from their homes in Nova Scotia) and then, late in the winter, on to the Horn and north to Chile. The shakedown phase of the expedition had been a success. No sickness on either vessel. La Pérouse wrote, "We had taken the greatest care to make sure that sprits remained high by having the crew dance every evening, weather permitting, between eight and ten."

Then from Chile to Easter Island and Maui.

* * *

From Hawai'i they sailed north and within a week were deep in fog. Another two weeks and they saw the snowy peaks of Mt. St. Elias, which marked the arena of the ruthless torment and devastation of fur-bearing animals begun by the Russians in mid-century, then continued by the Spaniards and English. Cook had claimed the coast in 1778 and charted parts of it.

At the beginning of July they found a bay that was on no chart. La Pérouse thought that probably no Europeans had ever sighted it. It provided a wide, sheltered anchorage, but the way into it was narrow and dangerous, with a winding channel and rocks just under the surface. Writing about their entrance once they were inside, he said, "Never in my thirty years at sea have I seen two ships so close to being destroyed." Yet he thought at first that the place might make a fine trading post for the French, and named it Port des Français (now Lituya Bay). The vessels stayed there for a month and the scientists had a chance to examine the flora and fauna and geology of the place, and the men replenished the vessels, water and firewood. They had been away from France for almost a year.

Because the entrance to the bay was so hazardous, as they were about to leave La Pérouse sent two boats ahead to sound the channel, which had a dangerous bar, and a tide-race between the rocks. La Pérouse repeatedly warned Charles-Gabriel D'Escure, the officer in charge of the boats, to keep his distance from the rocks, until D'Escure asked him whether La Pérouse took him for a child. But the boats went too close, were snatched by the tide-race and flipped over, and were lost within minutes, with six officers and fifteen men.

In the proposed itinerary he had been asked to look for the long-sought northwest passage, but it had not taken long for him to see how huge a task it would be to explore the whole coast of Alaska. He had profound doubts about the existence of any such passage. They sailed slowly south, mapping and taking observations as they went, constantly impeded by fog and low cloud. He wanted to complete Cook's survey of the coast. He continued charting along the Oregon coast, when the fog did not prevent it, and on south as far as Monterey, where they anchored, in mid-September, to stay for ten days.

The fur trade was a prominent enterprise of the place. The governor had received instructions to get all the otter skins he could. His goal was to supply thirty thousand skins to the China market. To La Pérouse, California looked like a paradise. The Spaniards were endlessly hospitable, and when he sailed, on September 23, the vessels were loaded with "an infinity of vegetables."

* * *

He headed west across the Pacific and after his near-escape at French Frigate Shoals travelled on to the Marianas.

Relations between the scientists on board and the officers had been strained and abrasive from the beginning. They grumbled, understandably, about shipboards' conditions and they were vexed by the brevity of some of the landings and the limitations on their field trips. It would be hard for anyone to endure a hundred days at a time at sea, in uncomfortable close quarters, much of the time in enforced idleness, with seamless patience. At the island of Tenerife, one of their first stops, the Chevalier de Lamanon wanted to climb the great volcanic peak, and resented it when he was told that the expedition would not pay for a mule train to take him up there. La Pérouse wrote about the argument to Fleurieu, saying that Lamanon "is a man who is full of zeal but as ignorant as a monk about everything except systematic physics. He thinks he knows better than M. Buffon how the world was formed. . . . there isn't a fifteen year old girl in Paris who does not know more about the globe than this doctor who has kept looking for the tropic with his spyglass ever since the student pilots told him that it could be seen from a hundred leagues away."

By mid-December the tensions between La Pérouse and the scientists broke into the open. After a brief stop in the Marianas the frigates sailed on to Macao, the entrance port to China, where they found forty-one foreign ships at anchor, and where La Pérouse was welcomed by the Portuguese governor, whom he had met twelve years before in India. Several of the scientists took lodgings in town, without giving him their addresses. A few threatened to leave the expedition and stay in China. In the end, La Pérouse had them brought back to the ships and they were placed under arrest for twenty-four hours.

* * *

His instructions called for another trek north, on the western side of the Pacific. He took on ten Chinese sailors to help replace the men lost in Alaska, and in February sailed to Manila, to have the vessels overhauled there in the port of Cavite. While they were there they picked up stomach parasites and lost one officer to dysentery.

In early April he sailed north to Formosa and Japan, though he had been warned of the monsoons, which were due to continue well into May. He had got away from the parasites of the Philippines, but the winds slowed him and it took him two weeks to reach Formosa. The weather remained hostile and the Chinese were landing troops to put down a rebellion on the island. La Pérouse said he had never seen seas as heavy as those in the channel to the west of Formosa, and he turned back and sailed up the east coast of the island to the Korea Strait and the Sea of Japan. Neither the Koreans nor the Japanese welcomed foreigners. He kept on northward, charting the coasts of Korea and Japan when he could. Once again they were hampered by fog. They managed to measure the width of the Sea of Japan, but they did not risk a landing.

They sailed on north to the site of the present-day Vladivostok, the land known as Tartary, and to dense fog once more. It was a region that Cook had never seen. In the third week in June they found an anchorage on the coast. They saw deer, bears, and a tomb beside a stream with two human bodies wrapped in bearskins. There were tools and a bag of rice beside them. They stayed there four days and then sailed farther north through the Strait of Tartary to Sakhalin where they had an amiable meeting with the inhabitants. When they sailed on, the strait grew shallow and they could find no safe channel, so they turned south again, turned the corner of Sakhalin and sailed across the Sea of Kamchatka to anchor at Petropavlovsk, the only town in Kamchatka, at the end of August. The landscape was bleak, but the hundred or so residents—forty soldiers in the garrison, a few native people, and Russians serving out terms of exile—were friendly.

They had expected mail at Macao but there had been none there. They had hoped to find some waiting for them at Kamchatka too, but there was none. Then a few days after they got there a courier arrived with mail. La Pérouse had been promoted to commodore. And de Castries sent word that the English were said to be starting a settlement in New South Wales, and asked La Pérouse to find out what he could about it. This would mean a change from the route they had planned. On September 28 he wrote to de Castries that he would sail at once for Botany Bay, avoiding the dangerous waters around the Solomons and New Hebrides that had been part of the original itinerary.

He entrusted his reports, letters, journals, and the other letters from the company, to twenty-one-year-old Barthélémy de Lesseps, who was with them as their Russian interpreter. He had grown up partly in St. Petersburg, where his father had been the French

Consul-General. De Lesseps was to carry these documents overland across Siberia and the rest of Russia, in winter, then in the spring thaw and the summer, to St. Petersburg and on to Paris. His journey, which took over a year, is a saga of its own. The decision to send the journals by land, and from Kamchatka, had a precedent in Cook's voyages. After Cook's death in 1779, the news and Cook's journals had been sent from there, overland, to St. Petersburg and London. As La Pérouse gave de Lesseps the last letters and journals snow was already falling and it was time to head south. They sailed on September 30, 1787. By the time de Lesseps reached Paris La Pérouse and his expedition had vanished.

*   *   *

The cold gave way to the heat of the tropics. They headed for Australia.

*   *   *

Their first stop on the way south was in the islands of Samoa. It was two years and two months since they had set out from Brest, and La Pérouse and his crew were worn down by months at sea. The vessels, sails, and rigging were in urgent need of repairs. They needed fresh water, fresh vegetables and food. On December 6, 1787, they anchored off Tutuila.

On New Year's Day of that year the Chevalier de Lamanon, physician to the expedition, had written, "what will always distinguish this voyage and will be the glory of the French nation in the eyes of philosophers, our contemporaries and posterity, will be to have frequented peoples who are reputed to be barbarians without having shed a drop of blood "

The best anchorage they could find, off Tutuila, offered little protection from the sea, and they did not plan to stay long, but a fleet of dugouts had come out to greet them with pigs and fruit to barter, and La Pérouse and de Langle agreed to send shore parties to barter for food and to fill the water barrels. La Pérouse proposed to weigh anchor and sail on as soon as they got back to the ships. He went with two armed longboats to a small bay slightly upwind of their anchorage. There were some two hundred natives in the village there, and they were persuaded to sit down under the cocoanut trees with their chickens and pigs and piles of fruit and vegetables and conduct a reasonably orderly market, with the women, some of whom, La Pérouse said, were very pretty, offering their favors to anyone who would give them beads. Europeans, La Pérouse noted, have no defense against such attacks, and the French least of all. Men whom he assumed were chiefs restored order.

There was a single occurrence that seemed hostile. A native had climbed into one of the boats and picked up a mallet with which he began to beat a sailor. La Pérouse wrote that he had wanted to resolve the matter without bloodshed, and he had ordered four men to pick up the Indian and throw him overboard, which they did, and that seemed to end the problem. The other islanders, La Pérouse wrote, appeared to disapprove of the man's behavior, and the incident went no further.

But he noted that the Samoans were taller than the French, and extremely massive and strong, and obviously were unimpressed by the physical endowments of the Europeans. In order to give them some idea of the power the French had at their disposal he bought three pigeons, released them, and the soldiers shot them in mid-air with the villagers watching.

But the encounter on the whole was peaceful. La Pérouse went to visit the nearby village set in a grove of fruit trees, the houses arranged in a circle, with a beautiful green in the middle. Women, children, old people walked along with him and invited him into their houses, spreading finely woven mats on the floor in front of him. He entered the most attractive of them and was amazed at the beauty of the architectural design and the skill of the construction "as well executed as any in the neighborhood of Paris."

He marvelled too at the abundance of the islands, the fertility of the soil, the plentiful fruits, pigs, chickens, the nearby fish in the sea.

"They were so rich," he wrote, "that they scorned the iron tools and clothes we offered them, and were interested only in beads. They had more than they needed of practical things and were interested only in useless things."

In the market, the people sold them more than two hundred pigeons so tame that they preferred to eat from the hand, and doves and parrakeets as tame as the pigeons. "These islanders," he wrote, "we kept saying to each other, are the most fortunate people on earth. With their wives and children around them they drift peacefully through pure tranquil days, with no other care than bringing up their birds and picking, without further effort, the fruit growing above their heads." But they noticed that the men's bodies were covered with scars, the evidence of frequent warfare and disputes, and the men's faces had a fierceness quite unlike the women's expressions.

And there had been a few more, relatively minor, run-ins with the men. Someone had thrown stones at M. Rollin, the surgeon, and one native, while admiring the engineer Paul de Monneron's saber, had tried to snatch it out of its sheath and run off with it.

When the water butts and food had been loaded onto the longboats they sailed back to the *Boussole*, around noon, and La Pérouse was relieved to think that there had been no real trouble ashore. They could hardly board their own frigate for the native canoes massed around it. He had left an officer on board with orders to allow a few islanders on board at a time, or to keep them off entirely as he saw fit. La Pérouse found seven or eight Samoans on the foredeck. He thought the eldest of them must be the chief. The officer whom he had left in charge said that nothing but shooting would have kept the natives from boarding. They were so much bigger than the French that they utterly ignored any attempts to restrain them physically. They laughed at threats and simply pushed the guards aside, and "knowing my principles of moderation," La Pérouse wrote, "he had not wanted to resort to violence, which alone would have held them back." And once the chief had come aboard, the others had quieted down and been less insolent.

La Pérouse gave the chief many presents and tried to express good will in every way he could think of. He provided a display of the French weapons, which appeared to leave the chief unimpressed: He seemed to believe the guns were merely for shooting birds. The water barrels were stowed and the frigate was made ready to sail.

In the meantime de Langle had gone in a smaller boat to another bay downwind, at some distance from the watering party and out of sight of the frigates. He came back enchanted by the beauty of the village he had found, its waterfall of crystal water, and the friendly inhabitants. He agreed with La Pérouse that the anchorage was unsafe and that they should sail on, but he wanted to return to the village to fill the remaining barrels at the waterfall. La Pérouse said they had no need of more water, but de Langle cited Cook's opinion that fresh water was always to be preferred to what was already in the hold. On his own vessel he had a few slight cases of scurvy and wanted to do what he could to cure them. And he said he had never seen an island like this one for the sheer abundance of everything.

Yet La Pérouse felt what he called a secret apprehension. He said he had found the people there too "turbulent" for him to want to risk sending a shore party to a place out of sight of the frigates, where they would have no protection from the ships' guns. Up until that point, he argued, the attempts by the French to hold back the islanders, based only on physical restraint, had merely made the natives bolder.

But de Langle argued that if he were denied this chance for fresh water, and the scurvy got worse, La Pérouse would be responsible. The two men had sailed together for a long time in difficult and dangerous places from the Canadian Arctic and Hudson Bay to the Pacific, and La Pérouse respected de Langle's experience and judgment. He gave in, despite his misgivings, agreeing to spend the night offshore, and wait while de Langle took a party ashore for water the next morning. Their anchorage was precarious and they prepared to move further offshore for the night. When they weighed anchor they found that the coral had sawed part way through one of the cables.

The night was wild and stormy. They moved closer to shore again in the morning, but the anchorage they found was still out of sight of the bay where de Langle wanted to take the boats. Those who were to go on the shore party included the few who were beginning to suffer from scurvy, among them the physician, the Chevalier de Lamanon. There were, in all, sixty-one in the boats and they included, La Pérouse wrote "the elite of our company." He reassured himself as best he could, as he waited. De Langle was taking more than twenty barrels to refill.

One of those who went ashore with de Langle, Jerome de Vaujuas, left a first-hand narrative of what happened. M. de Langle had thought the bay he had found, which the two longboats and two smaller boats were heading for, was preferable to the place where La Pérouse had gone with his boats, partly because there had been fewer natives there, the day before. But once his own boats started for the shore they saw, to their dismay, that many of the dugouts that had been clustered around the ships were following them toward the bay and that many other natives were lining the rocks along the shore and more were gathering, coming along the trails through the forest.

When he had been to the bay the day before it had been at high tide, and the boat had beached far up on the sand and shingle. In the morning the tide was out and still ebbing. De Langle was surprised to see that the tides were so high, there in the islands. The way in to the beach was a narrow channel cutting through the reef. It was not deep enough for the boats to pass through. Half a musket shot from shore they could move forward only by digging their oars in to the bottom, and that was with the barrels empty. By the time they got the boats as close to shore as they could, seven or eight hundred natives had gathered around the bay. Some of them threw into the sea several branches of the kava plant, from which, as Vaujuas knew "they make their narcotic drink." He, and presumably de Langle, recognized that this was a gesture of welcome. It may have been a crucial, ceremonial moment to which none of them knew how to respond properly, or it may have been an offering representing only a faction among the hundreds who had gathered around their arrival. The shore party may have given offense at that moment without knowing it, or may have contributed to a dissension among those who had assembled to wait for them, or something about their return itself may have been an offense in the eyes of many of the onlookers.

Each boat was left guarded by one soldier and one sailor and the rest of the party waded ashore, the crew taking the barrels to fill them and bringing them back, all quite peacefully. Some of the women offered themselves to the visitors "and their advances were not universally rejected" (though we are left to guess where or in what circumstances they could have been accepted, in a crowd, on a hurried work detail engaged in muscling twenty-some barrels ashore and back to the boats again).

While they were struggling to load the barrels more natives arrived and some of them grew provocative, so that de Langle abandoned his original plan of bargaining for more food, and ordered his men to leave immediately. He paused to make a parting gift of beads to several of the Samoans he assumed to be chiefs, whom he had seen restraining the others, keeping them from crowding the French. However, "we were convinced," Vaujuas said, "that this restraint had been only for show, and that if these chiefs, or pretenders, exercised any real authority it was only over a very few." Giving them presents apparently displeased some of the others. A crowd made plain their annoyance and it was impossible to hold them back. Yet they did not try to keep the French from boarding the boats, though some of them followed alongside into the sea, and others on the shore started to pick up rocks.

The boats were drawn up at some distance from the shore line. The French had to wade in up to their waists in the surf to climb over the gunwales. Some got their muskets wet. Once they were aboard de Langle ordered them to cast off and take up the grapnel and at that point several of the biggest Samoans took hold of the cable to keep them from getting away and others started throwing rocks at the men in the boats. The captain fired a warning shot in the air but instead of checking them it acted as the signal for a general attack. A hail of rocks began to strike those in the boats. Those who had firearms shot at the assailants who were trying to climb aboard, and they downed a few, but others came on in numbers and the murderous rain of rocks continued, and there was no chance to reload the muskets that were still dry. The French who were struck by rocks and fell into the water were immediately clubbed to death.

One of the first to be killed was de Langle himself. The natives mobbed both longboats, killing those who were in them with rocks and clubs. A few of the French escaped by swimming to the smaller boats which the natives were ignoring. Vaujuas had leapt into the water and reached one of the smaller boats. He watched the massacre helplessly. Both of the smaller boats got away. They brought away no officers, and almost everyone on board had been injured by rocks. Most of the natives stayed behind to plunder the longboats and the bodies of the victims, but one canoe sailed past the boats to warn the natives around the frigates, and as they passed they shouted insults. Vaujuas reported the terrible news to La Pérouse. "If the passion for pillaging had not held them, distracting the savages from their fury, none of us would have escaped," he wrote later.

This disaster, he said, vividly recalling that of July 13, 1786, in Alaska, poured bitterness on the whole expedition. When the news reached de Langle's vessel, the *Astrolabe,* there were natives on board who did not know what had happened. It was only with the greatest difficulty that the crew was kept from taking vengeance upon them.

"Everyone who was there," Vaujuas wrote finally, "can bear witness that no violence and no imprudence on our part preceded the savages' attack."

La Pérouse wrote that when the boats came back at five o'clock with the news the frigates were surrounded by native canoes bartering food with an assurance that proved their innocence. He realized that they must be brothers, children, compatriots of the barbarous assassins, "and I confess it took all my reason to contain my anger and keep our crew from slaughtering them. The soldiers immediately picked up their weapons, and some had rushed to the cannons." La Pérouse restrained them, and fired a single cannon shot loaded only with powder, to warn the canoes away from the frigates.

On the following day he considered sending in another party to recover what might be left of the longboats and to avenge those who had been killed—twelve had died, and many others had been injured, some so seriously that they would die of their wounds. Altogether, thirty-two members of the expedition were out of service. Charles Boutin, one of the survivors, explained how impractical, and how suicidal it would be to try another landing. La Pérouse cruised back and forth off the mouth of the bay for two days, in close enough to be able to see the remains of the longboats on the shore, and crowds of natives around them.

And during those two days half a dozen canoes came out with pigs and pigeons and cocoanuts for sale. Each time, he said, he had to restrain an impulse to order them sunk. When they saw that the French did not fire at them but would not trade with them, they started to shout insults, and more canoes were seen coming to join them. It seemed plain to La Pérouse that the natives had some idea of the range of the muskets but no idea of the range of the cannons, and "as everything seemed to be warning me that I would soon be compelled to set aside my principles of moderation, I ordered a single cannon shot to be fired in among the canoes, and my orders were carried out precisely. The water thrown up by the ball splashed into the canoes and they hurried back to shore as fast as they could, and all the others with them." He had had the chance, he wrote, to act vengefully and fire on the massed canoes, but the victims would probably not have been those responsible for the massacre, and "the cry of my conscience spared their lives."

In calmer moments he believed that resorting to reprisals lowered one morally to the level of the original assailants. But again, he saw no reason to suppose that native peoples were basically any better behaved than Europeans, whose destructive impulses he knew very well. "I am a hundred times more angry at the philosophers who praise them (i.e. the 'Noble Savages') than at the savages themselves. Lamanon, whom they murdered, was saying the day before that they are nobler than we are."

Years later, Europeans visiting Samoa were told that Tutuilans had not been responsible for the attack. According to some of the Samoans, generations afterwards, Tutuila had been subject at that time to the neighboring island of Upolu, and it was men from Upolu who had started the battle. The origin of that story is not certain.

There are descendants of de Langle who are convinced that the reason he was so eager to return to A'asu—the name (which he may not have known) of the bay and the village—was not the crystal waterfall but a beautiful woman whom he had met on his first visit and whom he wanted to come and see again. Her husband, who was a high chief, had learned about their meeting, knew the reason for de Langle's return visit as soon as the boats left the frigates, and he was determined to prevent another meeting, and to punish the strangers for his humiliation. If there is any basis for this romantic story it is hard to understand why the French were allowed to fill and load their water barrels before the eyes of many hundreds of assembled men, even if there was division among the assembled Samoans. La Pérouse clearly did not seem to suspect any such tryst, either at the time or afterward when he returned to the painful memory, trying to come to terms with his having consented to de Langle's ill-fated shore party.

* * *

"It was hard to tear myself away," he wrote, "from the place that had filled us with misery, and to leave behind the bodies of our massacred companions. I lost an old friend, a man of great intelligence, judgment and knowledge, and one of the finest officers in the French navy." La Pérouse told himself at that point that if de Langle had acted as others might have done and fired a volley into the assailants at the first sign of serious belligerence it might have driven them off, and he wrote, "His own humanity was the cause of his death."

In his own journal the name of the place was Massacre Bay.

The Chevalier de Monti was put in command of the *Astrolabe*, to replace de Langle, and with the crews thus depleted, the longboats lost, the ships, sails and rigging in dangerously weakened condition after months of voyaging in all climates, they sailed west to other islands of the chain, bartered for provisions again, but kept the islanders they met at a distance with displays of firearms, and did not allow them on board. They paused to map the coasts of the islands they passed, where the charts were inadequate. But their spirits were low.

One of the navigators, Joseph Dagelet, wrote in his journal, "The last months of a voyage are, honestly, the hardest to endure. The body's resistance has been worn down. The food goes bad . . ." It rained constantly. Everything was soaked, above and below decks. The journal of La Pérouse betrays his own depression and fatigue. On New Year's Day, 1788, a year after Lamanon (killed at A'asu) had written so optimistically about an expedition that would not have shed a drop of blood, La Pérouse left the islands, those known and those still unknown to Europeans, and altered course for Botany Bay in Australia, which they reached twenty-four days later.

* * *

They approached the land with the wind shifting, and were swept southward constantly by powerful currents. La Pérouse noted that Cook had encountered the same currents there. They saw a low-lying shore, and as they came in closer they could make out something they had not seen since they left Manila: a fleet of English vessels at anchor.

"Europeans," La Pérouse wrote, "are all compatriots when they are that far from their own country" and the French were impatient to reach the anchorage, but the winds and currents held them offshore for three days. Captain Hunter, of the English frigate *Sirius*, sent a lieutenant and midshipman to welcome the French vessels and offer whatever services he could provide. But he then explained that he himself was on the point of leaving for the north, and so would not be able to furnish them with food or ammunition or sails. "So their offers of help were reduced to good wishes for the ultimate success of our voyage." La Pérouse sent an officer to Hunter "who already had his topsails rigged," to thank him.

It was obvious to them that the English were there to start a colony in the area. They learned that the commodore of the fleet had already left for somewhere to the north, with four transport vessels, to look for a more promising spot. The English were "very mysterious" about the commodore's plans, but the French believed that the place the commodore had in mind was not far away. La Pérouse could see longboats coming and going under sail, and judged that they were not going any great distance. Then a few of the English sailors let the secret out to some of the French crewmen. They were all sailing to Port Jackson, only a few miles up the coast, where Commodore Philip had found a good harbor. "In time," La Pérouse wrote, "one would have all too many chances to be aware of the English settlement. Deserters from it were a considerable nuisance and embarrassment to us." He was speaking of escaped convicts who caused trouble to both the English and the French. La Pérouse was careful to return those who tried to join the French.

His two frigates stayed at Botany Bay for over six weeks, with the English anchored just around the headland, ten miles away by land. The French crews set to work building two longboats to replace the ones they had lost at Tutuila. They had brought the parts with them from Brest, already shaped and numbered and ready to be assembled in the equipment of the expedition, ready for just such a situation. As they settled in and began work they built a palisade around their camp, against the "Indians." After Samoa, La Pérouse was not in a trusting mood with natives anywhere, and the ones there "threw spears at us after receiving our presents and caresses."

Father Receveur, a French priest who had accompanied the expedition, a gentle, quiet man, generally beloved, died on February 17. It was said that he died as a result of wounds received at A'asu, where a rock had nearly destroyed one of his eyes. He had sent a letter to his brother saying that he was nearly recovered and hoped to see him in France, in the spring. Ten days later he was dead.

At Botany Bay, La Pérouse entrusted his journals, and the letters he wrote there, to Lieutenant Shortland, the agent of the British fleet, who was planning to sail for Europe on July 14. Among his letters was one to the Maritime Minister, outlining his plans for the next, and final, phase of the expedition.

"I shall go up to the Friendly Islands and do just what my instructions require with regard to the southern part of New Caledonia, the island of Santa Cruz of Mendana, the south coats of Surville's Arsacides (now the Solomon Islands) and Bougainville's Louisiades, trying to make sure whether the latter are part of New Guinea or not. Toward the end of July, 1788, I shall sail between New Guinea and New Holland (now Australia) by a different channel than the one the *Endeavour* took, if there is one. In September and part of October I shall visit the Gulf of Carpentaria and the whole west coast of New Holland as far as Diemen's Land, but in a way that will allow me to reach the Ile de France in December, 1788."

He was still planning a whole year's arduous exploration of the South Pacific, with ships and rigging half rotted by the long voyages they had endured, with a soured view of the indigenous people he was likely to encounter, and with a company whose spirits and health must have resembled his own, as he described them in a letter to a friend, Lecoulteux de La Noraye, on February 7, 1788, some ten days after landing in Botany Bay.

"Whatever professional advantages this expedition may have brought me, you can be sure that few would want them at such cost, and the fatigues of such a voyage cannot be put into words. When I return you will take me for a centenarian. I have no teeth and no hair left and I think it will not be long before I become senile."

When he wrote the letter he was forty-seven. It was two and a half years since they had left Brest, and almost three and a half since he had seen Eléonore. Drawings made of him six months earlier, in Sakhalin, show that in the months on shipboard he had put on weight. The waistcoat, which may have fitted him at the beginning of the expedition, is straining at the buttons and his stomach bulges and sags. It is hard to imagine the cumulative strains of such a voyage, and perhaps at the time of writing the letter he was struggling not to think of what another whole year of it would be like.

On March 10 the two frigates, with their newly built longboats, but their old sails and rigging, left Botany Bay. The British, on their own ships, and those at the settlement, watched them pass, just off the coast, and proceed on their way to the north. They were the last Europeans who would ever see them.

* * *

Another indication of what may have touched off the catastrophe in Samoa, besides those in the written accounts, was relayed after the frigates had sailed from Botany Bay. M. Lavaux, the surgeon of the *Astrolabe*, wounded at A'asu, told his English colleague there, the surgeon Worgan, from the *Sirius*, that the French thought their own crewmen had done something to offend the Samoans, so that when they saw another shore party heading for them, they had gathered to attack them. That version was supported, still later, by George Turner, an English missionary who spent nineteen years in Samoa. A Samoan had told him that another islander, either caught stealing or, as he said, suspected of theft (however that would have been expressed), had been wounded by a shot from a firearm on one of the vessels, and the attack was a reprisal, after the man's bleeding body was brought to shore. Something of the kind, of course, was possible, though it raises the question of timing, and why, if it happened like that, the shore party was allowed to fill and load the water barrels before the attack began.

* * *

The plans that La Pérouse had sent to the Ministry said he hoped to arrive at the Ile de France around the end of that year—1788. He did not propose to touch other European outposts before then, and it would be six months after that date—the summer of 1789—before news of him could be expected in France.

That time came and passed without a word. It was almost another year before Fleurieu, at the Ministry, began to make plans for an expedition to try to find him and rescue him. Eléonore, who had been living in Albi, waiting for him, as she had spent so much of her life doing, moved to Paris to be nearer to the Ministry, in case there was any news, and to exert whatever influence she could to get the government to do something.

It was a bad time for organizing anything. The Revolution had begun. The Bastille had been taken, the abolition of the aristocracy was under way, and the government was falling apart.

In the spring of 1790, more than two years after the British at Botany Bay had watched the *Boussole* and the *Astrolabe* disappear up the coast, Fleurieu, La Pérouse's friend at the Ministry, drew up a summary of the known facts about the expedition and discussed them with the King. At the same time the Academy of Sciences pondered what action could be taken, and decided to send Bougainville himself to "meet" La Pérouse. The members, of course, continued to assume that La Perouse was alive until they had evidence that he was not.

In February 1791, Fleurieu, who was then Maritime Minister, officially declared the expedition lost as of the last day of December 1788, over two years before, since that was the time when La Pérouse had planned to reach the Ile de France. The National Assembly voted to send a rescue expedition, though it would be months before it could be ready to start. On April 22 the Assembly published a decree ordering the publication of the journals and letters of La Pérouse "at the expense of the nation, and announcing that he would remain on the rolls as an officer until the return of the rescue operation, and that his salary would continue to be paid to his wife, according to the agreement made before he left."

The rescue expedition, under Bruny d'Entrecasteaux, sailed in September, with two heavy vessels. D'Entrecasteaux was an officer of great experience and intelligence, but along with the equipment for the voyage that he was carrying with him, his company brought with them the political dissensions that were tearing France apart at that moment.

There were delays, and it took the expedition four months to reach the Cape of Good Hope, where they heard third-hand reports of wreckage sighted in the Admiralty Islands, that might have come from the French vessels. D'Entrecasteaux made for the Admiralty Islands but the winds were against him and he changed course for Tasmania. It was not until May 1792 that he sailed on toward New Caledonia and the route that La Pérouse supposedly had followed, after leaving Botany Bay. From there he went on to the Solomons, and finally the Admiralty Islands. When they looked for wreckage there all they found was driftwood, the bleached remains of trees that had washed up on the reefs.

He gave that up, went on around Australia and back to Tasmania, then north again in the direction of Tonga. In May 1793 they sailed toward Santa Cruz, at the northern end of the New Hebrides chain, and sighted another island southeast of Santa Cruz, which was not on the charts. They noted its position on their maps, naming it Recherche Island.

Both the health and morale of the expedition by that time were appalling. The captain of the second vessel, Huon de Kermadec, had died. D'Entrecasteaux himself was terminally ill, supplies were very low, the political bitterness in the company had abraded, at close quarters, until it seemed daily to be on the point of violence. They did not approach the island but sailed on.

What they had seen, and called Recherche Island, was Vanikoro, where La Pérouse had been shipwrecked more than five years before, and where survivors from the wreck may still have been alive. Sickness and fevers had overwhelmed d'Entrecasteaux and many in his company, and it seemed to him that he had no choice but to suspend the search and sail for Java. But he remained troubled by the fact that

they had not explored the unknown island more carefully. "We saw
it from so far away," he wrote, "that we could not draw it on the map
with any certainty, though we verified its longitude and latitude." He
never knew that it had been the object of his expedition. Two months
later he died and was buried at sea.

*   *   *

Three months after that, the expedition had lost ninety men to disease and deprivation. At Surabaya, as d'Entrecasteaux's successor,
d'Auribeau, was waiting for permission from the Dutch to enter the
harbor, he received a message from de Trobriant, the governor of
the French Company of the Indies, saying, "I am a prisoner of war.
France is at war with Holland and with all the powers of Europe. The
National Assembly has been dissolved and replaced by a Convention
that has assumed supreme powers without being given them by the
nation. Our country, half overrun by foreign armies, is a prey to anar-
chy and the rending of civil war. The King has had his head cut off."

D'Auribeau died in Surabaya. There was a rumor that in despair
he had poisoned himself. In time the Dutch took the survivors to
London, where they separated at last, four years after they had set out
on their doomed expedition. The whole of Europe had changed in
their absence. The animosities of the age they had left had remained
with them all the way, festering into implacable hatreds. The ironic
memorial of their years of wandering and rancor was a series of
superb maps of every place they had been, by Beautemps-Beaupré,
which set the example for modern cartography.

*   *   *

Though all the families of the La Pérouse expedition were to have
been paid until the return of the rescue voyage, the economy of
France was in ruins, inflation was ballooning, and finally a decision
was made to pay Eléonore out of the proceeds of the publication of

La Pérouse's journals and letters. There were troubles about that, too. The rôle of the King in the organization of the expedition embarrassed the editor, the Baron Milet de Mureau, an army general who had dropped the "de" in his name, in an effort to conceal his aristocratic lineage, and who was intensely aware that the references to the royal influence, and the names of noblemen in the text he was preparing, might lead to the loss of his own head. He raised the matter with the Naval Office and it was passed on from department to department of the government, while time dragged on and the government itself changed, and the day came when the Terror was over, the Directory was in, the three-volume compilation could be published. By that time it was 1797 and so many things had changed that interest in the subject had waned. The book did not sell nearly as well as it had been expected to. Eléonore was given 1800 copies, priced at 80 francs each, the whole theoretically worth a good sum at the time. But in 1804 a note added to a report made for Napoleon said, "The edition was handed over to a bookseller at a bargain rate." In other words it was remaindered. Napoleon gave Eléonore a pension of 2400 francs a month and a grace-and-favor apartment at the Château de Vincennes, a setting so dreary that she preferred to find somewhere for herself in Paris, though her pension barely provided for her needs. She died there three years later, on April 3, 1807. She was fifty-two.

Almost two centuries afterwards, in 1988, at a gathering in celebration of the bicentennial of the landing of La Pérouse at Botany Bay, Jacques Thomas, the founder and president of the La Pérouse Boomerang Club of France, was the one representative of France there, and he was moved by the occasion to do something to honor Eléonore. But no one even knew where she was buried, beyond the fact that it was on private property in Louveciennes, not far from Paris. It was known that she had been befriended in her last years by a certain Mme. Pourrat. M. Thomas enlisted the help of a retired naval officer living in Versailles, Jacques Bodin, and he in turn obtained the assistance of M. Lay, the historian of Louveciennes. Mme. Pourrat turned out to have been the owner at one time of the Château des Voisins in Louveciennes, where Andre Chenier, Benjamin Constant, and Mme. de Stael had stayed. Eléonore had been buried in the family cemetery, in the park of the chateau. The property had been sold in 1857, and the new owner had had the graves exhumed and the remains transferred to Père La Chaise cemetery in Paris.

Commander Bodin took the family names to the office responsible for the cemetery and was given the coordinates of a tomb. There was no name on it. He continued his research and discovered that the paths of the cemetery, on which the coordinates were based, had been changed. Making his own adjustments, like a careful navigator, he found himself at last before an inscription that read ELÉONORE BROUDOU, FEMME DE MONSIEUR DE LAPÉROUSE, CHEF D'ESCADRE DES ARMEES NAVALES DE FRANCE, DECEDEE 3 ARIL 1807. He sent Jacques Thomas a telegram reading "Eléonore retrouvée—Amitiés".

* * *

The year Eléonore died a passage from an English officer's journal told of a Portuguese ship rescuing one of the unfortunate companions of La Pérouse, the astronomer Dagelet. He had been near death but had said that the *Astrolabe* had run aground and the *Boussole* had accidentally caught fire, and that La Pérouse and some of his officers had stayed in New Zealand for nine years before building a small boat. The natives had ambushed them before they could launch it, and only Dagelet had escaped in a small boat and reached the island where the Portuguese found him. He died a few days later, refusing to believe that the King had been guillotined and that France was a republic.

Nine years later an anonymous journal was published, also citing the report of an English captain who had claimed to have picked up the astronomer Dagelet on May 11, 1792, and heard the same story of the *Boussole* catching fire. In this version, the French who had made it ashore had lived for several months on good terms with the natives, but finally had been attacked as they were cutting wood to build a boat. Their gunpowder was all gone, and all of them had been killed except for Dagelet and eight others who had escaped in a small boat and made their way to a deserted island, swampy and infested with insects. There all the others had died from the terrible conditions of the place, and Dagelet, the last survivor, died too, a few days after he was taken on board.

Nobody could tell whether there was any truth in these stories, which were unsubstantiated by any evidence.

The first real clue to the fate of La Pérouse and his expedition did not come until 1826. It was found by Peter Dillon, who was officially a British subject but was Irish by blood and by family tradition, and more closely allied to French than to English interests. The Dillon family had had its own regiments in Ireland and had fought against Cromwell, and later for the French in the time of Louis XV. Arthur Dillon, one of Peter's forbears, had accompanied Lafayette, to fight against the English in the American Revolution. Afterward, he and his regiment had settled in Martinique, where he lived on a sugar plantation owned by the Comtesse de la Touche, the widow of a French naval officer. Arthur and she had a daughter named Fanny, who married a French officer, a close friend of Napoleon's, whom they accompanied to St. Helena. Several members of the Dillon family stayed on Martinique through the British occupation, and one of them was Peter's father, who was serving in the British garrison when Peter was born, in 1785, the year that La Pérouse set out on his expedition.

Peter's parents decided to return to Ireland, and he grew up there. At fifteen he went to sea in the English navy, and in 1808 embarked for the East Indies on an English vessel with an Irish captain, to start his life in the South Pacific.

The sandalwood trade was in its first years. It was a moment, and a world, open for adventurers.

Sandalwood, produced by several species of the genus *Santalum*, which consists of evergreen trees and shrubs native to parts of India, Malaysia, Australia and Polynesia, had been used as incense for an indeterminate length of time in India, where it grows—or grew—on the Malabar and Coromandel coasts. The entire slow-growing bush or tree must be cut down for a relatively short section of the heartwood near ground level, so that wild populations of the most coveted species have been rapidly eliminated, and the genus is not easily propagated or cultivated. The Chinese prized sandalwood but produced none of their own, and imported the "amber gold" from India. As it grew scarcer it became steadily more expensive.

Around 1800 the Chinese began to export tea to the English and to the new settlements in Australia, and both suddenly wanted it in great quantities. After 1800 many of the Chinese exporters would accept payment for tea only in sandalwood.

At about the same time an American, Oscar Slater, captain of the *Argo,* found sandalwood in Fiji and told people in Sydney about it, sending a rush of ships to the south shore of Vanua Levu in Fiji.

The wood could not be cut and removed easily. The inhabitants were hostile, and they were cannibals. Arrangements with local chiefs were tenuous and the crews were exposed to deadly attacks. No European power had claimed the islands of Fiji at that time. Despite the risks a growing number of "beach combers" had made their way to the shore of Fiji. Some were escaped convicts from the New South Wales penal colony. They gathered sea cucumbers, which were considered a delicacy in China, and anything else they could sell to the ships that came in search of sandalwood. Their number increased when the word got around that the American brig *Eliza* had been wrecked on the coast of Fiji and the crew had seized forty thousand Spanish piastres which the vessel was carrying.

For their own good the beach combers had arrived at a kind of gang organization. They put themselves under the protection of local chiefs who saw how useful they could be in dealing with sea captains avid for sandalwood, and in the use and repairs of firearms to help in wars with other chiefs. They were allowed to take one or several wives. One of them, Charles Savage, an American survivor of the *Eliza,* became well known as the advisor of one of the head chiefs.

In 1808 Peter Dillon, aged twenty-three, sailed from Sydney on the *General Wellington,* bound for Fiji. There in the village of Bua the crew learned of the wreck of the *Eliza,* and of the survivors living in the area, with whatever they had managed to take from the wreck. Some of the sailors on the English vessels anchored there jumped ship to stay and try their luck in the place, and Dillon decided to do the same. He hoped to win the confidence of native chiefs and acquire sandalwood to sell to the ships that came for it. He managed to learn Fijian, survived for ten months there, and in January 1809, when the *Perseverance* arrived—a vessel from the same firm as the one on which he had sailed there—he sold his sandalwood to the captain and returned to Sydney with him.

His acquaintance with the people of Fiji, and later with the Maoris of New Zealand, fostered a strong sympathy for Polynesians, and he deplored the way they were treated by some of the English captains. His respect survived a deadly confrontation with the massed warriors of one part of Vanua Levu, in which the Fijians had tried to seize the cutter *Elizabeth.* The attempt was a move in a conflict between local chiefs. A party of English sailors and beach combers, Dillon among them, assembled to protect the cutter. The English officer in command of the sailors foolishly divided his band into small groups. In the fight that followed, only Dillon's own group, which included the famous beach comber Charles Savage, survived being ambushed by the warriors hiding in the scrub growth above the beach. Six of them retreated to the top of a pinnacle of rock with their remaining guns and ammunition. Only three of them made it to the top, and from there they watched the bodies of their companions being butchered for the coming meal.

They escaped only because Dillon seized a priest who had come to try to talk them into surrendering, and they marched him, with their muskets at his head, to the single boat on the shore, where they pushed off and rowed away out of a storm of stones and arrows.

In 1813 he had visited the island of Tikopia, but had not noticed the iron objects that had been brought there from the site of the wreck of the La Pérouse expedition at Vanikoro. It would be another thirteen years before he returned to Tikopia, after marrying and starting a family in Sydney and sailing in command of his own vessel back and forth across the Pacific from Cape Horn to China as a seal hunter and merchantman. When he went back the next time he was glad to see an old friend of his, Lascar Joe, who had stayed there at his own request when Dillon had first visited the island. Hanging around Joe's neck as an ornament Dillon saw a silver sword guard. When he asked where it came from, several of the elders of the island told him that in their youth two big ships had been smashed on the reefs of the island of Vanikoro, a hundred miles northwest of them. Lascar Joe said he had met two survivors of the wreck. The elders had said that no other vessel had touched their island since the ships had been wrecked there. Dillon was sure that what they were talking about was the La Pérouse expedition. But his own vessel at that moment had just been badly damaged by a storm and was barely seaworthy and almost out of food, and he had to sail back to his home base in Calcutta, planning to come again when he could.

It had been almost forty years, by then, since La Pérouse had been wrecked at Vanikoro. The enigma of his disappearance had stayed in the minds of the Europeans and Americans who sailed the south Pacific, and Dillon had long dreamed of discovering what had happened to the vanished expedition. He was eager to get back to Vanikoro, and in Calcutta he planned a return voyage with the help of the British East India Company and the Asiatic Society. He was given a ship, *The Research*. The East India Company would pay the crew.

He learned that the French were also sending an expedition, under the command of Dumont d'Urville, to look for remains of the La Pérouse expedition. The news further goaded Dillon to get back to Vanikoro. Circumstances seemed to conspire to delay his journey, and it was a full year before he anchored again at Tikopia. There he managed to enlist a Tikopean interpreter who spoke the language of Vanikoro (perhaps not quite as well as he pretended to) and a sword blade, a razor, small bells, and another silver sword guard like the first one, from the wrecks at Vanikoro. Rathea, the interpreter, talked incessantly, rattling on about the shipwreck and the survivors. The more he talked the less Dillon believed him. While Dillon loaded on provisions at his anchorage off Tikopia he picked up further rumors about Vanikoro. As far as he could tell, the only Europeans the inhabitants of that island had ever seen were the survivors of the La Pérouse expedition.

The Research approached Vanikoro on September 7, 1827. Dillon looked cautiously for a safe anchorage. Rathea, the interpreter, and Bushart, one of Dillon's closest companions, made a preliminary, friendly contact with the islanders, whom they could see had arrowheads and adzes made of iron, and they felt sure they knew where the iron had come from. Further conversations with the inhabitants were impeded rather than helped by the interpreter, Rathea, who answered Dillon's questions himself without translating them to those of the elders who had been alive at the time of the shipwrecks. It was clear that the elders were anxious, even that many years later, remembering the massacre of some of the survivors of the wrecked vessels. Dillon plied them with presents and entertained them with fife and drum music, and gradually pieced together an account. As Dillon understood it, the first elder's story—allowing for flourishes of Rathea's—went like this:

"A long time ago the people living on this island came out of their houses one morning and saw part of a ship on the reef outside Paiou. It was there until the middle of the day and then the sea broke it up. Big pieces of it floated in to the shore. The ship had been driven onto the reef during the night by a terrible hurricane that destroyed many of our fruit trees. Four men survived and got to shore here. We thought they were evil spirits and were going to kill them, but they gave our chief a present, which saved their lives. They stayed with us for a while and then they went to join their companions in Paiou, where they built a small vessel and went away in it. None of those four men was the chief. They were all inferiors. The things we can sell you came from the ship that went aground on the reef. Our people would go out there at low tide and dive and bring back whatever they found, and some things washed ashore and we kept them, but it has been a long time since we got anything from that ship because it rotted and was washed away by the sea. We did not kill any of those men, but a number of bodies washed ashore with their legs and arms mutilated by sharks.

"That same night another ship struck the reef near Whanou and sank. Some of the men survived and they built a small boat and sailed away five moons after the big one was lost. While they were building the small boat they put up a strong fence of tree trunks around them, to protect them from the people of the island, who were afraid of them, so they did not have much to do with each other.

"The whites used to look at the sun through things they had. I cannot say what they were because we do not have anything like them. When the others left, two men stayed behind. One was a chief, the other was his servant. The first one died about three years ago. Around six months later the chief of the place where the other one was living had to leave the island, and the white man went with him. We do not know what happened to them "

Dillon and Bushart found bits of iron being used in every household into which they were invited, after all those years, and after what must have been put into the construction of the smaller vessel, and after all that the inhabitants must have used for barter with people from other islands. In the next few days they were brought other relics from the frigates, among them pieces of porcelain from Macao, where La Pérouse had stopped in January 1787.

On the basis of his bartering experience, Dillon made a list of what the natives prized most, in order of value. Most precious in their eyes was red cloth, then axes, scissors, adzes, empty bottles, beads, fish hooks. Barrel hoops were a valuable medium of exchange. Firearms and ammunition were treasures given to particular chiefs to help them against their rivals, with a view to facilitating, on those islands where it was found, the acquisition of sandalwood.

On Vanikoro he visited the head chief, which was a diplomatic success, and he continued to barter for objects from the wrecks and to garner scraps of information about the survivors, insofar as he could understand them. He had learned the site of the first wreck, and three days after anchoring he went with the longboats to see the exact place. He still had hopes of finding some indication of where to look for the last remaining survivor, who had left the island so short a time before he got there.

The natives guided the longboats along the coast to the mouth of the small river and the spot where they said the French had made their camp with its palisade, and where they had built the smaller ship. Storms and tropical rains had washed away almost all traces of them except for ax marks still visible on the trunks of some of the trees, under the vines.

Their guides showed Dillon's companions the places on the reefs where each of the ships had been wrecked. At the village of Ammah, on the west coast, they were told the same story of the wreck and the survivors, and among other relics they were sold a small bell and a small bronze cannon stamped with a fleur-de-lys. At the village of Lavaka they found a man planting taro who was wearing, as a nose ornament, a glass thermometer that had come from near the French camp. In another village they were brought part of a silver chandelier engraved with the arms of Jean Nicolas Collignon, the botanist of the La Pérouse expedition. (He was the young man who had sowed seeds of vegetables and fruit trees on Easter Island.)

Dillon managed to examine, and take more relics from the site of the first wreck, and to determine the spot where the second frigate had been destroyed. Before he left Vanikoro in early October, he made a remarkably accurate map of the island. He sailed from there to the island of Santa Cruz, hoping to find the last survivor, but discovered no trace of him. Before the end of the year his interpreter, Rathea, whom in the end he had grown quite fond of, died.

Back in Sydney, he invited representatives of the East India Company, and officers of the vessels in the harbor, to an exhibit of the relics. Their discoveries were written up in *The Sydney Gazette*, which gave Dillon some of the public recognition of them that he wanted, in order to confirm his achievements in the eyes of the East India Company, and provide a record, in case he, or his vessel, were to come to grief.

He learned there that d'Urville, with his vessel which was also named the *Astrolabe,* was in Hobart, on the way north to Tikopia. Dillon sailed back to Calcutta, to discover that the company that had been handling his finances, Baretta and Sons, had just gone bankrupt, and that as a result he had lost his ship, its cargo, and the savings of all his years as a merchant captain. But the governor general asked him to display the Vanikoro relics at Government House, he was lionized, and the French officials were among those who applauded what he had accomplished. With a loan from a friend, and the encouragement of French and English authorities, he sailed for England.

The French ambassador in London offered him more practical encouragement than the English. In 1791 the French government had offered a reward of four thousand francs in gold to the first person to find proof of what had become of La Pérouse. Dillon took the Vanikoro relics to France to present them to King Charles X. They were displayed in a major exhibit, with a commentary on La Pérouse and on Dillon's discoveries about the fate of the expedition. He learned that he would be given not only the reward but a sum to cover the expenses he had incurred and a pension of four thousand francs, half of which would revert to his wife, and that he would be given the Order of the Legion d'Honneur.

But in 1830 a new government in France reduced the small pension. There were delays in the publication of his *Narrative* of his explorations in French. He was overlooked on both sides of the Channel. He signed on with another captain for a commercial voyage to New Zealand with a cargo of linen, and then sailed back to London, with little reward for his years of danger and labor. His wife died there in 1840. He and his daughter Martha moved to France. He died in Paris in 1847.

* * *

Besides searching for survivors or traces of the La Pérouse expedition, Admiral Dumont d'Urville's voyage, begun in 1826, was intended to provide improved charts of New Zealand, New Guinea, Tonga, Viti, and Fiji. In his sailing instructions, the Maritime Minister noted that an American captain had said he had met natives on an island near New Caledonia who had a cross of St. Louis and several medals which appeared to have come from the wreck of the famous navigator. This, he said, afforded slight grounds for hope, but "it would afford His Majesty great pleasure if you were able to return any of those poor survivors to their homeland, after so many years of misery and exile."

His expedition was delayed by storms. He spent some time mapping the New Zealand coast before sailing north to Tonga, where he met the high chief, the Tamaha, a superb woman in her sixties, who remembered very clearly the passage of the ships of d'Entrecasteaux's expedition and, more remotely, Cook's, which had been there when she was nine or ten. Then, a few years before d'Entrecasteaux, she recalled two other vessels like his, with a white flag. They had anchored at Anamouka when she was there with her family, and had stayed ten days before sailing off to the west. Her brother, five years younger, remembered visiting the ships several times. La Pérouse had written that he planned to visit Tonga after he left Botany Bay, and d'Urville was sure that he had stopped there, and that they were on the right track. But after Tonga they found no other traces and went back to Tasmania.

There he learned that a Captain Dillon had been there six months earlier and had claimed to have discovered relics of the La Pérouse expedition on an island on the Pacific whose exact location he had not divulged. D'Urville was seized with mixed feelings. He was excited to think that the fate of La Pérouse may have been discovered at last, but of course disappointed that it was not he but "some unknown Englishman" who had suddenly happened upon "the theater of this great catastrophe. How I envy his luck," he wrote. Though he had no direct knowledge of the whereabouts of Tikopia or Vanikoro, he knew enough about the prevailing winds among the islands in that part of the Pacific to guess that he should make his way to the area around Santa Cruz in the Solomons. While he was still in Hobart another captain arrived with news that Dillon had come from Vanikoro with a number of objects from the La Pérouse expedition.

D'Urville learned the names and locations of the islands and sailed north to Tikopia and then to Vanikoro. At first he found the natives extremely reserved. Evidently they understood that the visitors were from the same country as the two ships that had been wrecked there. Finally they were persuaded to speak, and their story, as he understood it, was that they had shot arrows at the strangers, to begin with, and the others had shot back with firearms, killing several of the islanders. Then the strangers had all died and had been buried there in the village. They had used some of the skulls to make arrowheads.

For a gift of red cloth one of the islanders led a longboat out to the reef to a spot where they found cannons, anchors, lead plaques, musket balls, all in ten or twelve feet of water, and in the next days they brought a number of heavy objects and pieces of porcelain to the surface there. They set up a monument on the shore to La Pérouse and the *Boussole* and the first *Astrolabe*.

From the account that he had been able to piece together, with the help of interpreters who knew the language better than Dillon's Rathea, he put forward his own version of what he thought had happened to La Pérouse and his expedition:

"After a dark night with a violent southeast wind, at first light the islanders saw, on the south coast off the Tanema area, a huge canoe grounded on the reefs. Only a few of the men on it escaped in a smaller boat and reached shore. The next day, also in the morning, they saw that another big canoe had run aground off Paiou. That one was in the lee of the island and was beached on level sand, and it was there much longer before it broke up. The strangers on it came ashore at Paiou where they used parts of the big canoe to build a small one."

They called the French *marahs* (from *marin?)* and said they had respected them and approached them with lowered hands, a ceremonial gesture. But there had been some disputes with them. The islanders had lost several warriors, three of them chiefs, and two of the French had been killed. Finally, after six months of work, the smaller boat was finished and, according to most of them, all the *marahs* sailed away. Some of them said that two of the *marahs* stayed behind but did not live long afterward. Few of them believed that there were any of the French still alive either on Vanikoro or on any of the islands in the region.

D'Urville believed that, after New Caledonia, La Pérouse had turned northwest toward Santa Cruz and on his way there had struck the reefs of Vanikoro, the *Boussole* first, and then the *Astrolabe,* coming to its rescue and trying to make its way through what appeared to be a passage through the reef, discovering too late how shallow it was.

He thought that the poorly equipped "vessel of fortune" which the survivors built would have headed for the Moluccas and the Philippines, and that he might find traces of them in the western part of the Solomons. But forty of his company were sick, by that time, to the point of being "out of service," and he had little choice but to sail for the nearest port where they could be cared for, which was Guam in the Marianas. He never managed to return to search for news of the survivors. He was further tormented by the realization that in 1823, when he had been second officer on a voyage of circumnavigation, his vessel had passed within a few miles of Vanikoro at a time when some of the survivors of the La Pérouse expedition may still have been alive there.

He himself was in bad health when he left Vanikoro. The tolls of life in the tropics, for Europeans, particularly on shipboard, were terrible, and fevers, viruses, dysentery, sooner or later seemed to attack virtually everyone. D'Urville's achievements were not properly recognized or rewarded in his lifetime, and he did not long survive the voyage. For reasons that are not clear—perhaps merely because it was not he who had discovered the place where the La Pérouse expedition had ended—he is said to have spent the last months of his life "in semi-disgrace."

* * *

A series of voyages trying to learn more about the end of the expedition followed, from d'Urville's day to ours. In 1828 the French ship *Bayonnaise* anchored off Vanikoro and stayed twelve days, collecting basically the same story that d'Urville had heard, and a number of relics. In 1883 a French expedition brought back an anchor that became part of the La Pérouse monument in Albi. (By that time, in the middle of the nineteenth century, an official meddler had changed the spelling of the explorer's name to Lapérouse, though that was not the way he or anyone he ever knew spelled it.)

In the twentieth century the list of research vessels lengthened. Ships set out from the New Hebrides for that purpose in 1901 and from New Caledonia in 1938. After World War II underwater research vessels, the *Lotus* in 1953, the *Tiaré* in 1958, sailed from the New Hebrides and divers went down to the wreck of the *Astrolabe*. In 1962 a New Zealand diver, Reece Discombe, who was then returning to the reef with other divers every year to continue the exploration, found a fault in the outer reef that proved to be a pocket filled with pieces from the wreck, and in 1964 he and other divers, on two separate visits, discovered many remnants of the *Boussole*. There were diving expeditions, under the direction of Alain Conan of Noumea, in 1981 and 1986, 1988, 1990, 1999.

The archaeological excavation of the French camp, where the smaller vessel had been built, also yielded objects and some idea of what may have happened there, but the work was made difficult by years of jungle growth, and by the establishment there, earlier in the twentieth century, of the Kaori Timber Company (named for a great tree) and its heavy machinery.

In the opinion of the divers of the 1990 New Caledonian expedition, what happened to the two frigates of the La Pérouse expedition was probably this. They were sailing at night, the *Boussole* in advance. Heavy wind from the west. Suddenly the reef was dead ahead. The *Boussole* tried to turn but lost seaway, and it was too late. The vessel was helpless, driven by the waves and wind. Apparently they cast an anchor but it failed to hold them. The cable may have been cut by the coral. They struck the reef stern first and were caught in the break in the coral. There was a violent crash. The rigging collapsed, the vessel was battered and smashed by the surf, the cannons broke loose and caromed around the gun deck. Men were crushed, pinned, held in place to drown.

The *Astrolabe* saw the wreck or heard a warning shot and managed to swerve out to sea. They sighted a break in the reef and edged in toward it. They may have sent two boats ahead to sound the passage but the surf must have been wild and it would have been hard for the boats to determine the depths, in such a sea. On the outside the break in the reef is fairly deep, but a little way in it shelves upward. The *Astrolabe* ran aground. They dropped an anchor to keep from being driven in farther, and they were able to stay there for a while, wait out the storm, send boats to pick up any survivors from the *Boussole*, and get to shore, to confront the islanders and start to set up a camp, before the *Astrolabe* too was broken up by the surf.

The natives were suspicious, probably hostile, and cannibals. Three hundred inches of rain a year fell on the island, and mosquitoes and malaria were certainly an incessant problem, and for some must have proved fatal. Food was another problem. If indeed they finished building a boat, as they had done in Botany Bay, those who were able to embark from Vanikoro must have been few in number and not in robust health.

After all the research there is still doubt as to whether a smaller vessel ever left Vanikoro, but the islanders who had been there at the time said that it sailed away. The archaeologists continue to hope that they may find some record, some written log or message left behind, telling of plans for a last voyage. If there was such a sailing, we do not know who was on board, or where the final disaster was waiting for them. No vestige of it has been found.

*   *   *

Beside the bay that is named for him on Maui there has been a monument, since 1994, to La Pérouse and his expedition, and there is one to him and his company at Vanikoro, and one in Sakhalin, and one in A'asu Bay in Samoa, one in the La Pérouse district of Sydney near Botany Bay, and the traffic swirls at the base of the monument and the statue in Albi. (The La Pérouse Museum was opened there, across the river, in 1988.) There are markers like gravestones around the world, but there is no grave.

The Stone Boat

The windows are wide open to the hazed light and soft shadows of the first morning of September, in which the leaves of ash and plum and maple, still green after a rainy summer, are stirring slightly in the cool breath of day. It is a sight as familiar to me as that of anywhere in the world, one that I have known for the greater part of my life. Such is memory that I see it as though it had always looked just as it does at this moment, although it has changed every time I have seen it, from morning to evening, from day to day, from season to season. I have watched the plum trees flower early in the spring, and then, as their white petals darken, the green beads that would be plums emerge from under them, to turn plump and blue with the coming of the summer. I have noticed the trees aging, drawing into themselves, the bark splitting, limbs dying, and I have watched the birds at home in them year after year, but fewer of them every year, both their numbers and their kinds. I dream now that I hear the oriole, and it wakes me in the night, but I have not heard it this season, and this is the first year when the swallows did not come back. Yet I go on seeing it all as I saw it first, when so many birds were here.

Through the ash trees and wild plums along the lower edge of the small field I see, far below, what held me long ago, in the middle of the century. There is the broad sweep of valley on the far side of the river, and beyond that the ridges shading into each other, to the north. The river does not appear to be moving at all, and the blue shadows of clouds on the slopes and valley seem to have stopped and settled there. They are all suspended in the hush of morning.

I hear the train crossing the iron bridge over the river miles away down at Puybrun, and from the sound I can tell that it will be a fine day. As I listen, the still valley seems to be rising through itself like untold depths under a misty surface, a palimpsest. Below the near fields with their walnut trees the sheep move as slowly as mackerel clouds. There may have been sheep on that slope seven hundred years ago when Uc de Saint Cirq, the troubadour who was born a few miles away on the upland to a family of landless nobility, looked out across the valley from the village or from a lane that leads down to the river, one that is said to have been built and used by the Romans. Uc would have been on his way to the massive dark red castle set dramatically on the steep spur thrusting through a scrim of mist, down in the valley: the *château fort* of Castelnau, which may have been a Roman *castrum* at one time, perhaps built on the site of a Gaulish stronghold. The castle walls were raised higher in the sixth century at the orders of the waning Visigothic queen Brunehaut. There is a local belief, for which I have no written corroboration, that the fortifications were added to, and the name became Castelnau, or new castle, in the eighth century after Charles Martel stopped the northern advance of the Arabs, in 732, at Poitiers, and began to drive them back south toward the Pyrenees. Henry II of England occupied the château for a while in the twelfth century in support of his wife, Eleanor of Aquitaine's, claim to the domain of Toulouse. Throughout the twelfth and thirteenth centuries the barons of Castelnau were known for their hospitality to troubadours and minstrels. Uc de Saint Cirq, who came from their own lands, apparently lived at Castelnau for extended periods, as a guest. Hundreds of years later, before the Revolution, the château library was known to contain a collection of manuscripts of troubadour poems and music that ran to many volumes.

On the far side of the river, down to the west, I can see the long palisade of cliffs that, centuries before there were walls at Castelnau, provided the natural bastion of the Gauls in their final battle with Julius Caesar. The small plateau above the cliffs had been inhabited since Paleolithic times, and in the late Bronze Age there had been a settlement of some size there, and ramparts of huge stones had been set in place to fortify the heights.

In the summer of 52 B.C. the Romans had decisively defeated the Gauls at Alesia, and the Gauls' great leader Vercingetorix had been captured and would die in Rome in a foul dungeon connected to the sewers of the city. After the defeat the Gaulish forces scattered, and during the winter Caesar pursued them in the north and along the Loire, inflicting heavy losses. Two surviving Gaulish leaders, Drappes and Lucterios, decided to head south. It is not known how many followers they had with them—five to ten thousand, perhaps. Pursued by Roman legions with three or four times their number, they made a stand at Uxellodonum, known later as the Puy d'Issolud, the fortified village at the top of the cliffs, where the Romans could not take them by assault. Caninius, the Roman general, set up camps around the hilltop and began a siege, while waiting for Caesar to join him from the north. After Caesar arrived the Romans spent the rest of the winter building high dikes to divert the streams from around the base of the hill, and eventually succeeded in cutting off the last spring that provided water to Uxellodonum. When the inhabitants and the warriors on top of the cliffs began to die of thirst they surrendered.

"Caesar," wrote his admiring chronicler Hirtius, "was sure that his goodness of heart was well known, and that no one would attribute a severe sentence to cruelty on his part." He decided to make an example of these obstinate Gauls who persisted in defending themselves against the Romans, and he spared the warriors' lives but cut off their hands.

The streams on the far side of the hill returned in time to their own channels. One of them, the Sourdoire, runs through the small village of La Chapelle-aux-Saints, where I used to go every autumn to see a man a generation or so older than I was, who had a nursery of fruit trees there, which he tended by himself, "in the old way" as he assured me. I went, in fact, as much for his horticultural lore and reminiscences as for the few trees that I bought each year to plant in the shallow, unwelcoming soil here on the limestone upland. Some of his pear trees are still growing, and the fruit that I imagined decades ago is ripening now, at this season.

He talked about his years as an apprentice to an old nursery-man somewhere over along the river. Later, when I thought about it, I supposed he had been just too young to be called up in the first World War, and the nurseryman must have been too old for it, so they escaped it and grew fruit trees. He paused to talk as he chose the trees for me and dislodged them from the loose soil where they had been planted temporarily, and prepared them for me to take away in my antiquated delivery van. He was lean and not tall, a little stooped, his beret faded to a cobweb gray at the edges. Worn black jacket and trousers, *sabots* caked with mud. A thin, patient, confident face, and a quiet voice, measuring his words. He stood the uprooted trees in a wash basin of soupy mud before wrapping the roots, and he explained to me why it was that one could never buy fruit trees now that were as sturdy and resistant to disease as those of his youth. Back then, he said, he was sent out to the growers, to get seeds of the best kinds of plums and pears, apples, and the four sorts of cherries, when they were ripe, and then at the nursery the seeds were sown in drills like peas or beans, and were treated in much the same way. They were hoed and weeded, and as the seedlings grew, if any of them were stunted or sickly or malformed, or were attacked by insects or mold, they were pulled out and burned. In the autumn the survivors would all be dug up and transplanted, with the seedlings spaced farther apart, and the same culling-out was repeated the next year, and then the seedlings were again transplanted with more room. The cycle was repeated for three years and the remaining seedlings were the ones that were considered fit to use as rootstock onto which the desired varieties would be grafted. But now, he said, they simply spray them all, from the start, and grow the ones with the weaknesses along with all the rest, and can't tell the difference between them. That way the weaknesses are passed on to the next generation, and so on, and to the variety as a whole.

"When you get these home," he said, "make them a slurry like this"—and he gave me the recipe, the proportions of heavy mud, and manure, and milk, and a few other things. But he warned me each time that the trees reared in the valley might not thrive on the limestone upland.

I had heard about a burial site, bones, an ancient skeleton, that had been discovered near the village, and I asked him about it. He bent over the trees, not answering at first.

"Oh yes," he said at last, with his voice dropping slightly, suggesting that it was a subject he was not eager to pursue. I asked whether it was possible for anyone to see the skeleton, and he mumbled something about that being unlikely. "It's not encouraged," he said, by way of explanation, with a small, wry smile. "In the village," he added. "It's the church," he said. He shook his head, as though it were some recent scandal that the local authorities wanted to sweep under the rug. I thought it would not be tactful to press him further.

Others in the region had heard of the skeleton, but I did not find anyone for a while who was clear about the details. No one whom I asked claimed to have seen the bones. They had been sent, as I learned in due course, to Paris, almost as soon as they were found, and it would be over twenty years after my autumnal meetings with my friend at La Chapelle-aux-Saints before the small museum resembling a rural clinic was erected to house a replica of the original burial site, and charts and maps, near the place where the skeleton had remained undisturbed while invasions and civilizations and plagues and plows and harvests had come and gone a few feet above it.

The scandal, or controversy, had not been quite as recent as my friend's mumblings had suggested. The skull that revealed the grave had been exposed to the light of day, by the glancing blow of a pickax, six years before the first World War.

* * *

The skeleton had been found on August 3, 1908, some 5909 years after the moment when God—as Archbishop Usher assured the faithful, in 18th century England—created the world, and man, at nine o'clock in the morning, on the original 23rd of October. On the day when the grave was discovered Darwin's *Origin of Species* had been in print for almost fifty years, and its theory of evolution was widely accepted in the scientific world, but Christian literalists from William Jennings Bryan to many devout Catholic parishioners in southwest France still clung to a view of creation that resembled Archbishop Usher's. My father nursed a similar creed, and so, I expect, do many fundamentalists to the present day. In view of the bones' significance in the long dispute there is a certain irony in the fact that two of the three brothers who found them were priests.

But, as it was said of them then, they were priests "unlike the others." The eldest, Amedée Bouyssonie, forty-one at the time of the discovery, taught philosophy at the Petit Seminaire in Brive. His younger brother, Jean, thirty-one, taught physics and the natural sciences there. Both of them were devoted to the study of paleontology and prehistory, and had been for a decade, ever since Jean, in 1897, had been a theology student at the seminary of Saint Sulpice, at Issyles-Moulineaux, where his roommate was Henri Breuil, who within a few years would be the leading authority in Europe on the cave paintings of the Magdalenian Age. In that same year, 1897, Jean had invited Breuil to Brive to meet his brother Amedée.

When Breuil came, they all went exploring the valleys of the Courolle and the Planchetorte, near Brive, where Breuil found some of the first known prehistoric sites in the region. All three of the priests were ardent students of the writings of the Abbé J. Guibert, who advanced (with the blessing of the humanist pope at the time, Leo XIII) a "modernist" approach to science, Darwinism, human origins, and biblical interpretation. The social and political views of

Breuil and of the brothers were extremely liberal and in many respects were sympathetic with the political left.

The brothers continued to spend their vacations hunting for prehistoric remains in the countryside south of Brive, on their bicycles. They made important discoveries in a cave at Noailles and in one at Fon-Robert, and since the summer of 1905 they had been returning to visit cousins of theirs at Ginès, near La Chapelle-aux-Saints. Their youngest brother, Paul, was a farmer nearby. There, along the banks of the Sourdoire, they came to focus on a series of caves known as *bouffia*. Some of them, over the centuries, had been used in a variety of ways, as the surviving names suggested. One, for instance, was called the *Grotte des Contrebandiers* (Smugglers' Cave). But the brothers' careful examination revealed evidence of more ancient uses. There were stone implements and fragments whose forms and age they recognized. Their investigations narrowed to the approaches to one cave where the findings were particularly rich. It was known locally as the Bouffia Bonneval, for the contemporary owner of the property who was called the *Bonhomme* Bonneval. He was happy to give them his permission to dig in the cave, which at that time was the only permission they needed.

When they began digging there in 1905, the years of the modernist movement among some of the more learned French clergy had been paralleled by a secular surge of anti-clericalism. The year when their first finds at the Bouffia Bonneval had fixed their attentions there, the French legislature had passed the law separating church and state, and in 1907, when the new pope (who represented a reaction to Leo XIII), Pius X, refused to accept their ruling, they voted to impound church properties. The Petit Seminaire in Brive was forced out of the building it had occupied, and had to move out of Brive to a village where its name was changed to the École Bossuet. By 1908 both brothers were teaching there again, and Amedée was appointed to be the principal. That same year he was awarded a position as the honorary canon at the cathedral of Tulle. Both brothers realized that his new responsibilities would give him less time for prehistoric fieldwork, and when they had a chance they returned to Ginès and the Bouffia Bonneval, hoping to complete their explorations of the site.

Their excavations are considered now to have been admirably careful and methodical for the time, when often the digging of sites was scarcely better than looting, poorly recorded or not recorded at all, with the exact sources of individual pieces lost or obliterated, and the stratifications and arrangements of sites, and all clues to chronology, disturbed beyond reconstruction. The brothers, in their early exploration of the Bouffia, had concentrated on the entrance, where they found stone implements and fragments of bones of game animals, of the same period as the weapons. Farther inside the cave, they found that the floor had been hollowed out, and almost at the threshold of the hollow they found a bison horn, and then the neck bones of the same animal, then a stone spearhead or arrowhead, then many chipped pieces of flint, and broken bones, principally of reindeer.

The youngest brother, Paul, was the one who was farthest inside the cave, doing most of the actual digging. Caution as well as frugality discouraged the brothers from making use of paid labor, as some of the other site explorers did. Paul said something about coming upon a piece of bone that was much bigger than usual. It came out in his hand and he turned and passed it to Amedée, who was standing behind him, and he in turn passed it to Jean, out in the daylight. It was covered with mud, but they all remembered later that Jean gasped at the sight of what he was holding in his hands, and said at once, "It's the top of a skull, with heavy eyebrows—a Neanderthal man!" He set it down carefully, mud and all, and began to take photographs of it.

Both Amedée and Jean had some idea, at once, of the repercussions their find would cause as soon as it was announced and made public. They stored the remains of the site carefully while they conferred with their close friends who were prehistorians: the Abbés Bardon, Breuil and Carthaillac, all of whom would soon become eminent authorities in the field. None of their friends wanted to take the responsibility for announcing the discovery and describing it in a manner that would attest to its significance. Henri Breuil arranged for Marcellin Boule, a professor at the Museum of Natural History in Paris, author of an extremely influential work, *An Essay on the Stratigraphic Paleontology of Man,* to take charge of the relics and their public debut. They all knew that the discovery would set off the old post-Darwin wrangle about creationism (the belief that the world and all living things were created once and for all) and evolution.

The skull his brothers had handed out to Jean Bouyssonie was indeed Neanderthal—that was not the basis of the argument it aroused. There had been discoveries of Neanderthal skulls or pieces of skulls since the middle of the nineteenth century, notably at Gibraltar in 1848, in the Neander valley (for which it was named) in Germany in 1856, and at Spy in Belgium in 1868. By 1908 the age of Neanderthal man had also been reasonably well established. It is generally agreed that the Neanderthal people inhabited the valleys around La Chapelle-aux-Saints between 80,000 and 35,000 years ago. The crucial disagreement was about whether or not this creature could be considered human. The "La Chapelle-aux-Saints man" would become the type specimen of the species, partly because earlier Neanderthal finds had been relatively fragmentary whereas not only the La Chapelle-aux-Saints skull but the whole skeleton were virtually complete. It was the first discovery of its kind in which the base of the skull was intact, a fact that eventually figured in arguments as to whether this ancient's posture had or had not been fully erect. Marcellin Boule did not doubt the animal origins of the genus *Homo* but in writing about the discovery he stated with some care that there was no certainty of a direct genetic descent from Neanderthal man to Cro-Magnon and modern man. (His learned reservation—which would be proven sound by later studies—was exploited by some of the anti-evolutionary publications after the announcement of the discovery. Indeed, if one reads some of those articles it would seem as though the whole wrangle over evolution had just begun. It died away before long, but not, of course, everywhere.)

In the replica of the remains of the skeleton and its burial site, in the museum at La Chapelle-aux-Saints, we see a reproduction of the whole interment as the brothers Bouyssonie could never have seen it, for they found the bones one by one and removed them to be noted down and photographed. Nevertheless they knew what was there. It was a carefully placed burial, with the body lying on its back, the head to the west, and raised so that it was facing east. With the skeleton in the grave are the remains of other animals that were hunted by the inhabitants of the valley at the time and of the weapons the inhabitants used. It has been suggested that the animals or parts of animals were placed there as provisions for the person buried there, in the after-life. In view of the complex relation between hunter and hunted that is suggested by the later cave paintings of animals in the same region it seems reasonable to suggest that perhaps the remains of animals were also placed in the grave as guides in the after-world. The hunter had followed them, and their knowledge, in this world, and might go on doing so in the next. In any case the presence of animal parts and of weapons carefully placed in the grave were understood at once to be indications of a belief in a life after death. Some of the creationists who were troubled by the evident antiquity of the skeleton contended that it was, after all, an animal, not human, and not fully erect, but the signs that the La Chapelle-aux-Saints burial indicated a belief in an after-life, a spirit, were widely accepted as evidence that Neanderthal man was, in fact, human, and in the course of the century and of the rapid progress of paleontology from the '30s on, some paleontologists would classify Neanderthal man as *Homo sapiens— Homo sapiens Neanderthalensis*—though others would continue to consider him a separate species.

The burial, and eventually the discovery of others that could be compared with it, suggested other things about the customs and culture they represented. It seemed highly unlikely that this was the usual manner of burial for everyone in the society at that time, and far more probable that it was a kind of ceremonial interment reserved for eminent figures. The position of the body, like that of someone lying in bed, with the knees not straight but slightly bent, suggested a custom described as voluntary inhumation, which both Neanderthal and Cro-Magnon man are thought to have practiced for a very long time. Such a custom, it is assumed, would have been a great honor, with the dying figure continuing to represent the living in the world after death. It would have been reserved for great chiefs or others of high rank. Presumably the ceremonial interment would have taken place at a moment when the distinguished elder's life appeared to have almost reached its natural end, and he would have been laid to rest, still breathing, in his final position.

The body in the La Chapelle-aux-Saints grave had been that of a man, about fifty-five years old (almost certainly an advanced age at the time). He was just over five feet tall, and stocky in build. His health was not good. Besides a number of chronic ailments he suffered from severe arthritis in his neck vertebrae, which had affected his posture. One of his ribs had been broken not long before the burial and whatever caused that may have led to his death or to the expectation of his death. He had a crushed bone in one of his toes, and had only two teeth left in his head, one top, one bottom. Most of the teeth, it seemed, had fallen out some time earlier. The sockets showed signs of advanced gum disease and infection.

He had lived some 50,000 years ago, in an age much closer to the ice than ours. Only a very small part of the landscape he knew had trees on it. Most of the rest, over half of it, was open tundra, dry and arctic. Reindeer and bison were the animals he hunted on the uplands, and deer and pigs in the valleys.

In the decades after the discovery of his grave, paleontologists and paleoanthropologists learned considerably more about the evolution of the genus *Homo*. It did not originate in Europe but in Africa, probably (according to Donald Johanson and Timothy White in 1981) evolving from a hominid they named *Australopithecus afarensis* that existed between three and three and a half million years ago. They believe that the first member of the genus *Homo*, the maker of stone tools, *Homo habilis,* was a descendant of this species, dating from something over two million years ago, in the rift zone of east

Africa. Descendants of *Homo habilis,* now known as *Homo erectus,* are now thought to have been the first members of the genus to find their way to Europe. The oldest bone relic left by one of them is a jaw, found in Germany, that may be 650,000 years old. More remains of this ancestral species, from Hungary, Germany, Greece, and southern France, date from somewhere around 400,000 years ago. Traits indicative of Neanderthal man begin to appear in bones found in Europe that date from around 200,000 years ago, and the classic Neanderthal forms typical of Europe emerge about 80,000 years ago.

The Neanderthal humans of the valley of the Dordogne date from between then and 35,000 years ago. They appear to have lived mostly in southern Europe, confined there perhaps by the fluctuations of the last (Wurm) Ice Age. Their branch of the genus *Homo* seems to have been virtually isolated for millennia, without contact with relatives across the straits of Gibraltar or in the Near East. They had adapted to the climate and conditions of Europe and had become the first Europeans. It is one of them whose grave remained untouched beside the Sourdoire through the harsh latter end of the Ice Age. His own culture and whatever rituals, beliefs, mores, languages and arts it developed went on for another 15,000 years or so after the darkness closed over him—more than seven times the length of time between Caesar's presence there and our own day— before another species of the genus began to appear in the region, out of the Near East. That was Cro-Magnon man, essentially modern man, *Homo sapiens sapiens.*

We do not know what the relations between the two were, at any point. A few decades ago it was generally assumed that Cro-Magnon man simply wiped out his predecessor. Certainly his coming coincided with the gradual disappearance of the Neanderthals. But there is evidence which seems to indicate that the two species lived side by side in some places, perhaps for many thousands of years, until the Neanderthals died out. What caused that is not known. Neanderthal man was not physically inferior to his successor. In fact he was stronger. Nor can we assume, as once was done readily, that Cro-

Magnon man was more intelligent. The brain size of Neanderthal man was larger than that of the Cro-Magnons, but his intelligence must have functioned in different ways which are now lost beyond reach. If the two species lived near each other it is hard to imagine that they did not learn from each other. But for some reason that is not known there appears to have been little or no genetic mingling between them. The first indigenous humans finally became extinct. The remains of tools and paintings in one cave, at Chatelperron, in the Corrèze, are thought to represent the cultural transition from Neanderthal to Cro-Magnon. The Cro-Magnons who remained after the Neanderthals were gone, who made the great paintings in the caverns along the valleys, and left equally exquisite carvings of animals and human figures on bones and horn, eventually disappeared in their turn. They are no longer believed, as once they were, to be direct ancestors of modern inhabitants of Europe. Those forbears came at a later date, from somewhere to the east of the Mediterranean, but no fossil records have yet been found that determine where their migrations began. It may have been the glacial movements of the last Ice Age that drove them west into Europe.

*   *   *

Once the eminent elder had been laid in the long hollow and left there, with flat bones of animals laid over his face to protect it, he must have heard chants for a while, in the dark—words that he himself had learned in earlier years—before he stopped hearing anything. Later, the voices of every human he had known would fall silent, one by one, and then the language in which they had spoken to each other would be forgotten. It would grow steadily colder along the river and on the uplands. After many thousands of winters the last descendants of the people he had known would stop breathing, just as he had done, and the last of the animals they had hunted would be gone, and his entire way of recognizing the world would no longer be known.

After the distant rumble of the train crossing the bridge over the river down there, no sound reaches me from the valley. The silence of the morning is reassuring, as I have often found it to be here. It is all of a piece. It is where the morning is coming from.

Printed in the United States
by Baker & Taylor Publisher Services